News *from the* Village

News *from the* Village

Aegean Friends

David Mason

 RED HEN PRESS | *Pasadena, California*

NEWS FROM THE VILLAGE
Copyright © 2010 by David Mason
All rights reserved

Book design by Mark E. Cull
Book layout by Sydney Nichols
Cover photograph by Anne Lennox

Library of Congress Cataloging-in-Publication Data
Mason, David, 1954–
    News from the village : Aegean friends / David Mason.—1st ed.
        p. cm.
    ISBN 978-1-59709-471-9
    1. Mani Peninsula (Greece)—Description and travel. 2. Mason, David, 1954—Travel—Greece—Mani Peninsula. 3. Mason, David, 1954—Friends and associates. 4. Mani Peninsula (Greece)—Social life and customs. 5. Mani Peninsula (Greece)—Biography. I. Title.
DF901.M34M37 2010
949.5'22—dc22
[B]
                                  2009051132

The Annenberg Foundation, the Los Angeles County Arts Commission, and the National Endowment for the Arts partially support Red Hen Press.

First Edition
Published by Red Hen Press / www.redhen.org
Pasadena, CA

ACKNOWLEDGEMENTS

Portions of this book appeared previously in *Connecticut Review*, *The Hudson Review*, *Mondo Greco* and *The Sewanee Review*. Some poems and translations used in this book appeared first in *The Dark Horse*, *The Dirty Goat*, *The Hudson Review*, *Mediterraneans*, *Osiris*, *Pequod*, *Poetry*, and *The Times Literary Supplement*.

For Friends in Greece

Friends in Turkey

And for Anne Lennox
With whom I have made a home

CONTENTS

I

The Lotos-Eaters

. . . but those who ate this honeyed plant, the Lotos,
never cared to report, nor to return:
they longed to stay forever, browsing on
that native bloom, forgetful of their homeland.

—The *Odyssey*, trans. by Robert Fitzgerald

1

What did you expect?

The rain had stopped. I walked south of the village and found the path down from the road. It curved along a low stone wall among the dripping olive trees. And then I saw the little house where we had lived, the gate . . .

You have to understand: I thought I would never see these things again and it crushed me, as if a realm of happiness were inaccessible forever. Sixteen years had passed since I had last been in the village, and in that time I had lost my footing in the world. Losing the village, losing Greece was only part of that. I could see something of the past, nothing of the future, another fourteen years in which I would try to get this down.

And now I stood on the bluff above the rocks at Kalamitsi, my clothes wet from the rain, the winter sea green-blue and foaming on volcanic rocks below. The cypress tree, the tangled sage and thorns on the cliff edge were no bar to my coming back.

What did you expect?

I thought this was a story I could write, back in Greece after so much distance in time and space, and people known when I was young were still alive. The village was alive, still going on, and it was enough to know I had not lost them, not entirely. And it was not an ending any more than the village was mine to lose. It was just another circling back, another attempt to pick up the broken thread of things and follow where it led. Now I would be coming back and would write in earnest about my friends, trying to bring them all into the circle and tell the story as I saw it, and tell it again until I got it right. But the story was still unfolding. It has taken a long time to get this down and everything has changed as I have written. Revising a book, revising a life. . . .

I might as well begin at a beginning.

It was 1980. Jonna and I were living in Friend's house in the village in Mani. Friend's real name was Fred, but it sounded like Friend in Greek pronunciation. Our living there at all was accidental, and it has since occurred to me that accident and chance have shaped my life more than I care to admit. How could I know that Aegean friendships would shape my life and influence my work so profoundly? We almost did not go to Greece. Our original plan had been to settle in Scotland. We lived in Upstate New York on my gardener's pay and saved my wife's hefty saleperson's salary and thought of a year of freedom in another country, some chilly croft where I would write and Jonna would—what? What would she do? That was the rub. She saw herself in this frozen croft where I would soak in Celtic atmosphere, hammering out poems and stories, and she, perhaps, would knit.

You can see the dilemma. She was bright and did not want to spend a winter knitting in a croft while I withdrew in my customary way and wrote. So she said no, let's go someplace warm. And someone knew someone who had a house in Greece, a professor in Buffalo, so we called the professor and went to his house where he showed us photos of the village, and a week later we were in Greece, knowing not a word of the language or quite what we intended to do. I would write a novel, of course. The Scottish novel became the Greek novel. I changed the names. And I was young enough not to notice the riskiness of my ambitions, or that something about being a writer made being a husband doubly hard. A married couple are sometimes the last to know they are headed for the rocks.

2

It must have been autumn when we met Wolfgang and Isabella, because we had been harvesting an Englishman's olives in a village far south of ours, and the rainy season had begun. We hitched a ride from his hilltop village to Stoupa on the Gulf of Messinias and were walking home to our village along the narrow coastal road when a car whooshed around the corner, nearly flattening us. At that speed, it was a miracle we were recognized at all, let alone by Vassiliki, a woman we knew only slightly. Or maybe it was the mysterious Niki who recognized us—a beautiful woman with a brood of children by various fathers who was called a witch in our village and whose current lover was Stamatis, the village doctor. They backed up, rolled a window down and greeted us by name.

"Come with us," they said. "We're going to meet some friends." Out of the blue, we dropped our exhaustion and desire to go home for clean clothes and a hot shower. We quite uncharacteristically abandoned north, got into this panting little bug of a car and went south. And that was how the great friendship began—entirely by chance and luck.

We got in the car and headed south. A storm dropped down out of the Taygetos Mountains, driving rain over the terraced olive groves, the whipped grass and gray stone walls. Huddled in the flimsy car, we spoke in tatters of Greek and English. I was awkward at meeting people, my gift for solitude reinforced by two years as a gardener, and before that by time alone in Alaska and hitchhiking the perimeter of the British Isles.

Perhaps we all look back on early versions of ourselves and see the raw forms like unfinished compositions, full of misspellings and clumsy phrases. Jonna and I were two rough sketches, hardly people it would seem, secret, hidden even to ourselves. I was twenty-five at the time, my wife a year younger, and villagers often mistook us for brother and sister, unable to believe that such young people could be married to each other. We were college-educated and, in practical terms, ignorant as babes. My wife was heart-stoppingly beautiful and I was hard-working; otherwise we were hopeless cases, adrift in a Greek village where we provided local amusement. The villagers called us *ta paidiá*, the children, excusing our almost daily faux pas.

This must have been one of the first hard rains of the season. The dry terraces were just turning green; at every level the olive trees were thrashed by the wind into a green-silver froth. They looked like furies tossing out their arms in an ecstatic dance, defying village custom. The afternoon darkened and the spare stone towers of the villages paled in the rainlight. The peaks of the Taygetos disappeared under smoky clouds, and it seemed the Mani had reverted to its past of wounded *filótimo* and violence.

We drove uphill to the village of Riglia and parked the car near the last house. From there we had to dash to the upper village, stone houses hunkering under their rough tile roofs on a hilltop with an apron of walled and terraced gardens spread out below. We passed through a gate between a stable and a tiny church (later I would see the smoky and pocked wall paintings inside it), and stepped up to the house of Wolfgang and Isabella.

How different we were from the Austrian couple who came down the steps in the rain. Isabella, with bare and blackened feet, was dressed in Hindu cotton and an old sweater. She walked with tiny, mock-pious steps, murmuring, hugging and kissing in a way I found startling. Wolfgang was a huge, sandy-haired mountain of a man with a flimsy mustache. He giggled when he greeted us. Niki, Stamatis and Vassiliki melted into these known embraces, while Jonna and I stood by like cigar-store Indians.

I remember the Spartan simplicity of their house, a table and a few chairs, straw mats on a stone floor, the open kitchen fire under a smoke hole in the roof, so much more primitive than Friend's house, the rain-pelted front window with its view of the pale sea and faraway Koroni, the bells of a neighbor's goats as they were put away in the stable next door, then the utter silence of a village some distance from the main road. I remember tea and awkwardness. Jonna and I wore new nylon jackets chosen for efficient travel; Wolfgang and Isabella wore sweaters and rags.

Somehow they found out I was a writer. Though I had published only a few poems, an agent in New York was trying to sell my novel about workers I had known in Alaska.

Wolfgang leaned toward me. "You have been to Alaska?"

"The Aleutians. I unloaded crab boats."

"What kind of crabs are these?"

"King crab. They're kept alive with seawater in the holds of the boats."

"Did you hear this?" Wolfgang made everyone stop talking and listen. "Crabs, they are kept alive in these boats. Amazing."

"Or else they'd become poisonous."

"This is amazing! So you are unloading these living crabs from the seawater?"

"The water is pumped out. There are, say, ten thousand crab in a hold a big as this room, and you're standing on their backs. They move very slowly, so you can pick them up, two at a time, and throw them into these huge mesh bags."

"This I have never seen," Wolfgang said. "Isy, he has been to Alaska. This is incredible!"

It wasn't incredible to me. Growing up in Washington State, I knew many young men and women who fished or worked for the processors in Alaska. But it made Wolfgang expansive with sudden interest. That was how the accident of friendship began—in a room smelling of damp wool, wood smoke and thin oriental tea, in a patchwork language accompanied by silences. When we left Ano Riglia that evening, I doubted I would ever see the Austrians again. How little I knew about people, or about winter in Mani.

3

If you called Mani the Sicily of Greece, you would not be far wrong. After all, Maniots are said to have colonized Sicily in the old days. When we first flew into Athens, a girl on the plane warned us that Maniots were bad people, pirates and thieves and fascists. They were certainly a rugged lot, earthy and frequently dour, shut off from the rest of Greece by the high mountains of the Taygetos. They were never conquered by the Turks and were among the fiercest fighters in the War of Independence. Their land was covered with dry foliage: sage and scrub oak, asphodel and oleander, the occasional plane tree in the villages, cypresses like exclamation points in the stunning hills. It was a steep land cut into terraces for the olives. Visitors to Mani now find a more prosperous place, accustomed to tourists, but in 1980 the old Mani was still visible in its people and rough villages.

The house we used for the first eight of our thirteen months in Greece was one of the modern concrete and stone piles with a walled garden and several astonishing modern conveniences like a refrigerator and a washing machine. Two walls contained tall windows (screens in summer) with varnished jalousies to keep out intense sunlight or sudden storms.

We had arrived in late summer and had grown used to the easy weather, days spent swimming and learning Greek and walking in the fragrant hills. But as winter approached we discovered how cold a stone house could be. Many days we huddled close to the *mangáli*, a small Turkish brazier in which we burned crushed olive pits, or we squandered a few drachmas on propane for the gas heater, turning ourselves in front of it like slow-cooking meat.

Frequently in the evenings we went to the home of our dear friend, Anna. Because she was in mourning for her husband, Christos, who had died just months before, she refused to leave her house. Anna had a fireplace and a television. We learned a fair amount of Greek in conversation with Anna, whose operatic gestures clarified, or oversimplified, all ambiguities. And from her father, Theodoros, with his gold-toothed smile. I remember our first night in the village, how Theodoros walked us to Friend's house and, unlocking the gate, pointed at the moon: "*Fengari,*" he said. "*To fengari.*" The moon. "*Entaxi?*" Okay? This was how we would learn: point and speak.

We also learned from their television, watching Greek soap operas. *Methismeni Politeia* was "Drunken Town." Or subtitled American TV shows like *To Ploio tis Agapis*: "Boat of Love." When we were sick, Anna made us tea with brandy, into which we dipped *paximáthia*, or rusks. She mothered us, coached us in matters of local behavior. Other women from the village stopped in to gossip beside Anna's fire and to cajole her into leaving her widow's weeds, and Anna would sprout tears and relive the drama of countless losses while her hands fretted at her knitting. There were stories of extreme poverty, of murder and revenge, courtship and the dowry system in which land was the supreme measure of wealth; of the Italian Occupation, and the Germans, resistance and reprisals, the Civil War, massacres, hangings; of the saintliness of Christos and the endlessness of work for a woman in Greece, and how the dead became vampires if improperly mourned. And there were the constant permutations of politics.

"David?"

"Yes, Anna."

"Why does America not love Greece?"

"But Anna, we love Greece very much."

"Then why let Turkey take Cyprus away from us? Why does America love our enemies more? We Greeks have given you so much. Democracy and science and poetry. Aristotle and Plato, Homer, Sophocles. . . ."

"And Seferis?"

"Yes, and Seferis. Do you know when Seferis was here in the village he heard my sister sing?"

"Seferis was *here?*"

"Yes, he came to visit Fermor, and one day in the olives he heard Voula singing. She has a beautiful voice, like an angel. And he called her a little songbird and wanted to hear her again. But the Turks—" in a flash she returned to her former topic— "they are barbarians and murderers. Why does America love them more?"

I learned to steer clear of controversy in these conversations. A nervous American boy with my own reasons for avoiding conflict, I would listen politely even when I disagreed, and Anna played the elder sister to us. She was a natural over-actress. As long as we kept to the confines of our roles as *ta paidiá*, ignorance was bliss. She taught Jonna to knit, so our avoidance of the Scottish croft had in one sense changed nothing at all.

At the end of the evening, Anna would jokingly tell me to fetch my *tsánta*, or bag. This was an old olive oil tin with its lid cut off and a wire handle—a homemade bucket. I slung the bucket on a knobbed stick she had given me, and brought it to the fire. Setting her knitting aside, Anna filled our bucket with several shovelfulls of hot coals from the fireplace and bid us good night. Jonna and I walked home through the darkened village with a bucket of red-hot coals swinging on the stick between us. We walked quickly because of the cold, and I remember the wind swirling sparks from our portable fire and trailing them out behind us in the night. We carried that bit of warmth from Anna's house to ours, so that the cold stone house would not be quite so cold when we were ready for bed.

4

One afternoon, Wolfgang and Isabella paid a surprise visit to our house. We talked, and perhaps we had a meal and agreed to visit them in Ano Riglia. By November there were very few foreigners in Mani; we quickly grew to rely on each other for relief from our circumscribed village roles. Anna would not have approved of their gypsy dress, so we could not share them with her. One had to keep acquaintances distinct. With Anna we were friendly innocents, with other foreigners we were formal acquaintances and fellow readers. But with Wolfie and Isy a rarer plant began to grow through the winter: friendship based on mutual discovery rather than role-playing. Wolfie and I had both been gardeners—I for a wealthy Upstate New York couple, he for an Austrian aristocrat—so we had both known the meditative work of pruning and planting. For Jonna and Isy there was the rich terrain of young womanhood to explore. Jonna had grown up in a prosperous Rochester family, the eldest of three children. She was very sensitive, conscious that others found her beautiful with her thick hair lightened by the sun, her long legs and unblemished skin, the exotic beauty of her eyes and mouth. For her there was always a struggle to get beyond or beneath the conventional life she had led. She admired creativity and felt little of it in herself. Isy, by contrast, seemed utterly sure of herself, naturally creative, and this was something Jonna wished she could find in her own life.

The weather warmed for one of their early visits to our house. We hiked up a limestone footpath to a village higher on the mountainside. How slowly Wolfie and Isy moved, because Isy wanted to notice every plant poking from the rocks; she knotted late blossoms into the dark curls of her hair. Wolfie walked with his long arms hanging loosely, smiling at the woman beside him whose shawls were constantly loosening so that, by the time we were halfway up the path, Isy was half-naked. She seemed unconscious of these unravelings, amused by our mild shock at the bronzed exposure of her breasts. In those days more tightly-wound than I am now, I came from a rather chaotic family, and perhaps that doomed me to seek tradition and stability in the world. My chief concern about Isy's nudity was not, alas, its loveliness, but what the villagers would think. Not wanting it known that *ta paidiá* were seen frolicking in the hills with wicked foreigners, I was becoming more Maniot than the Maniots.

Isy was Viennese, the daughter of a businessman. She had met Wolfie at a commune among the organic vegetables—or "wegtables," as Wolfie would have called them. He was recovering from a catastrophic marriage and a sequence of spiritual quests, and Isy must have seen in him her way out of a life in which even the communards were conventional. They were journeying east when we met them; this was only a way station in their path. Then they went east and we went west, and if their lives have changed as much as ours there is no telling where they have landed.

5

Our winter with Wolfie and Isy was spent telling stories. I told stories of Alaska, or of growing up in the American West, meeting Jonna in Colorado, moving back to be near her family in Rochester, making money to get away from making money. Wolfgang found my tales of American expansiveness fascinating, which must have flattered me. His was a Lawrentian spirit, sloppy and mildly crazed, but hot on the trail, we thought, of substantial truths. Where Isy had grown up among the baroque perfections of Vienna, Wolfie was from a village near Salzburg, a mountain boy who had learned about mendacity when, at sixteen, he found that his mother had concealed her Jewishness from him, from the whole community. She had survived the war by hiding out somewhere in Poland, but she was not fooled by the Allied victory into thinking anti-Semitism had been defeated. So she had kept her secret, and somehow Wolfie had discovered it and learned what for him was an important lesson, that people are living lies. He spoke of it in amateur anthropological terms: societies as tissues of lies, arbitrary signifiers detached from the private unhappiness of citizens. No one was living the life he or she wanted to lead; everyone was bound by the insane expectations of his or her own culture. The result was a planet of sick people, taking out their unhappiness on each other. Wolfie wanted to escape the vicious trap of self-abuse into which the world had fallen.

Perhaps we were sitting on mats by their kitchen fire when he discoursed in this way. We ate the charred flatbread Isy warmed on the coals, olives and cheese, and various greens plucked from the footpaths or from their walled garden plot, while Wolfie told us the story of his life. A professional chemist, white coat, office keys, name on the door, he had sickened of ambition at a time when it was common to do so, and he left it all behind to make his spiritual pilgrimage. He had read Hesse, so of course he went to India, accompanied by a woman with Saxon-red hair. They got married. Now Wolfie referred to her as "the bitch, this fucking bitch that I was married to."

"You must meet this woman to believe her," Isy added. "She is always controlling everything. She has this craziness of control."

"I was crazy in those days," Wolfie said, "otherwise how can I marry such a fucking, fucking bitch as this?"

On their way to India in the 1970s, Wolfie and his wife lived briefly in Greece. Land in Mani was very cheap, so they bought a ruined house in Ano Riglia. The ex-wife still owned half the house, in fact, and at one point in the winter Wolfie and Isy stayed with us because the bitch had come to visit and had driven them out with her passion for cleanliness.

India was the quest for *dharma* in a world of *maya*. I had an older brother, Doug, who made similar travels, but his quest was more political than spiritual. After living in Africa, he traveled east to make his own investigation of American involvement in Southeast Asia at the end of the Viet Nam War. When I was in high school I got letters from Doug in Cambodia at about the time Wolfie would have been in India. Wolfie had also been a mountain climber when he was younger. I had climbed with Doug in Colorado. He had climbed in several countries, but it was on a mountain near our hometown in Washington State that he fell to his death in 1979. He was twenty-eight years old. Only a year later I was in Greece, listening to Wolfie's spontaneous sermons.

Perhaps I was still numb from grief. Maybe that was part of what closed me down, made me difficult to know. I spent so much time alone, trying to write, trying to control the universe between my temples, and this Herculean effort shut out other people, including Jonna. All these years later I look back on myself and wince at my strange obsessiveness, an unedifying stupidity about other people. I was naïve enough to think I could escape the part of life I hade not yet come to understand, the part we refer to as "the real world."

Anyway, Wolfie and the bitch ended up studying with a guru in Indonesia. Rather, the bitch studied, but Wolfie was transformed. I don't know what happened to him there, though I heard stories from others about frightening moments, such as a time when they still lived in Greece and he had tried to fly, breaking his leg in a fall off the balcony.

For Wolfie it wasn't madness, of course. It was connection. It was intimacy. It was life. It was truth. The bitch did not agree. She tricked him into going to Singapore, where she had him committed. Doctors in Singapore gave him electroshock treatments. Wolfie's spiritual quest ended with a series of artificially-induced seizures that produced a temporary state of normality.

There followed a few ghost years, gardening back in Austria for an aristo-cratic family, pacific years in which he broke with the bitch and found solace in communal living. Then he met Isy and moved back to Greece. When the summer came, Wolfie would return to his teacher in Indonesia and try to learn what he had lost to electroshock.

He was a wounded man, but he never lost the romantic conviction that civilization was at fault. "Look at all these people," he would say, waving his huge hands as he spoke. "The young people in these willages, they cannot mate with each other because of tradition, they must have all this dowry shit. Their mothers wear black all of their lives because of tradition, or if the fathers are alive they beat the mothers because of tradition. And look at this American house where you live. What is this for, this clothes washer and this modern stove? What good is such a house where you don't touch the things that are feeding you? All of this is crazy. The old way and the new way are both crazy. In every country people are all the time working for money so they can have the key to the office and the name on the door and the little white coat, and in their hearts they are crying because they know this is all bullshit.

"I mean," he would say, "I can look out from my window here and see Kostas taking his goats up on the mountain like he is doing for fifty years, and his father and grandfather and great-grandfather, and it looks like paradise. I think of myself, God damn, where I am! Where I am! Did I ever think I would be in such a place? In this fucking beautiful place where people are all the time making their own little hell out of nothing. I think of this place that is so beautiful, and everyone hates his life here and follows fucking tradition. It's crazy!"

He had grown a wispy beard for winter, his unwashed hair hung to his shoulders, and his great bear's frame rocked to and fro when he spoke. "Where I am," he would say. "Where I am!" He improvised an English learned from rock and countercultural books, a jerryrigged philosophy of mysticism, loose historical data and ecology. From the lab in Austria he had moved to a kind of missionary life; he taught me how to build a compost pile and how to recognize edible plants around the house or in the fields. Sometimes we argued. When we argued politics he took the side of the terrorists, I the cause of the ordinary people who were their usual victims. When I showed him my Greek novel he was outraged by its fraudulence and he told me so to my face. When I showed him my Alaskan novel he told me it was a real story, he was impressed. He taught me something about genuineness, I suppose. He giggled like a little boy when we visited, and his embrace was like that of a mountain, swallowing me up.

Isy made culinary masterpieces out of nothing. Her salads were glazed with sugar and decorated with tiny edible flowers from the hills. She made *spanakópitta* with nettles instead of spinach, and when she discovered apricots in our yard, treated us to apricot dumplings coated with sugar. Wolfie brought out his guitar and his two songbooks: Leonard Cohen and Judy Collins. Of the four of us, Jonna sang best, but she was shy about singing in front of others. She had little confidence in her own emotions. Maybe that was one of the problems silently dooming our marriage. I was trapped in an overactive brain, an emotional escape-artist, and she was afraid to blot the air with her lovely voice. We croaked Leonard Cohen by the fire and slept on mats in their smoky little house.

I remember one lingering evening in spring when Isy had moved her cooking fire to the terrace in front of the house with its view of the village rooftops and the sea below—*san ládi*, the Greeks would say, "like oil." We were eating Isy's flatbread and looking out on the sea when two owls suddenly perched on the crooked roof of the old church below. As we watched, the owls mated furiously, emitting sharp little cries. Just as suddenly they flew away, and all was silent again.

We looked at each other with a wild surmise. The quiet had descended upon us and allowed us to witness this astounding event. There was nothing else we could do but laugh.

The red sun hovered over the oily sea. Kostas called his goats, and the village settled down to its uneasy truce, a whole history of feuds and alliances hidden behind its gray stone walls.

Jonna, 1981
PHOTO BY DON MASON

6

We did not worry about money, we worked only when we wanted to and slept the deep sleep of people recovering from some mysterious illness. Greece itself was not the cure. No country is a cure. As Wolfie would say, all countries are crazy. No, this was merely an opportunity to get away from our families, to see our homeland from a distance, to slough off accumulated anxieties and inhabit dreams remembered from the long, long nights.

In the spring we had to leave the modern house to its owners, and the result was something far more beautiful than we had anticipated. Anna had an uncle by marriage, Barba Yiorgi, who owned land south of the village in a little bay called Kalamitsi. There were olive groves and polled mulberry trees, and there was a one-room stone house that had stood empty for years. In exchange for some work on the land, Barba Yiorgi let us live there through the warm months.

Kalamitsi was a miraculous place, primitive enough to please Wolfie and Isy, but blessed with every natural convenience that a *nouveau sauvage* could desire. In ancient times, one story went, a shrine to the Nereids had stood on the headland near the bay. Some previous resident had discovered a freshwater spring on the land, and had chiseled a bowl in the rock where the water collected before draining into a slime-covered cistern. Whenever I wanted fresh water, I had merely to scrape the dead bugs off the surface of the spring and dip my pan for clear liquid that seemed blessed by the gods. From the cistern I fed my large vegetable garden, where I had used a rough mattock to hack plots for tomatoes, cucumbers, peppers, zucchini, onions, garlic, okra and potatoes. I fertilized the soil with dried pig manure scraped from a nearby shed. We grew herbs as well, and kept pots of basil about to ward off bugs.

My teacher in this activity was Petros, whose wife, Lela, cooked for the writer, Patrick Leigh Fermor. Petros had told me what to buy at the market in Kalamata, had showed me how to plant and tend my garden, and we shared the water from the cistern fed by the sacred spring.

The little stone house had a roof made of kalamus reeds, a sort of bamboo, and the tiles common to that part of the world. Mice scurried at all hours between the reeds and tiles. I screened the two windows and painted their frames and limed the walls so they looked like melted white icing. We swept the house clean, stuffed the mouse-torn mattress with grass and herbs, hung our provisions in a cage from the rafters, used an old blanket for a front door. We read by candlelight (which gave me a profound appreciation for electricity) and cooked on a one-burner gas stove Anna had loaned us. We used soap made from olive oil when we needed to wash clothes or dishes, heating water in the sun, and when we wanted to bathe we dove into the sea.

Below our little house there was a cluster of dark boulders from which we could swim. A trickle of fresh water, perhaps from the same marvelous spring that fed our garden, filled a bucket under one of the rocks. We used this gallon of fresh water to wash the salt off our skin and out of our hair when we had finished bathing in the sea.

It was a slow life. We wore few clothes and regressed to a simpler state, which was easy to do in the warm weather. Even as close as we were to the main road, we felt cut off from the tourist traffic. There was a small stand of bananas (someone's agricultural experiment) near which we had hung a hammock, and I remember lying in the hammock, reading and watching huge rats on the swaying banana leaves. They never bothered us and we never bothered them. Our only neighbors in the bay were the Leigh Fermors, and one night I heard their opera recording drifting from their villa, over the olives and cypresses to where I lay, imagining the rats enraptured by an aria. It was a gentle life, our five months in Kalamitsi. Even our toilet, a pit with a stone seat, had a glorious view of the sea. I began to feel like Wolfie, shouting, "Where I am! Where I Am!"

The author writing at Friend's house
Photo by Jonna Mason

7

Wolfie and Isy sat with us at siesta in the shade of a cypress tree, where we hoped to catch a few rags of midsummer breeze. We ate our main meal on a makeshift bench out there above the bay, falling asleep or stepping down the hot stones for a dip in the sea. The hot, motionless air rang with cicadas, and sometimes the only escape was to submerge ourselves in the bluegreen water. This was a lazy life of eating, talking, swimming, sleeping some nights under the stars, the cicadas having finally silenced when the breeze soughed down from the mountains. Days so hot and slow we were like dogs panting on a porch. Make no movement that is not absolutely necessary. Watch the ants crawl through the dry grass on their busy little workroads. Peel open a fig and spread it on your fingertips, sucking the red flesh inside. Then sleep and wait for the night to come, when the olive trees looked like Nereids.

Of course we were intoxicated. Greece became our dream of freedom and ease. We wrote to friends in America, telling them—just as Henry Miller had once told his friends in New York—to drop everything and come to the land of truth and beauty, the Peloponnesos, "a soft, quick stab to the heart." It was a lotos-eating life in which we were stoned on sea and sunlight. We were *ta paidiá* in more ways than we knew, ignorant of responsibility, forgetful of the deeper rewards of work. For Jonna and me, it would take great suffering, divorce and marriage to others to begin to place ourselves in the real world, and when I returned to Greece sixteen years later it would be almost as another man, hopefully better equipped to love the place for what it is, to accept its many changes, and not to desire it only for my own gratification.

When the time came for Wolfie to leave, he and Isy stopped at Kalamitsi to visit us, and to say farewell. It had all been planned; Wolfie would go off alone and make his way to Indonesia. Money had come from Austria, perhaps from the book he intended to publish. Isy would stay a few more weeks in Greece, then return to her mother's house in Vienna.

We sat up late by lamplight, talking and telling stories. We had been through the winter together, had larked in meadows when the spring came and lazed through summer. We had become friends. That huge gulf I felt between us when we first met had disappeared, and I felt a brotherly bond with Wolfie that I missed with my own dead brother. The year had changed all of us, as if the scattered notes of our characters were finding the thread of a story, and in the story a new sort of homeland.

In the morning Wolfie said he wanted no good-byes. We were to stay put by the house where we could see him walking away. Isy could start on the path with him, but then she was to turn around and come back. He seemed eager to be on the road again, and his step was light as he carried his rucksack into the olive groves, an unkempt bear of a man who waved a huge hand and disappeared into the trees.

We saw him a last time when he stepped onto the road that curved away into the village, where he would catch the Athens bus. We were calling his name and blowing kisses. Then he was gone. Isy came back to us, sobbing, and stood a long time in Jonna's embrace.

Who knows how long we might have stayed in such a position, waving as Wolfie disappeared or embracing Isy or sitting without talking in our little house? I can imagine us frozen there in the dream of expatriate freedom, the almost insane belief that we could be other than ourselves. As it happened, we did not stay. I was offered a screenwriting job in the U.S., adapting my unpublished novel about Alaska, and suddenly became quite drunk on the idea of writerly success. I would go back to America, I thought, and live a life of unfettered bliss, writing and being paid pots of money for it.

So we went back in the fall of 1981, and I worked at the writer's trade and for a time I did make money. Then the company that hired me folded like a house of cards in a hurricane. I was still the same troubled pile of unfinished notes, only now I was older, and Jonna was moving slowly but inexorably away on a path of her own. Everything we thought we had escaped by living in the village had only been put on hold. Within four years our marriage had failed, and I had failed to make a living as a writer.

Every now and then, word came from Wolfie and Isy. She had left Austria to join him in Indonesia, where he completed his course with the guru. Then he took an interest in the chemistry of rice cultivation, and went to work for the Indonesian agricultural ministry. I read these brief reports as I labored in graduate school, having decided in my thirties to teach. Finally, there was a card saying that they would come to America—Canada, actually—and they hoped to see us, not knowing we were divorced.

I have not heard from them since.

I remember Wolfie's big, flat-toothed smile when he listened to stories around the fire, his long-fingered hands dancing in air when he talked. He spoke of human behavior with the freewheeling curiosity of a self-made anthropologist. He once told me that he was able to walk among shy Indonesian crabs without frightening them by moving in steps of tai chi slowness, as if he weren't moving at all. I wonder who he has moved among now, and whether anyone can see him watching.

Did they ever come to the New World? I almost dreaded their seeing the conventional creature I had become. What a gulf there might be between us. A broken marriage and a new life later, would I be able to let down my guard and meet them again? Our first meeting was by accident, or fate if you believe in such things, and now I do not know how to reach them anymore, or even whether they are alive. Many days go by when I do not think of Wolfie and Isy. Perhaps they have become conventional, like me—house, car, job, name on the door, the whole show. Perhaps they too have discovered a kind of ordinary happiness.

What would Wolfie say if he knew I was thinking such things?

II

GREEK FEVER

This is not a cage and you are not a lion.

—Melina Mercouri in *Topkapi*

1

But all that awful future hadn't happened when we first arrived in the village and fell in love with Anna. A friend of Friend and Margarita for many years, she was our savior in those early days.

I wrote about her in my journal when we had been in the village a few weeks:

> She is a sturdy woman, dressed in mourning for her husband, Christos, who died only last summer (her father wears a black band on his left arm). She has bright eyes when she talks, a bit of a mustache. She commands her end of town from the window above her hand-turned sewing machine (where she seems constantly at work), and yet she can be so simple and soft to us, knowing we need all the help we can get.

We were learning Greek, but not at a satisfactory pace, so Anna's natural thespianism came in handy:

> Words are only half of it—phrases of Greek, syllables of English. The rest is the dramatic range of her voice and body—and the fact that she is careful to speak slowly. Whenever we come to her house there is food—retsina, olives, salad, bread, strips of smoked meat, cooked vegetables like beans and eggplant and onions. Somehow, in our pidgin Greek and her pidgin English, we have discussed the American election, its possible effect on Greco-Turkish

relations, and the long, tragic history of her sister Voula's love affairs before her happy marriage.

The house of Anna and her father, Theodoros, was a stone, two-story square that stood right at the juncture of the old and new villages. Though she rarely left those walls for much of a year—out-mourning the best mourners anyone had ever known—Anna seemed to absorb every burp and hiccup of village life. Nothing happened that she did not know about. We visited almost daily and often ate meals with her and Theodoros, who became our "professor," helping us with words from our Greek dictionary. Sometimes we cooked a meal in our modern kitchen and carried it to their home on the opposite end of the agora, and they graciously bore the gesture, pointing out later where we had failed to use enough olive oil or garlic in our cooking. Every meal was a lesson time, a lesson in the history of privations in their lives or a lesson in war or civil war or songs or the little fables called *paramythia*. Anna, who said she would kill herself sooner than live through another war, told us of killings once while cleaning okra in a bowl on her lap, a knife clenched in one fist, then drawn across her throat, her face going dark in the firelight.

Since Anna would not go out, village women often came to her and sat before her fire in the colder evenings, gossiping. Sometimes Lela was among them, and we learned through Lela about Kyrie Michali, the great writer who lived in the villa at Kalamitsi—this was Patrick Leigh Fermor's name among the Greeks. We learned that many of the foreign tourists who passed through the village were whores and devils, exposing their flesh to the world out on the beach. Bah, they were fornicators who didn't care who saw them—even the priest! The deep conservatism of the Mani could be seen in the crow-like women who darted about, descrying changes and the horrors now visible on television sets in the *kafeneía*. Anna and Theodoros had their own television, no doubt due to their connection with Friend, and sometimes neighbors came by to join us watching the news or the evening soap operas. As the lone man of the household, Theodoros sat nervously outside the circle of conversation, now and then growling orders at his daughter. Anna's hands were always busy. If she wasn't sewing or preparing food she was knitting, or unraveling an old sweater to knit a new one.

Jonna started knitting under her tutelage. We went to Kalamata to buy yarn for a sweater, and there we learned that the word for soft, *malaká*, was perilously close to the word for someone soft in the head, self-polluted through masturbation: *maláka*. Change an accent mark in Greek and you can give yourself a lot of trouble. *Malakía* is masturbation, but also, as it were, the condition of masturbatoriness. One can joke that everything's in a state of *malakía*, and sometimes that seems just the right word. In any case, we succeeded in scandalizing the old woman selling yarn in the Kalamata market, and the yarn we got was not very soft. Months later, Jonna presented me with a sweater as dense and heavy as a coat of mail.

I adapted quickly to a lazy life of reading, writing, walking in the hills or snorkling in the sea, watching quiver-fulls of small fish dart before my eyes. But Jonna saw how limiting our condition was, and insisted that we try to learn better Greek. Anna arranged for a teenaged girl, Aleka, to come to our house several nights a week over three months to give us lessons for a small fee. Though she had trouble with her own lessons at the local *gymnasio* and was desperate to escape the confines of the village, Aleka turned out to be the best language teacher I have ever had in my life.

Shy at first, she quickly perceived that we needed discipline. When she stopped by the house we served her coffee or tea, and she drilled us in the alphabet, then in reading from the school primers we found in Friend's library, books that started with *Na to*—There it is—and led us to *paramythia*, a sort of Hellenic Mother Goose. The three of us often engaged in pantomime, trying to explain abstract concepts, or drew pictures of what we meant, and ended up laughing hysterically over our errors. For example, a young man in the village name Stratis was sometimes called *O trelós*, the crazy fellow, because he could be heard singing at all hours despite the inbred dourness of Mani, and was sentimental about the cats that bred about his parents' house. He was married to a beautiful young woman from another village, Elefthería, or Freedom. Once Jonna got her tongue twisted on the name and called her *Efimerída*—Newspaper.

As task-mistress and schoolmarm, Aleka loved our mistakes, and gently chided us with them while she ran us through verb conjugations and noun declensions. Joan Didion once wrote that grammar was a piano she played by ear, and I was just that sort of language learner—everything from context rather than rote. So I learned fluently but badly, and it was not until I met writers Yiorgos Chouliaras and Katerina Anghelaki-Rooke in later years that I began to face up to my bad grammar in Greek.

Aleka's older brother was away in England as a graduate student, eventually becoming a professor, but Aleka herself had no intention of going on in school. For her, as for most young people in the village, escape to Kalamata or Athens was the dream. Her father spent much of the year away in the merchant navy, and her mother, Pipitsa, held hearth and home together with the sinews of her personality. In summer, when her father returned for a few months' vacation with the family, Aleka's joy was radiant. She invited us to the midday meal with her family. We had rabbit, and I noticed Pipitsa's enthusiasm for the skull and its contents while her youngest daughter, Evangelia, sobbed in her chair.

We were eating the little girl's pet.

Soon a visiting relative brought out his guitar, and the fierceness vanished from the mustached face of Aleka's father, and we all sang or hummed under the vine leaves of their narrow terrace.

So Aleka's lessons were softened by friendship and reinforced by daily dealings in the village. We shopped at the markets of both Petros and Vassili, bought wine and ouzo in six-litre bottles from Michali, decanting the liquids into smaller bottles at home. Mani is an olive-growing region, but wine grapes are not grown there, so wine makers buy the must from other regions. It was considered a stupid extravagance to buy wine with the famous labels. In tavernas we bought "local" wine in cans. The pine resin flavor of the wine could be subtle or strong, depending on its maker, while the *ouzo's* sweet licorice deceived you and left you with a wicked hangover.

Our language lessons revolved around food, its preparation, its manners. Theodoros sent me for seed potatoes at the Kalamata market, and I loosened a strip of soil in Friend's terraced yard with a mattock, planting a winter garden of potatoes, garlic and spinach. With most tourists gone, we were more openly acknowledged as residents by the villagers—or at least as people who had to be tolerated since we were not going away. We were known customers in the two tavernas that remained open in winter, their windows steamed and their wood stoves stoked, the heat radiating from long stove-pipes that crossed the room and exited through the wall. We ate whatever was in season or had come fresh from the sea. More and more frequently we were able to set aside our dictionary and converse about these elementary things, and our efforts to learn Greek demonstrated that we were sincere in our respect. If Jonna hadn't insisted we learn, our lives in the village would have been terribly diminished.

Jonna. Why did she have such trouble believing in her beauty? "Are you there?" she would say to me. "You're always locked away, always writing. I wonder where you are." There is so much to regret about the young man I was in those days, so much to wish I had done differently. Are all writers such monsters of egotism, so deaf to the people they love? How can someone who practices the art of paying attention to the world fail so completely to hear such a lovely voice?

"You're a poet," a friend has said to me. "Put some poems in your book."
"Okay," I said.
So here is a folksong I translated years after our lessons with Aleka:

I kissed red lips and my lips too were dyed,
and the handkerchief I wiped them with turned red,
and the running stream where I washed the kerchief
colored the shoreline far out into mid-sea.
An eagle swooped down for a drink, and its wings
as it rose stained half the sun, all of the moon.

2

That winter we helped Anna and Theodoros harvest their olive crop. Anna was willing to leave the house for this because it counted as work and could not be perceived as an unmournful activity. We rose early and joined her and Theodoros, who let me push the wheelbarrow loaded with sacks and tools or carry the old wooden ladder until we got to one of their parcels of land in the terraced groves. There we unrolled tarps on the ground beneath a tree to be harvested. Then, some of us on the ladder or standing on the thicker limbs, others on the ground getting the tree's lower branches, we knocked olives onto the tarps or combed them out with little rakes called *lanária*. Sometimes the fruit was so ready to fall that a shake of a limb would send showers of green olives to the ground. Sometimes Theodoros brought out a cane and whacked the branches as if to punish them, muttering obscenities under his breath. When a tree appeared to be harvested, the ground tarps were gathered so we could spill their fruit into giant sacks and sew them up.

Standing among olive boughs one could pause to look down on the calm sea or up at the snow-capped peak of Prophitis Elias (named for the Patron Saint of mountains), listening to the chatter of other harvesters in surrounding groves, the occasional grind of a motorized cart hauling sacks of olives to the factory, the faint knock-knock-knocking of a fishing caique out on the sea, or the shepherd's flute theme music of *Trito Programma* or some more popular music from a radio. In the afternoon we would pause, sitting on the tarps for a meal of bread, cheese, olives, fruit and wine. Anna brought oil for us to dip the bread in. "This is the best food. Bread and oil. Nothing else." We ate much less meat in Greece. More fish, of course, and plenty of fruit and vegetables in season. As Americans who had grown up without vegetable gardens, we had never before tasted the full flavors of vegetables and fruit grown with minimal chemical interference, picked only when ripe. Though village food was hardly *haute cuisine*, it seemed to us the greatest fare in the world. One bought bread fresh almost daily from the village baker, a giant fellow who lived with his mother. When the American Thanksgiving came around, we arranged with Wolfie and Isy to buy half a turkey, which the baker cooked for us among the loaves in his oven. A real extravagance, the familiar taste of turkey was a particular comfort we tried explaining to our friends. Isy made one of her sugared salads of greens gathered in the hills to go with it. The tray coming out of the oven was also full of browned potatoes and carrots and onions in the bird's juices. It was a feast.

The olive harvest stretched from November well into the winter. When heavy rains came, few people worked in the groves. Old women would greet us in the *agorá* with one word, "*Heimónas!*"—Winter!—and raise their eyes in despair at the clouded peaks. It was remarkable how many of these women limped because they had taken falls from ladders during the harvest and broken their hips. They lurched like drunken crows with kerchiefed heads, muttering, "*Ti na kánoume?*"—What can we do? Weather was fate, and moods were bound to its fickle behaviors. But on harvest days the village emptied into the groves, and all night one heard the few motorized tractors pulling wagonloads of olive sacks to the factory.

The olives were ground between huge stone wheels, and the pressed oil gouted into tins to be hauled to Kalamata. The first pressing of oil was the most precious; people sometimes dipped their cups in it, drinking it straight.

I remember at Christmas we took a day off from the harvest. That night at Anna's we had octopus grilled over the fire, sawing off edible bits of leg with our knives as it cooked. And Anna relaxed her moral code enough to countenance card playing into the wee hours.

3

When we lived in Friend's house, our neighbor across the dirt road was a lone old woman, Erasmia. Her tiny concrete house sat atop a gully that became a gushing stream in winter thunderstorms. Erasmia had a subtle boundary dispute going with Friend over their property line marked by a row of stones. Some days I noticed that the stones had been moved, giving her a few feet more land, and I would wait until dark to move them back to their original position. Later I saw her puttering in her yard like a crow, dressed in black, an eye trained on me while I puttered in ours. Jonna and I tried to be good neighbors. I took her a present of some food, knowing that she had been to see some doctors in Kalamata, and asked after her health.

Erasmia gave me an inconsolable look. "I am not well."

"What's wrong. Do they know?"

She shrugged bitterly. "Something in my blood."

Then came the word that meant "white blood," *leukemia*. Erasmia went away to a hospital, asking me to feed her rabbits while she was gone.

Once I went to feed the rabbits in their makeshift cages and noticed that a brown one was missing. In a panic, I ran about Erasmia's yard, looking everywhere. The poor old woman, I thought. She was ill, she was poor, and now one of her rabbits had gone missing!

I had crossed the road to Friend's and started for the steps to the front door when I noticed some unusual movement among the rosemary and oleander. I looked, and there was the twitching little face, the pair of eyes.

When I reached for the scruff of its neck it lurched away. Soon I was chasing this rabbit all over Friend's yard. For a while I gave up. Jonna suggested I ask another neighbor what to do, so I walked down hill to the house of an elderly woman named Aphrodite. She opened the door a crack, peered out at me.

"Madame Aphrodite," I said with what must have seemed hilarious formality. "One of Madame Erasmia's rabbits got away. It's in the yard." I pointed. "I don't know what to do."

"It's nothing," said Aphrodite. "Kill it. Cut its throat. Cook it with onions and tomatoes. It's delicious."

"But it isn't mine. It's Erasmia's."

"Bah, it's in your yard. It's yours. Erasmia will be dead soon. What does she need a rabbit for? Kill it. It's nothing."

Aphrodite shut the door. I walked back up to Friend's yard, wondering what etiquette required of me now. I certainly didn't want to be hauled before the magistrate who periodically came to the village on a charge of stealing a rabbit.

This time, determined to catch the little beast, I snatched up a plastic laundry basket and stomped around the yard, hoping to spring a trap. Each time I hurled the basket at the rabbit, it hopped away. At last I cornered it, shivering and twitching under a rosemary shrub. Instead of coming at it from the side where it could see me, I reached down through the shoots of evergreen from above, got a firm grip on the fur collar and yanked it upward. The poor thing squirmed like a furry heartbeat. I dashed across the road with the rabbit and threw it into its cage, checking again to make sure all rabbits were present and accounted for. I had never butchered an animal in my life if you don't count seafood, and I wasn't about to start.

When Erasmia returned from the hospital she was clearly very ill, her movements slowed. She looked at me tearfully in our few conversations, but seemed to have no language for what was happening to her. Then one day the gray-bearded priest came to give her final unction, and before we knew it she was dead. Relatives arrived from somewhere. The coffin stood outside her door, and the activity of women meant that her body was being washed and dressed in preparation for the grave.

We began to hear laments. After the all-night vigil over the body, the voices of women singing in alternating choruses rose from inside the house. I waited a long time before going over, but when it seemed enough men had gathered outside the house, smoking and talking, I joined them. Jonna did not feel like going. It was too intrusive; we knew hardly anyone there. But I had had dealings with the deceased, and besides, I wanted to see a Greek funeral.

I spoke awkwardly with some of the men while we waited, and from inside the house came the wailing and singing, a constant incantation. It was the *mirolóyia*, the dirges for which Mani is famous. I had read about them in Paddy Leigh Fermor's book, *Mani*, and no doubt that overlay of literary reference gave the occasion a particular importance to me. I did not take notes on what I heard, which would have seemed rude to me if not to those present, but I was at least dimly aware of the privilege. These songs were spontaneous compositions in a long-established pattern, making use of conventional tropes about death as well as specific details about the deceased. They were an intimate and very real tie to the great oral tradition.

The priest arrived with the ikon for the funeral procession. He went indoors to recite the *Trisayio* over Erasmia's body. Then the coffin was closed and carried out of the house, and I followed the long march to the church for her funeral.

Sometime during the service I left the church, feeling out of place. No one ever chased me out of an Orthodox service in Greece, but my ignorance of ritual made it hard for me to stay the course through many of them. I was not brought up in any church, and at that point of my life had read parts of the Bible only in a college classroom, so I always felt like a fraud, despite my amateur interest in chants and manners.

After the service they would have marched out of town to the cemetery and buried her, then returned to the *plateia* by the church for *kólliva*, the boiled wheat mixed with sugar traditionally eaten after burials. Someone brought us cups of it later on. Indeed, I remember wandering past a mountain church later that year and having a perfect stranger tell me that someone had just been "planted" and hand me a little paper cup of *kólliva*. The anxiety about joining these rituals was all mine.

Erasmia's relatives wasted no time in planting themselves at her house to protect her few possessions from theft, like a scene from *Zorba the Greek*, the pillaging of Bouboulina's possessions.

By now Erasmia's bones have long since been exhumed, washed and stored in the village ossuary. By now the bones of Theodoros and so many others have joined them, put away in initialed boxes. It still strikes me that, with its ritualization of each stage of grief and its recognition of a connection to the dead for the rest of one's life, the Orthodox way of death is the most beautiful I have ever encountered. Not only is each grave plot recycled after exhumation, but the living can visit the bones of the dead. Of course I also remember the bone houses of tiny, almost deserted mountain villages, and how strange the uncared-for bones seemed, spilled out of cardboard boxes or scattered over the land. The atmosphere of transgression leaves a bitter taste, even in the mouth of a doubter.

Now another translation, or modification, this time adapted from the Greek of Yannis Ritsos:

Lean girls are gathering salt on the shore,
bending to bitterness, ignorant of the open sea.

A sail, a white sail, beckons from the blue,
and what they do not see in the distance
    darkens with longing.

4

At the end of the American academic year Friend returned to his house in the village, anxious to prepare for Margarita's arrival when she had finished teaching school. This was when we got to know Friend better, going with him to Kalamata when he bought a small sailboat, hearing about his experiences as a prisoner of war in World War II. He relaxed quickly, pouring himself a shot of ouzo with his first cigarette before breakfast. Jonna and I stayed with him to help in the preparations. We knew our time in the house was up, but by then we had decided to stay on in the village. The film rights to my unpublished Alaskan novel had been optioned and it didn't seem that money would be a problem.

Anna found a solution to our dilemma. She arranged with Barba Yiorgi that *ta paidiá* would live in the little stone house at Kalamitsi, rent free, in exchange for some work on the land. "It seems it is in my *moira*, or fate," I wrote to a friend, "to be a gardener." For weeks I trundled supplies out in Theodoros's wheelbarrow: paint, lime for whitewash, cooking supplies and borrowed garden tools. The little house had not been inhabited for years, and it took us a lot of work to clean and prepare it. Also in those days I began to plant my vegetable garden under the tutelage of Lela's husband, Petros, a laconic man with a pencil-thin mustache and a jaunty black beret.

This was when our warm weather idyll began, our hippie existence of sun-and-sea worship in the olive groves.

There was just one catch: Barba Yiorgi. In his eighties then, he had lived more than fifty years in America and had become rich, eventually owning a trucking company. While his money allowed his children and grandchildren to become educated Americans, the process of acquiring it turned Barba Yiorgi into a bitter old coot. His biggest fault, from my point of view, was that he didn't like living things, especially plants. On his return to Greece he built himself a cement pile over a sandy lot in Kalamata, and much of his waking energy was devoted to seeing that no living organism survived there but himself. He wanted barrenness. He liked the clean lines of concrete, considering them more efficient, less troublesome than the clutter of life. He even kept his silver hair as short as possible without actually shaving his head.

He approved of my work on the house. He hummed with pleasure that I had uprooted all the grass in front of the house to protect us from hiding snakes, but he wanted me to cut down an ancient mulberry tree on the land, and I refused.

I tried reason. I tried asking Anna to reason with him as well, but Yiorgi wouldn't budge. The tree was unsightly. It was useless. There was no silk industry now, so why have a mulberry tree?

"For berries?" I offered.

"It's only one tree, only a few berries. Cut it down. I'll be back next week and I want to see it cut."

I never did cut down that tree.

For the entire five months of our life in Kalamitsi, I dreaded any appearance by Barba Yiorgi with his axe and pruning sheers. We tried not to think of him all the time. Indeed, it was often relaxing there—whole days spent reading in the hammock, watching the ants march by. And what a year of reading that was! I remember devouring volume after volume without interruption: Homer, Seferis, Cavafy, Leigh Fermor, Chatwin, Dostoyevsky, Borges, Woolf, Twain, Shakespeare, I.B. Singer, Updike, Philip Sherrard, and Patrick White's spooky novel about an artist, *The Vivisector*. I read about Eskimos. I read about Napoleon's invasion of Russia. Only in Greece, liberated from job and other responsibilities, have I ever been free to read so widely and with such total immersion.

But then the dreaded call would come. Jonna spotted Barba Yiorgi's Volvo parked up at the road, the old man picking his way down the footpath. I dropped everything, flew across the terraced land to the bluff, where I scuttled down the rough and rugged rocks, and hid myself at the base of the cliff. More than once I could hear Barba Yiorgi asking about me on the ledge above—luckily he was too frail to risk the descent—and Jonna explaining that I had important film work to do and had gone to Kalamata to see someone.

5

That summer the old man's granddaughter, Christina, came from America for an extended stay, dividing her time between his monstrous house and Anna's home in the village. Christina was a recent college graduate, eager to become reacquainted with her ancestral country, and I remember her calm humor and lovely smile. She knew how to handle the old man.

Once, as Barba Yiorgi drove them on the Kalamata road, they had come to a bus broken down at a narrow hairpin turn.

"They shouldn't stop here," the old man said.

"Grandpa, I think they have some trouble."

"They're blocking the road. It's against the law."

"Grandpa, be patient. See, the driver is waving at us to wait."

"These drivers are too ignorant. I don't have time."

"Grandpa, you can't pass them, there isn't room. Grandpa, stop!"

The old man put his head down and stepped on the gas. Between the broken down bus and the precipice there was barely enough room to maneuver, so he nudged his Volvo against the bus and pushed ahead, scraping the passenger side of his car slowly and methodically along the entire length of the bus. By the time they screeched to the end of its siding, the bus driver stood screaming on the tarmac in front of them. "You crazy old man! You idiot! What are you doing? What have you done to my bus?"

"Your bus is too fat," Barba Yiorgi said.

"What? You donkey! You goat! You masturbator! How could you?"

"And the road is too narrow. They should make it wider."

Without quite neglecting her family responsibilities, Christina began to spend more of her time in the village, away from the old man. There was soon another reason for this. That summer she met a young man in the village whose family had recently returned from Australia. Known as Jimmy, he was a handsome, thickset fellow who spoke both Greek and English with a down-under accent. Christina grew fond of him, but they discovered that it was impossible to pursue any sort of courtship in the village. Between his family and other prying locals, privacy was too rare a luxury. Young people who wanted to court each other couldn't even hide in the hills for fear they would be found and punished, so they often escaped to Kalamata or Athens when money allowed.

There were stories of scandals in the past—teenagers who'd hung themselves in despair or been killed by fathers or brothers for dishonoring the family. And there had already been one scandal in the village that year. Elefthería had tired of her marriage to Stratis the fisherman, tired of living with his parents in a village not her own, and had run off with a boy from her own village, where she now lived under the protection of her family.

Christina and Jimmy had both experienced more liberal ways in other lands, so they took to visiting us at Kalamitsi, where the walled olive groves or the rocks by the sea gave them plenty of privacy. They couldn't be seen in public holding hands or kissing or even talking together without supervision. What we gave them was a place in which they could begin to get acquainted.

Slowly we learned of an odd side to Jimmy's character, a fondness for right wing politics that he voiced with a quiet, steady conviction. He seemed friendly enough. We never considered him dangerous and were happy for Christina that she seemed on the verge of finding genuine companionship. It was only after their engagement party that all hell broke loose.

But before that came my Greek fever.

6

I had never before lived in a place of such intense sunlight, and in the long, hot days of that summer often worked in my vegetable patch or swam in the sea without bothering to protect myself. I never liked hats. By then I had a full beard and mustache, and was vain of the way the sun had bleached them. Jonna's thick hair was sunstreaked, her skin smoothed by olive oil and darkened by sunlight.

We were both fond of wine. At some point late that summer of 1981—was it July or August?—the combination of sun and wine nearly did me in. Dehydration was part of it. One night after sunset, I sat with Jonna by the still-warm outer wall of the house, watching the eerie shapes of the olive trees. In daylight I was driven half mad by the high-pitched whine of cicadas, and I loved that moment after sundown when they suddenly fell silent. But that night I felt faint. We were drinking a bottle of sweet wine from Samos, a gift from friends, but the effect of the wine could not explain what was happening in my brain or the lethargy in my limbs. At one point I tried to stand and fell back against the wall. Thinking it must be exhaustion, I staggered inside to our bed under the mosquito net.

Neither of us took it seriously at first. Jonna slept beside me, and as I began to sweat from fever I tried not to wake her. Just a year before, in Mexico, when my father had gone to live there and we had a partial family gathering after my brother's death, I had come down with a case of *turista*. On that occasion the fever lasted only twenty-four hours, followed by several awkward days of liquefaction. Perhaps that night in Greece I thought I was catching a dose of the same thing. Remembering how I had hallucinated under the influence of that tropical fever—my soaked bedsheets becoming a mountain range and then a nest of snakes—I steeled myself.

Whether I slept that night I do not recall, but by morning the fever was very high and I was too weak to move.

Jonna nursed me through most of that day. Along toward sunset I was getting worried. Out at Kalamitsi, all alone, with a husband too weak to sit up in bed, Jonna decided it was time to move me into the village.

Somehow, leaning heavily on her shoulders, I managed the walk to Friend and Margarita's house, waiting exhausted on their steps while Jonna went inside to ask if we could use the beds in their basement. Our hosts welcomed us and helped us settle in, and I collapsed into the single bed from which I would hardly move for more than a week.

The fever continued that night. Again my sheets were soaked, my body oily with sweat. I stank. The look of my face apparently terrified everyone who saw it. If I got anything down at all, it was water and a few drops of soup.

The next day found me delirious, tossing and moaning, and Jonna sent for the doctor.

Niki's friend Stamatis had moved on, and we now had an attractive young woman in residence at the clinic. I remember her leaning over me in the dark of that room. Her beauty and health made me feel ashamed of my condition. It was like a scene from some hospital movie, the concerned faces of Jonna and our friends beside the young doctor's. I was barely conscious, and it had occurred to me that I might be dying. They certainly looked at me as if I were dying. I even considered that dying to end this misery was not such a bad bargain. Dying was easy compared to this.

Poked and prodded while the doctor questioned my wife, I heard that my fever was very high and my liver seemed enlarged. I was seriously dehydrated and sun-stroked and perhaps something else. She said there was little to do other than wait it out, taking water when I could and aspirin for the fever.

I spent that night certain I was dying, and could feel my brain like a shriveled melon inside my skull. My hair and beard were drenched with sweat. My own stench appalled me, and I drifted in and out of hallucinations—a bone house, skulls full of screaming cicadas. Time could not go fast enough. Other people came and went in a separate universe, while I was cocooned in this oily agony, this slow pain that would not go away.

On the third or fourth day the fever broke, but I was too weak even to raise my head from the wet pillow. Soon enough, though, I had to move, because I developed a colossal case of the runs. Luckily, Friend and Margarita had a modern flushing toilet in their basement, and Jonna stoically helped me to it every few minutes for another gush from my innards. This is not how a young, romantic husband wishes to be seen.

Whatever sort of dysentery I had contracted along with sunstroke, I was too weak to move further than the toilet for another ten days. If I were to compare miseries between the high fever and this dependent condition, I'm not sure which I would prefer. Though I soon realized that I was going to live, I was for several more days sick enough to desire death.

When I could make my own way to the toilet, Jonna was free to spend more time upstairs. I filled the lonely hours by reading a fat history book, watched over by slim little geckoes clinging to the walls. The French army was getting picked apart as it retreated from Moscow.

"Are you going to the *gléndi*?" Anna asked us. "Christina and Jimmy are engaged."

It was late September, and we had just returned from weeks of travel by bus and boat to Skyros and then across northern Greece to Yanina, finding the mountains of Epiros in autumn an entirely different aspect of the country. By that time we knew that I had been hired to write the screenplay about Alaska, and were planning our return home.

While we were away on our travels, Christina and Jimmy continued to meet at Kalamitsi, then their relationship took a serious turn. The families would not allow them to progress further without an official engagement, so a party in celebration was planned.

Now we found it difficult to see anything of the happy couple. She was whisked away on shopping expeditions or guarded by relatives, and Jimmy seemed almost in hiding, perhaps preparing himself for the big event.

The party was held at the school in a room large enough to fit much of the village, with food-laden tables surrounding a space left open for dancing. Music blared from a cassette player, and I conversed with a mustached goatherd at our table, who mixed his retsina with Coca-Cola. We ate and drank, and the volume rose as toasts were followed by dancing. By that time we had come to know the Leigh Fermors better and I saw Paddy across the room and went to speak with him, though my hero-worship still made me awkwardly deferential. He was having a good time. We were all at least one sheet to the wind.

I tried dancing but never got the footwork right. Paddy danced arm in arm in a ring of men, and was royally applauded for his skill. And then the wedding songs began, a series of choruses alternating between men and women in the room, taunting each other with outrageous ribaldry and laughter. Paddy sang in the thick of it, beating time with one sweatered arm.

We were looped when we staggered home that night, so I'm not sure I can trust any of my memories of the party. Years later, Paddy would gently ask me, "I say, can you tell me something? Did you and I carry the young woman home that night? I seem to remember she was too drunk to walk, but I'm not sure I haven't dreamed it."

I wished I could answer him. It would be a great story to tell—how with Paddy Leigh Fermor, perhaps the greatest living writer of English prose, legendary traveler and *bon vivant*, I carried the bride-to-be up some staircase in the dead of night. Unfortunately, I feel reasonably confident that I was not there.

III

GETTING TO KNOW MICHALI

Writers are like Odysseus sailing through the
siren-islands, insecurely lashed to the mast.

—Patrick Leigh Fermor, "The Aftermath of Travel"

1

Meeting Patrick Leigh Fermor in December 1980 proved one of the great gifts of my life. Of course there had been sightings before that—a man with matinee-idol looks walking the road into the village, erect in military sweater, going to fetch his mail. Or on the road down from the hills as he passed Friend's house. We had been staying in the seaside village since August, two aimless young Americans sampling life abroad, and as our Greek improved and this sunny coast came into focus we discerned much talk about Michali, who lived in the villa to the south in the bay called Kalamitsi. Much was made of names. The Irish "Patrick" worked no magic in the Orthodox world, so in the war he had adopted his middle name, Michael, and to the Greeks he was henceforth Michali. To English friends he was Paddy. The former name was the legend, you might say, while the latter belonged to the man.

It was in Friend's concrete and brick pile, not yet sufficiently hidden by fruit trees and climbing vines, that I found *Mani* and *Roumeli*, and began to read. Then I bought *A Time of Gifts* at a shop in Kalamata and was trebly hooked. Eventually I borrowed Paddy's other books from the author himself and read them all straight through. I distinctly remember that his prose made me hungry, and I had to get up for a plate of figs and cheese before returning to bed where, opening his book, I dove into pools of bright prose.

So I had seen and read him. I desired nothing more than to be in the company of writers, as if their *mojo* might rub off on me—as if I too could be a writer and live in such beautiful circles. I had met Bruce Chatwin in the village (a story for the next chapter) and knew he was a guest of the Fermors.

Now I nailed down a scrap of courage, jotted a note of appreciation, and waited. In due course a telephone call came from Joan, Paddy's wife, whose accent evoked an aristocratic universe I had experienced only in movies and books. Would we come to lunch? That would be lovely.

Admitting people like me into his life is one of Paddy's vices, the distraction of conviviality too often keeping him from his desk, but to this day I remain grateful to him for this small lapse in discipline. Over the years, Paddy and Joan have meant more to me than I could ever convey to them—as models of graciousness, always curious about the world. More than two decades later it would be pointed out to me that Paddy was a youthful spirit, Joan an older one. He was all energy, she more reserved, growing into a wisdom I began to appreciate more deeply over the years and miss terribly now that she is gone. But Paddy was the dashing hero in ways he couldn't help, and I was a star-struck young writer with a smart and beautiful wife, and perhaps this childless couple found some harmless charm in that.

Though we had passed the bay and their villa many times on our walks to other villages, we had never been down to it and nearly got lost thrashing about for the trail. At last we followed the high stone wall of their garden to the roofed gate and were admitted to that extraordinary compound of cobbled paths and a house that combined the best Mediterranean ideals, large sunny vistas and an artful containment of stone and tile. Old friends were there, including Xan and Magouche Fielding, and we were the young interlopers briefly admitted to their more intimate circle.

That first meal began as most others in fair weather have done, with drinks out on one of the terraces. Because it was winter we sat out in the sun, the bright sea visible beyond the narrow cypress trees of the garden. Paddy and Xan were robust in conversation and, for the benefit of their young American guests, quite fatherly. Joan and Magouche were less loquacious at first, but patient with our youth. The Fieldings lived in Spain (or was it Andora?) and I learned that Xan liked Almería, the city on the Costa Blanca, setting of so many spaghetti westerns. I remembered reading *Anna Karenina* in cafes there when Generalísimo Franco was still alive—my first hitchiking tour of Europe five years before.

I recently looked up Xan's London *Times* obituary and learned that he had been born (in 1918) Alexander Wallace Fielding in Ooteamund, India, to a military family. Brought up in the south of France (he would later make much of his living translating books by Pierre Boulle and others), he attended Charterhouse School in England—one of several mentioned by Robert Graves in *Goodbye to All That*. But like Paddy he was early infected with restlessness and a strong dislike of authority, and before the war he tried his hand at several professions, including running a bar. He happened to be on Cyprus when war broke out, and "found a not totally uncongenial berth in army intelligence."

After his exploits on Crete, Xan parachuted into France, where he was captured and imprisoned by the Gestapo. He then had one of those remarkable experiences you read about in lives like Dostoyevsky's. Sentenced to death, he was one day marched out of his cell convinced he would be shot, only to learn that his freedom had been secured through the wiles of "Pauline"—the famous spy Christine Granville, who was herself later executed. The trim and athletic man I was talking to, who seemed so eloquent and modest, had won both the D. S. O. and the Croix de Guerre, had written several books about travel, the war, casinos and other subjects, had translated *The Planet of the Apes* (which I had read) and *The Bridge Over the River Kwai* (I'd seen the movie), and was contemplating a new book about the winds. His second wife, "Magouche," was Agnes Phillips, daughter of an American admiral, though I'm sure I thought she was English at the time.

Paddy, I later learned, was also thinking about the winds. Houseguests noticed that he rose at six each morning and was seen pacing the garden, apparently raveling and unraveling his sentences—George Seferis once gently chided Paddy for "Penelope-izing" his prose. But he was actually pacing out the design of the magnificent compass he would build with a fountain for its rose and the Greek names of the winds designated around it in beach pebbles of different shades. This sort of distraction from work made Paddy a famously slow writer. To this day, in fact, his fans despair of ever seeing the final volume of his masterpiece, the travel memoir that began with *A Time of Gifts* and *Between the Woods and the Water*.

Paddy was at one time best known from movie legend. Dirk Bogarde had played him in *Ill Met By Moonlight* (1957), the film about his plot to capture the German commanding general on Crete. He was actually better looking than Bogarde, and less inclined to let aristocratic reserve subdue his youthful zest. I suppose what I most admired about Paddy from the start was that he seemed always to have lived life on his own terms. Money helped, of course, but I know he did not always have money. Translation work he had done in the 1930s (including a version of *Forever Ulysses*, by C. P. Rodocanachi) paid his way for a while, and the war would have temporarily made money the least of his worries. After the war he wrote the script for John Huston's *The Roots of Heaven* (1958), a movie that has been both lauded and excoriated by critics. Huston himself disliked it, though his autobiography contains praise for Paddy and hilarious anecdotes about their drinking on the set in Africa. I once asked Paddy about these stories and was told that Errol Flynn was great company, but that Trevor Howard couldn't hold his booze and would usually retire early. It's remarkable that Paddy kept up with the former and has out-lived even the latter. In any case, he has made money from time to time without having to commute to a dreary office, and he and Joan came into some money in the early sixties, which helped them build the villa, and his books have occasionally done well as the tide of travel writing rises.*

But luck with money is not his whole story, nor is the fact that he is clearly an aristocrat, which has put off some of his detractors. To a great degree, Paddy has progressed in life because of his own unkillable spirit, which Greeks might call *enthusiasmós*. Curious about everything, fluent in Latin, Greek, German, French and English, with no doubt pretty good Hungarian and a few other languages thrown into the mix, Paddy is a man of the world in the very best sense. I would pit his learning against that of any American trained Ph. D., yet he has had the advantage of retaining his joyful spirit along with his erudition. It hasn't been hammered out of him by routines of a working life.

---

* Paddy dislikes being called a "travel writer" and simply says that he is a writer who observes the world in front of him. He is much more than that.

But back to lunch. I remember that Lela served us salt cod and *skordaliá*, those eye-tearing garlic potatoes, and we drank a lot of wine, or I did anyway. A Greek gentleman was there with his American bride. Paddy would much later recall that it was the great painter, Nikos Ghikas, a close friend of his, but this gentleman in my memory was not bald and did not have Ghikas's mustache. I hope it was Ghikas, though it's a pity to meet a great man and not be able to recall it. I know that I chattered away in my usual manner, partly trying to show them what a smart fellow I was, and that Jonna impressed them with her beauty and quieter knowledge. I had not met many "famous" writers at that time, and this no doubt helped the wine do its work, lifting me to that light-headed mood the Greeks call *kéfi*, which remains one of the ineffable pleasures in life.

When we left that afternoon we took several books Joan had loaned us. We also had to find a spot in the roadside scrub to pee, which didn't prevent us from seeing the Leigh Fermors' station wagon dash by on the tarmac, Xan Fielding at the wheel, perhaps taking them off for a walk in the mountains.

2

One night in March 1997 I went with my friends Nikos and Ourania to hear Paddy lecture at the Gennadius Library in Athens. He later sent me the typescript of his talk, worked up from the notes he had used that evening, and this text proves a perfect way to introduce his career to the uninitiated. Titled "The Aftermath of Travel," the talk detailed "the restless and rather exciting wild goose chase . . . in pursuit of the perfect refuge, asylum or hermitage for getting the original journeys down on paper." The first of these journeys was his remarkable walk, starting in December 1933 at age eighteen, from the Hook of Holland across Europe. He arrived in Constantiople on New Year's Day 1935, having had spellbinding adventures in Germany, Austria, Czechoslovakia, Hungary, Rumania and Bulgaria. After Constantinople he went to Greece, always one of his fascinations, staying in monasteries at Mount Athos and following Greek royalist cavalry on horseback through Thrace and Macedonia during the last republican revolt before the Metaxas dictatorship. Then Athens, then the rest of Greece, including an idyll at Lemonodassos in the Argolid: "A waterfall rushed down through the cypresses and thousands of lemon-trees. No telephone and no electric light. It was a legend, and leaf-fringed, with only writing, painting and swimming all day, then sitting up late talking and singing with Spiro and the lemon-growers, and summer seemed to last forever."

After more Balkan travels and a love affair with a Romanian princess, Paddy returned to England to pursue translation work until the outbreak of war. At this point in his lecture Paddy paused, waiting for his audience to catch up, then said, "After the war. . . ."

The audience gasped. He had skipped his most famous exploits completely, as he has almost always done. Others have written of his involvement in the Cretan Resistance, some of them accusingly.[†] When a major Balkan front failed to open up in 1943 and the Allies invaded Italy instead, the air seemed to go out of the resistance movement in Crete. British officers like Tom Dunbabin, Xan and Paddy were often stuck with the job of organizing divided factions of fighters, which was harder to do without victories against the enemy. When the work began to seem pointless, Xan got himself transferred to France, where he nearly died. Paddy and others at British headquarters in Cairo began to plan a special strike against the Germans in Crete, partly to buck up local morale.

Their greatest fear concerned reprisals. Ever since the Battle of Crete, when so many crack German troops were shot as they parachuted down and the island's civilian population rose up with such determined courage, attacking Germans with ancient guns, mattocks, stones, knives or any other weapons they could muster, the Nazi military authorities were especially vicious in response. Anthony Beevor reports, "Of the 1,135 Cretans executed from the start of the invasion [20 May 1941] until 9 September 1941, only 224 were sentenced by military tribunal." It wasn't an eye for an eye; it was a whole village for an eye, and thousands more Cretans would be shot in Nazi reprisals. Villages were dynamited. Atrocities were committed. It was a nasty business. British stragglers left over from the rout following the battle joined officers who were parachuted in or dropped off by submarine, many of them disguised as mountain shepherds, their public school Greek slowly transmuted to modern Cretan dialect. Paddy, of course, already had good modern Greek and great affection for his Hellenic friends. Like Xan Fielding, he was not given to wasteful heroics, and had no desire to invite reprisals.

The plan to kidnap a German general now looks to some like a dangerous schoolboy stunt, and the fact that several villages were destroyed in

---

† One very good account is *The Cretan Runner* (1955) by George Psychoundakis, translated by Paddy. Another is Anthony Beevor's *Crete: The Battle and the Resistance* (1991).

reprisals months later leads them to accuse Paddy of cavalier judgment. But as Beevor demonstrates, "The objective of the operation was to achieve a dramatic yet bloodless coup which could not justify reprisals against Cretan civilians." Several things went wrong, Beevor reports, but Paddy should not be blamed for them.

Paddy, or Michali as he was now called, parachuted back onto Crete in February 1944 with a plan to go after the hated General Müller. Unfortunately, the operation had to be delayed until April, by which time Müller had been replaced by the rather less ruthless Heinrich Kreipe. The action, however, was remarkably well executed under changed circumstances. Wearing German uniforms, Paddy and another officer, Stanley Moss, with nine Cretan fighters in support, managed to stop Kreipe's staff car on the road between Knossos and Heraklion. They hauled out the driver, subdued the general, and packed him on the floor in the back of the car. Unfortunately, the driver's throat was slit by enthusiastic partisans despite Paddy's explicit order that the engagement be bloodless. Those in the car didn't know this at the time, and it was probably a lucky thing. They managed to keep cool as they passed through German roadblocks and drove slowly through the streets of Heraklion. Once through the city they ditched the car on the coast further west to make it look as though they had escaped by sea. But their escape route would take them over the mountains to the south coast of the island.

It was not only the driver's murder that brought on their bad luck. They couldn't have known that the Germans had just intercepted a shipment of arms and that reprisals had begun against several villages for harboring *ardártes*, or guerillas, and their weapons. Beevor quotes the German declaration concerning these reprisals, noting that it does not mention the kidnapped general. The capture of General Kreipe was embarrassing to them, assuredly, but Beevor's point is that if the Germans intended to use it as an official rationale they would not have hesitated to do so. Months later, when the town of Anoyia was destroyed, the principle reasons were again that Anoyians had murdered a German soldier, protected *ardártes* and participated in an attack at Damastas. But it is also mentioned that the kidnappers of General Kreipe "passed through Anoyia, using Anoyia as a stopping place." This accumulation of unlucky coincidences has led to accusations against Paddy for what followed. "Virtually the whole town was burnt," Beevor reports, "and thirty inhabitants were shot together with another fifteen men caught nearby. Another account claims that over a hundred houses in Damatas were destroyed and thirty people were shot there, but that only fifteen died in Anoyia."

I'm sure that Beevor's painstaking research will never silence those who wish to blame Paddy for these disasters, but it ought to. I don't mean only that the operation was conceived with good intentions. But it would have been carried out bloodlessly if his orders had been heeded, and it cannot be directly related to German reprisals except for that one mention, almost an afterthought, among the list of reasons given for destroying Anoyia months later. Paddy's concern for human life has been strong in everything he has done, but the fact that his heroics have been filmed and written about probably causes some people to assume he was a glory-seeker. When in *A Time of Gifts* he tells the famous story of General Kreipe reciting Horace in a cave on Mount Ida, and Paddy recalling the poem from school days and completing the recitation, I can assure readers that his memory is accurate—at least that I've heard him reciting the poem by heart. The resentment against these aristocratic images of education is real enough—think of the outdated German and French officers in the film *Grand Illusion*, their universe already made absurd by the realities of war. Paddy's point about the friendlier attitude that resulted between him and the general is not that the man's Nazism could be excused by his recitation of Horace; it's that one of the war's many ironies was the way it pitted people against each other who, despite their political differences, may have had similar educations.

After the war, the writer and film critic Dilys Powell visited Kreipe in Germany, as she wrote in *The Villa Ariadne* (1973), and the general reported liking Paddy very much, while fearing Stanley Moss, "'always with his pistol' (he made a gesture indicative of excessive enthusiasm in a guard addicted to prodding) 'it was childish.'" In any case, the escape over the White Mountains was harrowing for all involved, not just for the general. Soon after they made it safely to Egypt Paddy came down with rheumatic fever. His recovery took six months, and for a time he was paralyzed. He never mentioned this to me when I told him about my puny case of sunstroke in 1981. By that time Jonna and I were his neighbors, living in a tiny stone hut in Kalamitsi, where I shared a large garden with Petros, Lela's taciturn husband. This was our own "time of gifts," and in my mind the proximity to Paddy and Joan was one of the best of them.

The view from Paddy's villa
PHOTO BY DAVID MASON

3

But his lecture skipped the war entirely and moved on to the Caribbean, where, equipped with a book contract, he travelled with Joan and the Greek artist Costas Achillopoulos. *The Traveller's Tree*, which appeared in 1950, is probably the most dated of Paddy's books, though it contains lovely writing. He followed it with a brief novel, also set in the Caribbean, *The Violins of Saint-Jacques* (1953), then his translation of *The Cretan Runner*, followed by a marvelous short book about monasteries he had known, *A Time to Keep Silence* (1957). All of these books were composed while on the move, or when briefly settled in other peoples' houses in England, France and Italy. In a small town at the border of Tuscany and Umbria, he recalled,

> I moved into the little albergo-trattoria. But it was March, when a wind from Siberia blows into the Tuscan hills, and in a day or two, fingers were turning to icicles; no question of holding a pen; so I went down to the bar and found it full of woodsmoke and dramatically-cloaked herdsmen from the Abruzzi drinking *grappa* at high speed; it was the only thing to do. When I got back at last, the landlady said I would be nice and warm as she had just put a priest in my bed. I didn't like the sound of this, but stumbled upstairs. The bed had grown a hump in the middle, for the prete was an elaborate wooden framework under the top sheet and the blankets, holding a brazier full of live charcoal. When I had clumsily lifted the whole thing out, I felt lucky, after all that *grappa*, not to have set the beautiful little town on fire.

After more travels in Italy, including a tramp through the region known as Magna Grecia "to listen to the surviving Greek dialects of Apulia and Calabria," Paddy began to spend more time in Greece, at the home of Angelos Sikelianos in Salamis or the mountain lodge of Vangeli Averoff in Metsovo "with stacks of Pindus firewood and a library." There was also Nikos Ghikas's "fine family ziggurat on Hydra," an island minus the disruptive noise of automobiles, then the same artist's home on Corfu after the one on Hydra burned down. There were sojourns in Athens with Ghikas, Seferis and George Katsimbalis, the Colossus of Maroussi himself. They had to settle somewhere, but Paddy ruled out Crete, fearing that his "many war-time friends" there would prevent him from finding enough peace to do his writing. Also, "I knew I wouldn't be able to resist the temptation to sit up eating and drinking all night. If we had settled there I would have been dead and buried long ago."

Ultimately they chose the Mani, a rugged region of the southern Peloponnesos, then rarely visited by outsiders.

We found a piece of land on a peninsula and became godbrother and sister to a brilliant master-mason called Niko Kolokotronis, the last of seven generations of master-masons from Arcadia who had all played the violin; and then we collected a small team of builders and stone-cutters from a mountain village—things not even to be dreamed of now, but possible thirty years ago. Settled in tents, reading Vitrouvius and Palladio while we learnt what we could from old Mani buildings, and planned the house going up with our architect friend Niko Hadjimihalis, whenever he could get away from Athens. We were given the raw material free—grey, fawn, russet and apricot-coloured limestone—which we hacked, prized and blew out of the side of the Taygetus and roughly dressed with claw-chisels. Only a footpath led to the place, there were no machines, all had to come by mule and if anything were too heavy, we had to carry it on our shoulders. One morning, a heavy stone lintel seven feet long, salvaged from a demolition in Tripoli, had to be shifted from the road to the half-built house. Roping it to a ladder, twelve of us sweated and swore and stumbled under it for a quarter of a mile down the steep tiers of the olive-groves and through a flock of sheep. The simple-hearted shepherd asked us what we were going to do with it and our godbrother answered through clenched teeth: "We are going to chuck it in the sea, to see if it floats."

This marvelous paragraph, constructed almost as painstakingly as the house itself, is a characteristic bit of Paddy's prose. I have two photocopied type-scripts of his—the first he sent was an account of swimming the Hellespont in his seventies. Both are roughly typed, covered with scrawls and emendations, and decorated with the little clouds and seagulls Paddy likes to draw on his letters and inscriptions. The whole impression of a Leigh Fermor manuscript is of great verbal copiousness matched by constant and obsessive re-shaping.

Once, when I was fixing up the little hut at Kalamitsi, a gentle sprite of a man knocked on the back door I had left open in the outer wall and struck up a conversation with me. He was curious about my work, and no doubt pried a lot of my story from me before I found out who he was. This even-tempered fellow with big ears and slicked-back hair was none other than Paddy's publisher, and a descendent of Lord Byron's as well, John Murray. We talked for an hour about Paddy and his books, and Mr. Murray said to me, of all people, "Oh, do see if you can talk him into finishing, will you?"

The book in question was *Between the Woods and the Water*, the second volume of a proposed trilogy. In a long letter written to me on April 27, 1985, Paddy reported having finally written the last chapter of that book and sent it by bus to his typist in Athens: ". . . now for pruning, revision, scissors and paste, the moment I get it back." The book appeared in 1986 and occasioned a huge revival of interest in Paddy's writing. I've seen a film in which he was interviewed for British TV, and there too is good old Xan Fielding, then Mr. Murray talking about the trouble of getting Paddy to finish anything. Even that does not seem to have ruffled the publisher, who on film leafs through Paddy's meandering, scissored manuscripts with the tenderness of an old friend.

Among the "siren calls" that have prevented Paddy from completing the trilogy, in addition to visits from fans like me, were mountaineering trips in the Himalayas and Peru and the riches of his own library. His Gennadius lecture concludes:

> But when I got back, for some perverse and forgotten reason that had nothing to do with the Andes or the Himalayas, I was suddenly racked with curiosity about the distribution of crocodiles in the upper Volta River, where I had never been or ever wanted to go. I took down the right volume of the Encyclopedia, but must have opened it at the wrong page, for three weeks later I had read the complete works of Voltaire, but I still know nothing about the distribution of those crocodiles.

I sometimes think the most delectable journey would be to spend a few weeks vacationing in Paddy's brain.

4

Twice in those early days I climbed high on a southern shoulder of Prophetis Elias, emerging from pine forests to a promontory that afforded me a view as far as Cape Matapan, the southernmost point of the Greek mainland. Further off by thirty miles, a vague shape in sea mist, was Kythera, the island birthplace of Aphrodite. It was the sort of stunning view that still makes me melancholy, thinking of all I will never see, all I will never know.

I missed a bus on one of those mountain excursions with friends, and made the long, steep descent toward the sea. We ended up in the tiniest coastal village, perhaps Trahila, at the time more accessible by boat than by land. That bone-weary night I felt I had glimpsed Mani as Paddy and Joan might have seen it in the fifties.

Still, even if I had, why would that be remarkable? A great many other foreigners had seen Mani before Paddy and Joan. He was only unusual in having written about it so splendidly. This peculiar desire of human beings to see what few others have seen—what does it come from? Not all people of my acquaintance suffer from such neurotic hunger for the unknown, and most who do would admit that it is like a fever, delusional as a sailor's calenture.

I have never traveled to any new place without wishing I had seen it at least a generation before, as if the virginity of rocks and trees could be possessed, undefiled by tourism or overcrowding. Travel, in other words, is an act of the imagination as well as the body. Certainly it requires scholarship, a reporter's memory and eye for detail, research, an ability to sponge up the stories one encounters. But the travel narrative remains an imaginative act, an uncovering and forging of connections that might not occur to another person to be worth writing down.

Good writing produces experience, or makes us believe that it reproduces it. When I pick up one of Paddy's books, open it at random and start reading, it's hard not to find a gorgeous passage. Here is one from *Mani* (1958):

> Cypresses and poplars fluttered beside the climbing path above the oleanders of the torrent bed. All this random green seemed frivolous, reckless and miraculous after the harsh regions to which our eyes had become attuned; but beyond it the stern biblical rocks soared through the evening air. In the middle of them half a mile away a goatherd, with his flock scattered about him like cave-paintings, waved his crook in salutation. How large and distinct he looked! Almost as disturbing as the gigantic Eye of my imagination. This rocky world has the property of making all look momentous, for all is isolated, nothing congregates, everything becomes archetypal and, as it were, symbolic of its own essence, so that the landscape is very sparsely and . . . over-significantly furnished with archtrees, archthistles, archcactuses, archgoatherds and archgoats. . . . No wonder that Greeks of all centuries have populated these hills with a magical fauna and *dramatis personae* and a pantheon.

Yes, I think again as I copy these words—that's exactly it. Exactly. That's what you saw on a walk in the Mani, at least in the old days. The biblical land of thorn and rock, the archetypal goatherd, the goats like cave paintings—an atavistic vision as ordinary and surprising as the bite of Cretan *raki* on the tongue. Something that convinces even as it distorts. These highly imaginative associations do not arise out of nothing. When a village friend of ours read *Mani* in a Greek translation, she expressed her admiration for the book while calling it "fantasy." But she had in mind the roots of that word, the common-or-garden roots in the Greek language—a "making visible." She was not saying the book was fiction; she was saying it was like a dream. And so it is.

Of course Paddy is lumped with every writer who ever romanticized Greece from Byron on down, and critics love to point out the delusions and errors of romantics. But the experience that real writers give us is never, ever, simply the truth. One of his great gifts is the ability to convey sensory experience with freshness, whimsy, strangeness, and precision. No one else has, in English, so well conveyed that midsummer afternoon torpor, that after-lunch paralysis of the body settling on man and beast alike. No one conveys more pleasure in encounters with people, seeming to love the world exactly as he finds it. But that love is inseparable from the horrors he has known, the killings in wartime, and from the imaginative act of apprehending the world and translating it over time into words. Though in his modesty he would deny it, Paddy's knowledge of Greece is nearly encyclopedic, but one doesn't read his books only to get access to that knowledge. One reads them—I do, anyway—for their transformative powers. To call them travel books is far too limiting. They are works of imagination, a form of poetry.

In the fifties, looking at the village by the sea, he wrote, "It is too inaccessible and there is too little to do there, fortunately, for it ever to be seriously endangered by tourism." But time, that great ironist, has removed the barriers, and the village is now a common tourist destination. Paddy's entire literary legacy has been commodified by strangers, reduced to the lingo of package tours available from travel web sites. Follow in the footsteps of Patrick Leigh Fermor, they say, as if that were even remotely possible. As more wealth and population have come to the village, so have more crowds and kitsch. Some days Paddy must feel like a prisoner who has built his own baroque dungeon.

Now you can sit outside at Lela's taverna, eating a fine meal and feeling lucky to get a table, and you can see other solitary tourists reading Leigh Fermor by lamplight, intoxicated by his prose as well as their half-kilo of wine. Those readers might be unaware that their dinner was cooked by Lela herself, and that the small barefoot girl in a straw hat whose photograph appears opposite page 257 in the hardback edition of *Mani* is also Lela, looking into the lens of Joan, for whom she would eventually work for many years as cook and housekeeper. Dear hardworking Lela bustles in her kitchen into the wee hours each night, rising early to market and do laundry and start cooking again. I have almost never seen her relax—she is too much a woman of the old Mani for that.

The village's prosperity is unquestionably good. Protesters may lament globalization, which too often means Americanization and trivialization, and the rest of us might feel aghast at all the dreck of contemporary commodified culture, but it's better than starving. And it's better than dwelling in a world of medieval social values and brutish prejudices—a world where Lela is stuck more than her grandchildren will be. Yes, better. But sad at the same time, for all that dies away even as we ourselves are dying away.

Change is the great subject of Paddy's books. Even their acts of scholarly preservation are acknowledgments that nothing lasts. That's why the power of his imagination is so important. He makes the lost world vivid.

Arising from the dream of *Mani*, the change surrounding me now in America seems so rapid and meaningless that my imagination can hardly keep up with it. I can dimly remember Colorado before the Interstate highway, when it took forever to drive from Denver to my father's hometown of Trinidad on the New Mexican border. Sometimes I lament a world in which children grow up without memories like mine or without the freedom to play unsupervised in the woods and mountains. But my father could remember hitchhiking to Colorado Springs in the thirties to take flying lessons in a bi-plane, and his father recalled running off to Canada to join the Seaforth Highlanders in World War I (the Germans saw their kilts and called them the "ladies from hell"), and *his* father went down in the mines near Ludlow long before the massacre of miners there in 1914, and so on. We are doomed by the laws of change to lament lost worlds, no matter who or where we are.

I think of the changes in Mani, and what comes to mind is a circle of marble fragments—walls, columns—lying in the grass, one of the earliest Christian churches in the area, closer in appearance to a pagan temple. I think of the ancient kingdoms of Laconia, the offering of five of its cities to Achilles if he would come out of his tent and fight in a war that began when Paris stole the Spartan Queen, wife of Menelaus. Menelaus who wrestled the shape-changing Proteus. Menelaus who, according to Euripides and others, fought the ten year war for nothing, for an illusion, because Helen was safely waiting in Proteus's kingdom in Egypt. I think of Apollo's fiery chariot and that of Elias in Christian frescoes, gods and prophets conflated in the iconography of change. I think of the fierce Slavic tribe, the Meligs, who settled in Mani in the Fourth Century, the rise of Mistras among Byzantine cities to a place of uncanny civility. My mind leaps back and forth over the Taygetus Mountains from Mistras to pirate raids on the Mani coast in the Twelfth Century, leading to more fortifications and the rise of a protective aristocracy of families like that of Petrobey Mavromichalis, said to be partly descended from a nereid. Then the Frankish conquest of Kalamata in 1205, and how contempt for invaders is reflected to this day in the name for the ubitquitous cactus, *frangósika*, or Frankish fig. More coastal attacks in the Thirteenth Century from Normans, Venetians, Genoese. Attacks in the Fifteenth Century from the Turks, who never succeeded in ruling over Mani. The uprising of Mavromichalis and others that sparked the Greek War of Independence in the 1820s, the imposition of a Bavarian King, Otto. The Balkan War of 1912–13 that extended Greece's northern boundary, making Macedonia a controversial term even today. The *Megáli Idéa*, the "Great Idea" of a Greece that would assume its ancient boundaries, and how it led to the Asia Minor Catastrophe in 1922. The alternation of monarchy, republic, and dictatorship as Greece struggled for identity and stability. The onset of war, occupation by Italians and Germans, resistance. The Civil War arising from factions among the *andártes* as well as the meddling superpowers, Russia and the United States and Britain. The generations of poverty. The slow rise of democracy, the horrible set-back of the Junta (1967–74), the conservative but peaceful government of Konstantine Karamanlis. The election I saw in 1981, trucks blaring slogans in villages and tossing out thousands of leaflets. The marches I saw in Athens—all of Syntagma Square packed with red-flag-waving Communists, and a few supporters of New Democracy's George Rallis shouting *Embrós!*—Forward! Meaning forward into Europe, which seemed to spell financial agony for Greece. And the modest slogan of the ETHIK Party: "Neither left nor right—always forward." And the victorious socialist coalition, PASOK, with its slogan, "PASOK will bring change." And how the socialists won but the protests were not quelled—now it's globalization the young are fighting. And I notice how far this fantasy has moved from Mani, where despite all those changes the hobbled goats still lie down in the olive shade on a hot summer's day, and the fishermen's caiques still go tak-tak-takking on a sea smooth as oil, and a furry rat scuttles over Aphrodite's tiled roof. . . .

5

Tangents, distractions, friendships, connections. Paddy's books are expert at conveying the flotsam of history. They are grateful for gifts and shattered by loss at the same time, which is perhaps the only way we can react to change as we perceive it.

I remember more than once discussing the relative merits of Marcel Proust and Anthony Powell with Paddy and Joan. They knew Powell personally, of course, and loved his comic early novels, but were unmoved by the grand design of *A Dance to the Music of Time* because for them it was little more than a disguised memoir of their friends. They knew all the people Powell was writing about, and felt his prose had become pretentious. I countered that I had read all twelve novels while working as a gardener in Upstate New York, that I didn't know any of the people involved, that for me the cycle represented what fiction does best. More than any other art form, I said, fiction makes us feel the passage of time, the weight of it. Powell's novels made me feel, as it were, the tragic heft of the twentieth century.

I mention this because Paddy's nonfiction books, too, are transmitters of lost time. That is one of their primary gifts to readers. Even so slight a book as *Three Letters from the Andes* (1991), relating an expedition in 1971, has such moments. In one of them, late in the book, he relates a dinner with a character who might well have stepped out of Powell's novels, an English-woman married to a Peruvian and bearing the impressive moniker Doña Diana de Dibos:

Suddenly I realized who she was: the sister, that is, of Mike Cumberlege, that amazing buccaneerish figure (very funny, very well read, with a single gold earring) who used to smuggle us into German-occupied Crete in little boats; he was captured later by the Germans trying to blow up the Corinth Canal, held prisoner for three years in Flossenberg concentration camp and, tragically, shot four days before the armistice: a marvelous almost mythical figure; Xan and I knew him well. His sister Diana and I fell into each other's arms and I told her lots of stories about him she'd never heard. It was too extraordinary.

But in Paddy's life and work it's not at all extraordinary, in large part because he has the mind and experience to realize the importance of such encounters. The scene ends with him singing Bulgarian folksongs after "much wine," and it's typical of Paddy's myth and his reality. The man has absorbed so much of what he's seen in life and can wring it out with no apparent effort, all in a spirit of affectionate play.

In February 1997, when I went back to the village with my second wife, Annie, we visited Paddy and Joan one cloudy day for lunch indoors at their home. Together with their Austrian houseguest, we had much conversation over ouzo and the luncheon wine. We were catching up, Paddy and I remarking that neither of us had changed in sixteen years—truer of him than of me, I think. I was less the hero-worshipping boy, a bit more sure of myself as a scribbler, and was able to joke with him about those early meetings. I recalled an impression he once did of Marlin Brando in *The Godfather*, as if that American mumble could be imagined with an overlay of aristocratic English. Paddy was taken aback; he had no memory of it at all. But he could entertain us with a few bars of a Marlene Dietrich number he had taught himself to sing—backwards.

Joan spoke fondly of the early days in Athens, their friendships with Seferis and Katsimbalis, indicating the sense of estrangement she felt from the city in its present incarnation. I brought up old friends of theirs I had met, some in their home years before. Xan Fielding, Bruce Chatwin, Stephen Spender, perhaps Nikos Ghikas. Joan, in her typically understated manner, simply said, "They're all dead." But neither she nor Paddy were the sort to impose feelings of grief upon others, and we simply carried on. Annie, whose working-class Ayrshire childhood must have given her a unique way of seeing these two Old World aristocrats, found that she genuinely liked them for their kindness and humor. Their world was all but unimaginable to her, but her fondness for eccentricity was satisfied.

That night when I told Lela about our visit—we were renting one of the rooms over her taverna—she brought out her copy of *The Violins of Saint-Jacques* in translation, lovingly inscribed in Greek to her and Petros. I was touched by her pride at being able to read a little, though she had had to quit school as a girl when her father died and the war came along.

Next day Lela told us that Joan had phoned, inviting us to join them again for lunch, this time at Lela's taverna. We were the only customers that afternoon, sitting in winter sunlight out near the sea, and Lela served us the same dish—salt cod and garlic potatoes—that she had served when I first went to the villa at Kalamitsi, with the clean unresinated white wine made by a man in one of the mountain villages.

Annie's favorite memory of this lunch is the conversation started by Joan about the most exotic food any of us had eaten. Their Austrian friend had tried hedgehog cooked by gypsies, and he also tenderly mentioned having eaten what we in America call Rocky Mountain Oysters. Joan cut him off with a curt, "Oh that's nothing—everyone's eaten balls!" She and Paddy won that contest with the iguana they had eaten in El Salvador.

We talked about books as always, about odd things that crop up in all cultures. "Hair of the dog," I said, for some reason thinking of the folk remedy for a hangover. "How would you say that in Greek?"

"*Skyli pou se dágouse*," Paddy replied, "*vále ap' to mallí tou.* Dog that has bitten you, pour in (or put on) some of its fur." It was a Cretan saying he had recorded in his book, *Mani*, and he wrote it down for me. I still have that scrap of paper tucked in a file with his letters and typescripts.

Later that winter, while staying at Katerina Anghelaki-Rooke's on Aegina, I frequently went to Athens to see friends or to do some work at the Fulbright office. There I met another American, David Roessel, who has done remarkable scholarly writing about Greece. At the time David was helping to create an exhibit of Seferis's manuscripts at the Gennadius library, and he and I attended the opening where Edmund Keeley movingly ruminated about the great poet he had translated. Through David's connection at the library I was able to spend a happy afternoon reading Paddy's correspondence with Seferis, finding still more evidence of his genius for verbal play, including his verses called "Anglo-Romaic Pastorals"—apparent nonsense poems in which transliterated Greek words became English neologisms. There was also an unguarded letter from Joan to Seferis, asking him to intercede with Katsimbalis, who had taken sudden offense at their stance on the Cyprus issue.

I know how Joan felt. As an American, I know at times I represent a hated empire, just as Joan knew the Brits were sometimes hated in much of Greece—these hatreds are usually aimed at governments rather than individuals. Two years after I read her plea, my country was bombing Belgrade. Our motives were honorable—preventing the slaughter of Moslem Kosovars—but our methods were cold and detached, and our attacks upon Orthodox Serbs appalled most Greeks. Feeling one's personal friendships in the vise of history can be painful, to say the least.

It's Paddy's gift for friendship I want to honor now. The gift can be seen, too, in his support for a man he first met on Crete during the war, George Psychoundakis. Not only did Paddy translate and see to the publication of *The Cretan Runner*, but he has also supported another of Psychoudakis's forays into literature: his translation into modern Cretan dialect of both the *Iliad* and the *Odyssey*. In 1999 Paddy sent me a pamphlet published by the American college of Greece containing English and Greek versions of a letter he wrote in support of these translations. This letter is a small but fascinating rumination on types of translation, arguing that an autodidact of the Cretan hills deserved a place among scholarly and academic translators. Paddy pays due respect to the professors, but as one of the great autodidacts himself, his defense of accidental learning has much resonance. The pamphlet ends with a two-sentence coda written in 1998 that conveys the free spirit of an old friend:

A few months ago George was sitting under his vine trellis with his wife Sophia when he heard that Penguin were going to bring out *The Cretan Runner* in paperback. His face lit up and without a word, he dashed indoors, took down his rifle, smacked a clip into the magazine and emptied it over the olive trees and the sea.

IV

CHATWIN'S ASHES

I see men as trees, walking.

—Mark 8:24

1

Bruce Chatwin, though, I had never heard of, and when I first met him I did not know he was a writer. The first of my postcards from him is dated 30 October 1980:

> Nice talking to you at the bus stop. Sorry it couldn't go on longer. Best of luck with your work. I'm just off to New York to see about mine.
>> Regards, Bruce Chatwin
>> Copy of *In Patagonia* in post

Yes, I'm sure it was mid-October when we met. He had been dropped at the bus stop in the *agora* by his hosts, the Leigh Fermors, and had stepped into a grocery shop to use the phone.

In those days two brothers, Petros and Vassili, owned grocery shops at some distance from each other, and we learned that we were obligated to spread our business around as evenly as possible. I had stopped at Petros' and endured the melancholy darkness of his small store, and now I would finish the job at Vassili's, which was always brighter and more cheerful. Vassili was a wisp of a man whose mustache could not conceal an almost giddy smile. He seemed to take particular delight in our fledgling Greek. He was especially delighted, cackling and slapping his thigh, when I learned the word for shit—*skatá*. He told people about it for weeks. "The American boy's favorite word—*skatá*!"

Just as I stepped in among the shelves of Greek products (this was before the European Community loaded shelves with luxurious imports), I noticed another foreigner there. He was negotiating with Vassili to use the phone, and when he spoke into it I heard at once that he was English. "Yes, it's Bruce," he was saying. "I'm afraid I forgot my sweater."

He was a bit taller than I, wearing jeans and a blue workshirt and sturdy walking shoes. When he got off the phone, and I had purchased my few supplies from Vassili, Bruce saw me and struck up a conversation. He was waiting for the bus, which was late. The friends he had been visiting were driving back into the village with his sweater. Just then I saw a small white stationwagon pull up at the curb. Bruce dashed out, returning with a blue pullover. Only later did I realize that Leigh Fermor—whose book, *Mani*, I had just read—must have been at the wheel of that car.

Somehow Bruce divined that I was a writer, or an aspiring one, and we talked nonstop about literature. He knew and adored Leigh Fermor's books, told me which of them I should read next. In two solitary years as a gardener I had grown greedy for literary conversation, and I took to Chatwin like a beggar to a smorgasbord. I was desperate to be a writer, and this fellow, this stranger, seemed to know exactly how I felt. Jonna had always supported my ambitions, sometimes with a touch of jealousy, but her family didn't understand them. I had worked by myself all day, raking leaves, shoveling snow, planting and pruning on a large estate near Rochester, New York. Almost my only contact with things literary had been my conversations with Jonna, who loved to read, and my correspondence with friends like Dana Gioia, a poet who was working in business. We had not yet met, but his unfailing friendship and guidance via the mail sustained me as a writer through years of isolation. Dana has since sent me xeroxes of my letters from Greece as an aid to memory. In November 1980 I had written to him, "One day in our village I met a young English writer named Bruce Chatwin, very charming and loquacious. He has sent me his book, *In Patagonia*, which is delightful travel reading." But when I first met Bruce I didn't have the foggiest idea who he was.

We talked about travel writing, which was not then as popular as it has since become. When I criticized some of Paul Theroux's books, Bruce tilted his blond head, suddenly embarrassed, and said, "Well, he's rather a friend of mine."

Seeing I had overstepped, I offered that I had liked *The Consul's File* very much.

"Yes, that may be his best."

When we met, *In Patagonia* had been out for a few years. *The Viceroy of Ouidah* would soon be released, but somehow I had missed reading anything about him. He told me an amusing story of how an American editor came to accept his first book. The editor always took a stack of manuscripts home for bedtime reading, and when he noticed that *In Patagonia* had short chapters he decided it was just the right book to nod off with. Then he got caught up in it. "So you see," Bruce said. "Short chapters."

When the bus finally arrived, he wrote down his address for me, and I lugged my groceries back to Friend's house, where Jonna had begun to wonder what had happened to me. I burst through the door in a state of high excitement, saying I had just had a long talk with a writer. And that was it, really. In our very brief meeting, Bruce had taken me seriously as a writer—something few people had done. He was intrigued that I had lived and worked in Alaska, that an agent in New York was trying to sell my novel based on the experience. Though fourteen years my senior, he treated me as an equal, and I was flattered by this even before I became an admirer of his work.

There it is again—the head-down concentration of the writer who cannot see reality at the tip of his nose.

2

Paul Theroux has written that postcards are the vice of the self-advertiser. They certainly allowed Bruce to stay in touch with a great many people while avoiding the depth and commitment of letters. But the remarkable thing was how long Bruce stayed in touch. A second postcard, 16 February 1981, tells me he is "off to the Caribbean to work on Wales." A third from Yaddo contemplates a trip to the Aleutians, an archipelago I had described to him. To my knowledge, he never got there.

The fourth postcard is addressed to me in Rochester, New York, so the illegible postmark must have read 1982 or later. By then Jonna and I had returned to the States, where I worked briefly in the film business. I flew to Los Angeles for story consultations, read scripts in the library of the Academy of Motion Picture Arts and Sciences, stayed with my great-aunt, Mary Hertz, a former vaudeville dancer, and her flea-bitten cockapoodle named Snoopy. It was Mary who told me that her grandfather had fought in the Civil War and gave me stories I would later incorporate into a long, fictional poem, *The Country I Remember*. But in those days I was still convinced that fame as a novelist and filmwriter lay just ahead of me. When the feature film division of the company went bust we drove back to Rochester in our '63 Plymouth Valiant; we rented a cottage from her father while I took odd jobs and she worked in the city's art museum. It was the beginning of a bad time in our marriage. Bruce's life seemed very different; his card from London reads,

Rochester's a far cry from [the village]. It so happens that it looms large in my life: my in-laws (alas, now separated) live in the Genesee Valley. Above address is reasonably permanent. Have just been following the route of the Vikings down the Volga. Hence the card.

    As ever Bruce

On the flipside of this card is a Nicholas Roerich painting, "Overseas Guests," depicting Vikings staring over the rail of their bright ship at the Russian landscape. The words are all in Russian, but I have a translation of them in a book about Roerich, the Russian artist and mystic who painted sets for Diaghilev, because he is connected to my life in a different way. Less than a decade after I received Bruce's card, I published, at thirty-six, my own first book, a collection of poems that had won the Nicholas Roerich Poetry Prize. The coincidence is probably meaningless, but it still astonishes me.

    A fifth postcard from Bruce deepens the drama concerning his in-laws. Dated 30 August 1983, it reads,

Send a PC with your phone No. It's conceivable that I may come over [to] spend Christmas with my wife's family in Geneseo, N.Y. (Not 30 miles from you). If so, I would need some LOCAL moral support.

    As always Bruce

If he did come over, he never contacted me. And what was all this about his in-laws and moral support? Did he need the friendship of a fellow writer, or was there some other motive for his maintenance of this connection with me? I've since wondered whether Bruce's secret life, which eventually led to his death of AIDS in January 1989, was in any way involved, but I prefer to think not. Rather, he seems to have found it simply unthinkable that anyone should forget about him.

    This anxiety is not uncommon among writers because ours is such solitary work, leaving us acres of silence to fill with our own nagging voices. Some writers are genuinely reclusive. Not Bruce. His terse correspondence with acquaintances like me was surely the product of a gregarious sensibility. Some writers become self-advertisers out of a grating neediness. What I sensed from Bruce was more akin to uncontainable enthusiasm.

However one interprets all of this, the sheer nervousness of most writers surely makes us exasperating partners. I know, for example, that I both adored Jonna and neglected her. She was an uncommonly beautiful woman—"A thoroughbred," one friend noted. Heads turned when she entered any room, not only because of her body, but because of the exotic intelligence in her face. I was like some proud landowner, vain about the beauty of his fields but too unwise and inexperienced to properly care for them. And Jonna feared I would judge her desires too harshly, keeping more and more of her inner life secret from me. In private she suffered excruciating doubts about her talent and beauty. In those days she wanted to be an artist, yet struggled against herself no matter what she made. She never knew those intoxicating moments of unfettered creation that fool us into thinking art will be easy. On the terrace of Friend's house I helped her build a simple Navajo loom with lumber we bought in Kalamata. For months Jonna worked at her weaving, tearing it out not like cunning Penelope, but because nothing she made ever approached her high expectations.

"It's not working."

"You just have to keep at it."

"Nothing I do ever works. It's all so awful."

And there I was, constantly scribbling as if nothing could stop me. I was so wrapped up in my own ambitions that I can't possibly have given her what she needed. The fact that we lived for a time next door to her parents' mansion, to wealth that made my literary ambitions appear utterly ridiculous, certainly did not help.

As it happens, the last card I received from Bruce was sent to an address near the center of Rochester, where Jonna and I had moved, away from her parents, in an attempt to save our marriage. It was forwarded to a rather seedy apartment behind an urban hospital and a McDonalds, where I lived alone after our separation.

As I followed his career in the papers, Bruce's life could not have seemed more different from mine. To many of us, he rapidly became a literary hero.

His fine novel about Wales, *On the Black Hill*, was followed by a provocative bestseller, *The Songlines*. I had moved about so often in my life that I almost believed his thesis—that we are naturally migratory, and that our problems arise from the unnatural state of settlement.

Later revelations of Bruce's secret life came as a complete surprise to me. He seemed to have everything: a happy marriage, the freedom to travel where he pleased and write about it, a spirit of curiosity, vast stores of eccentric knowledge. At thirty, desperate for another kind of job, I was studying toward a doctorate in English, driving to the University of Rochester in the now battered Valiant held together with bungee cords, duct tape and bits of rope. I was living in a dusty apartment surrounded by wailing sirens and pervaded by the smell of hamburger grease.

In some small way, it helped to read writers like Bruce. The absence of bitterness and self-pity in his writing, even when he took on horrific subjects, buoyed my spirits. I buried my bruised ego and kept on working.

Disclosure

With blue official flap and legalese
the state acknowledges an end to what
began in privacy, in passing glances.
What I remember of your voice is not
an issue lawyers willingly address,
and I've avoided their neat document.
There was a time when the word "wife" warmed me,
but as you say I think too much of words.

Many nights I raised my head from the pillow,
watched you sleeping, wife in a girl's flannel,
there by the bed your window open.
Long-stemmed unnamable flower in whom
I was lost and saved for ten brief years,
my rancor can't contain these images:

your hair lightened to its roots by Greek sun,
my maps of married pleasure on your skin.

It's strange what we can make ourselves believe.
Memory saves; recrimination uses
every twisted syllable of the past.
Still, with all the errors I acknowledge
added to those I fail or refuse to see,
I say our marriage was a gentle thing,
a secret bargain children sometimes make
and then forget when the weather's changed.

Lawyers put it another way; they don't know
how small exchanges still take place, of gifts
collected long ago, drawings of a house
we lived in, letters from friends we haven't told.
How separately we stumble on some object,
a book I signed, a scarf you knitted,
and call to tell the other it is there,
wondering if it will be wanted back.

3

From a brief interview with Bruce, published in *The New York Times Book Review* (January 15, 1989) together with a review of *Utz*, his last novel:

> Travel itself can become a form of tyranny, he added. "As you go along, you literally collect places. I'm fed up with going to places. I shan't go to any more."

I was shocked by the despair in this. The surface life of the collector, the love of beautiful and rare objects as well as places, had gone sour. As he says in *Utz*, "Things are the changeless mirror in which we watch ourselves disintegrate." I had read the stories about an infection caused by something he had eaten in China—he published one account of this in *The New York Review of Books* that same month—but only vaguely suspected it was the fabrication of a dying man.

Bruce was forty-eight when he died. By then, my own life had taken a turn for the better after years of doubt and woundedness and error. I was living in Pittsburgh with my new wife, Annie, while I wrote my dissertation and she worked as a photojournalist. Annie with her tilt-of-the-head bemusement at the world, her way of living without expectation, her gardener's soul. Friends had introduced us, and I had been alone and had not realized she might be interested in me. I was always falling for any woman who showed an interest, but Annie seemed more grounded, down-to-earth, and she knew a life far removed from the frenetic egotism of literary pursuits. I had fallen in love not only with her beauty, but also with her curiosity, her attachment to things unliterary. Through her work as a photojournalist, she connected me to the world outside the university, kept me from feeling absorbed into nothing but mind. But it was really her whole manner that moved me: the way she cared for people, the way she could nurture any cut leaf into a full-blown plant, the way she remained friends with her ex-husband and other lovers, her gentleness and eloquent hands, her laughter like clear water. Born in Scotland, the daughter of a blacksmith's hammer man in a steel works, she had emigrated with her family when she was ten. Though he'd had little formal education, her father still had reams of poetry by heart—Robert Burns and the border ballads and more—and he honored my ambition to write where Jonna's family had belittled it. Deciding to marry Annie meant I would not have a family of my own, so we spoke often about what this would mean. I chose it, though. I chose a life with her because I knew we could make a home—something I had not bothered about when young.

The news of Bruce's death may not have surprised his close friends, but it hit me like a bullet. I turned up Public Radio and sat down, listening in stunned silence. It was impossible, impossible. How strange it is that we can be so powerfully affected by the deaths of people we barely know. I didn't shed tears over it—this was nothing like the death of my brother years before. But it felt like an emotional crossroads of sorts. Who was this man I had admired so much? How could he die so mysteriously, without finishing his work?

Soon enough the rumors proved true. It was AIDS. So there were many things I had not known about him, and the freedom I had envied was another kind of rootlessness. I had bought the myth, had emulated an illusion. Moralists would no doubt scold him for this, but to some extent all writers mythologize their lives. They cannot take reality unmixed with imagination. I am no different, and I read books for the same reasons. Only the worst sort of puritan would lecture us for doing so.

A Greek friend once said to me with absolute conviction, "The artist is not working class," and some strutting little snob within me might have agreed. But in the year after Bruce's death I would begin, at thirty-five, my first full-time job in northern Minnesota, a landscape that, while congenial to many, was as foreign to me as Flanders. I would learn that work, even the unglamorous work of a teacher in a provincial university, is its own value—not because it is virtuous, but because it is real. Nevertheless, I missed Greece painfully for the sixteen years I was away, and something in me remained unwilling to settle where I was. The idea of going back—especially to a place known in my first marriage, was unthinkable, yet somehow always there, under the surface of my daily life. I flirted with the language, dreamed of the food, of sunlight scattering off the sea, of friends I thought I would be too ashamed to face again (though I kept writing to some, like Paddy). By marrying Annie, an older woman with a grown daughter and a strong sense of her own identity, I was beginning to build the life I had once scorned. It was the life I had been given mixed with the life of choice, and I had to get on with it.

4

In 1997 I was the guest of the Fulbright Foundation, an artist-in-residence whose residence changed from Athens to Aegina and, finally, Friend's house in the village I had last seen in 1981.

The village had changed. It was wonderfully prosperous, with several new hotels and restaurants. Petros now owned a large market and was in furious competition with another large market not ten feet away from his. He was still melancholy. "My life has been ugly," he said to me one day. "My son was killed in a car crash on the mountain."

"But you have daughters."

"Yes, I have daughters, but that means nothing."

His brother, Vassilis, had gone into the hotel business, which had done nothing to steady his giddy spirits. Lela now ran a guesthouse and taverna down by the sea. Apparently the Mani no longer lived up to its reputation as a dour, violent place. Sotiris, the kindly gas station owner, had won a fortune in the lottery but changed nothing about his life. He was still the presiding angel of the agora, as Paddy called him, smiling at anyone who passed. Young people who had once dreamed passionately about getting away from village oppression were now married parents themselves, wishing they could return to the slower pace of life in a small community. My return to the village is symbolized for me by the nightly appearance of the Hale-Bopp comet in a star-filled sky, as if, suspended there in the heavens, it were showering good fortune on us all. Never mind the fact that, to a cult in far away America, the same comet signalled mass suicide. To me its appearance cast a happy spell: *This is it. Here we are. What luck!*

I found Paddy and Joan in great form. Lela told me that she had seen Paddy driving by one day, and that he had shouted to her out the car window, "Lela, I'm eighty-two today! Who says whiskey is bad for you?" Indeed, he still looked like a matinee idol. His hair was as full as ever, brushed back in waves. In his woolen knickerbockers and army sweater, he looked equally prepared for a walk in the hills and a meeting of generals. I noticed how thick and strong his wrists were as he handed me a glass of *ouzo*.

It was a rainy day in April, weeks before Annie would rejoin me in Greece. We sat at a round table indoors, between the *hayati*, an Ottoman sitting area with sash windows looking out on the sea, and the sofas by the fireplace. They had designed their extraordinary stone villa themselves, with elements borrowed from Byzantine, Persian and more recent island structures. The reference library stood on shelves around us, as Paddy had insisted, so dinnertime arguments could more easily be settled. I could see books in several languages and on many subjects along with dictionaries and an encyclopedia. On a low table in the *hayati* there always seemed to be a chess game going.

We talked about books, about the effects of hashish and the nargiles of old Athens—I found it hard to remember that my hosts were in their eighties, asked them about their meeting in Egypt during the war.

"You're not going to write about us, are you?" Joan said. She was a tall, slender woman, virtually unchanged from sixteen years before except for an arthritic hip. She presided easily over the serving of food at lunch, but whenever she got up from her chair she winced at the torture, never complaining.

"Not at all," I said. "Just curious."

"You are. You're planning to write something, I know." Her tone was gentle, but I felt I had intruded on her privacy. I shifted the subject to Bruce Chatwin, reminding them I had met him when he was their guest all those years ago. Paddy had already told me how he, Joan and Elizabeth Chatwin buried some of Bruce's ashes at a spot in the hills. Suddenly, he suggested that he take me there. The luncheon wine inclined me rather to go back to Friend's house for a nap, but this was an offer I could not refuse. Within minutes this robust octogenarian was driving me in his battered white station wagon (nicknamed Dapple Gray) toward villages higher in the hills.

As the road turned upward, Paddy spotted an elderly couple waiting for a bus, and stopped to give them a lift. After our greetings, I began to introduce myself and Paddy to them, only to see in their eyes that they knew him very well. These thin and sinewy elders, who would have met Paddy many dozens of times, smiled politely at my ignorance. At one point we were stopped by a few goats being urged across the road, and I could see the toothless goatherd cursing and waving his switch at the car. Then he, too, saw who was at the wheel and leaned in at Paddy's window, shaking our hands and offering blessings before he let us drive on.

We left the old couple in their hilltop village and continued to climb. Above us the Taygetos Mountains disappeared in a mist, though I could see traces of snow on high ridges. This was a landscape of gorge and precipice, constantly surprising to anyone accustomed to lazy days beside the sea. Some of these villages had not been accessible by car when I had lived there in the eighties, and I used to see donkey-loads of goods being whipped up the old stone footpaths. The paved road we traveled had been dirt then. It still ended in a dirt track hugging a cliff and vanishing in wet cloud. We turned downhill on another track squeezed between gray stone walls, and drove into the outer village, where Paddy parked the car. Reaching for his walking stick, he told me, "It's not far now."

The silence except for the scuttling chickens of a mountain village was astonishing. Smells of goat shit and wildflowers were sweet-bitter, revitalizing. The terraced olive groves appeared to float between the mountains and the sea, like an image from a Japanese painting. Land dropped away so suddenly that I imagined sheer cliffs below us.

In a small *plateia* next to a church, Paddy pointed his stick at a closed house, the paint long faded from its door and shutters. It was spectacularly positioned with a view down a long ravine to the Gulf of Messinias. This was the house Bruce had thought of buying, he said. So the writer obsessed with nomadism had contemplated a more rooted life, and Greece, a nation of wanderers as well as fiercely rooted people, had struck him as a possible home. He and Paddy used to come up here often, sometimes alone, sometimes with Joan and Elizabeth. Here they had taken many long walks in the hills, always conversing, stopping to identify flowers or watch a circling hawk. But the church we were headed for lay further down the hill, almost obscured by the little crowd of houses. You had to know where to step off the stone path at a wall with an old millstone leaned against it, and take the dirt trail through an olive grove to the tiny church of St. Nicholas, perched on the edge of its own acropolis, looking down on the threshing floors of another village, long abandoned. Later Annie and I tramped through those fields with a friend who knows the whole history of risen and fallen fortunes there. In old times, part of the land was called *Kalo*, Good, because its owners harvested two crops a year, but it was also a place where Slavs had been lured into a trap by local men dressed as women. In one of those bizarre transgressions of hospitality you read about in Greece, the locals slit the throats of their guests. I heard the story retold by an old man in the village. One wonders how much longer this violent communal memory will last. Maybe Bruce was right, and such horrific xenophobia is a product of unnatural settlement. Think of the hospitality enjoyed by the wandering Odysseus, the killing he encountered and initiated at home. Think of the many hatreds that have given us the verb *Balkanize*. Greece is a part of that horror, too.

The church of Ayios Nicholaos is itself emblematic of a long, complicated history. Though one stone dates it to the Eighteenth Century, a few of its features may be hundreds of years older. The saint's painted head watches from a little niche over the front door, which is held shut by an olive branch jammed through the handles. An old marble font, upturned in the grass, serves as a front step. One stoops through a doorway not much larger than an igloo's, and steps onto a worn bare floor. This seems to have been a sacred site for a very long time. Behind the frescoes of the iconostasis, which Paddy dated to the Sixteenth of Seventeenth Century, there is a marble slab on the altar. Striking a match, one can see that it is covered with Ancient Greek writing. Evidently it was "borrowed" from a classical site closer to the sea. At such moments the mind staggers in the damp, moldy air, as if drunk on historical associations, something Paddy has captured particularly well in his books.

While I poked around in the church, maintaining a reverent silence, Paddy sat cross-legged on the wall outside, his hands resting on the knob of his stick. I have never seen a man his age looking so fit and at ease in the world. When I rejoined him, he told me about Bruce's late conversion to the Orthodox faith, a genuine conversion that grew from a long-standing interest in Greek and Russian culture.

There was something I had always wanted to ask him: "Are you Orthodox?"

"No," he said, "I'm a sort of ordinary Protestant, you know, if I'm anything at all."

Down below us, a few feet over the wall to the north, lay a circle of grass and wildflowers with a solitary olive tree in their midst.

"That's where we buried poor Bruce," Paddy said. "Elizabeth, Joan and I. We used to picnic here years ago. It was one of his favorite spots. He thought of living here, you know."

I stepped down and stood for a while by the olive tree. Clouds were burning off, and I could almost see the peak of Prophetis Elias above, the windswept gulf spread out below. Few people have left even part of their remains in such a beautiful place. My family and I had scattered my brother's ashes in such a place, far away and long ago.

At some strange level I felt empty. I was moved, but not greatly moved. I felt pity that he had died so early, pride that Paddy had honored me with this excursion, but also a not unwarranted *nothing*. This was not my life. This was a life that had touched mine so briefly that perhaps I should hesitate to make the connection at all. Why do we like to pause at the graves of writers we have loved, whether we knew them or not? Why do we seek something more than what they give us in their books? Once, I stood in a Georgia downpour at the grave of Flannery O'Conner. I felt moved, but I also felt eager to get out of the rain. Perhaps there is a momentary honor in all of this, a small acknowledgement that words, too, have made us who we are. Beside Bruce's olive tree I whispered something that might have been a prayer, though I have never known how to pray. I said it to Bruce and to my own dead brother, then went to find Paddy, who waited on the wall above.

Annie, 1997
PHOTO BY DAVID MASON

5

We had just begun to drive back, and Paddy was pointing out *to pefko*, the tall pine tree landmark where so many of their hikes had started, when he turned to me abruptly and asked, "I say, do you fancy a walk? I can't do it now. Old age, you know. But I could show you where to go if you like."

I was still half-drowsy from wine, but this seemed another opportunity I could not let go. When one of the world's great walkers suggests an afternoon stroll, it would be churlish to say no.

"That would be wonderful."

"Good man. I'd do it myself, but it's all downhill and my knees aren't what they used to be."

He backed up to the pine and pointed to the trail.

"That's where you start. Look out for the important left turn on your way down."

He named the villages I would pass on my way to the sea, and described how the path would drop me right at Friend's house. He offered me his stick, but I declined and, thanking him profusely, set off downhill.

I have always felt light-hearted at the start of a walk, as if I were entering a new world of possibility and surprise. But when Paddy had driven off—"Don't forget that important left turn!"—and I had found the trail, I realized that I should have asked for a few more directions. Exactly which left turn did he mean? The one immediately onto the path? One further down the hill? Once on the trail, I saw what looked like a precipice to my left; assuming I had already made the important turn, I followed a well-traveled track through the olive groves. It should have been a simple matter; the sea was quite visible before me, the mountains had to be kept at my back, but soon enough I had lost sight of the village and found myself in a scrubby wilderness with a few thin goatpaths disappearing under giant thorn bushes.

Now the sun glanced off the sea far below. It was almost hot. My mouth was dry from the wine, and I seemed to find on all sides nothing but cliffs dropping away. I quickly realized that even here, with obvious landmarks in the distance and villages all around (though invisible at present), even in this ancient and apparently domesticated landscape, one could get lost.

The ilex trees were not so tall that they obscured my destination, but they hid the important middle ground where I might have seen a way to avoid the cliffs. This was a low jungle of sage, thistle and thorns. Soon enough I had been pricked and scratched and turned around by crisscrossing paths so often I could only stand still, trying to gather my wits. I grew up in the American west, and have spent much of my life in the mountains, but I had rarely before found a landscape and vegetation so perfectly suited to thwarting my progress. Only animals enjoyed walking here, and they were nowhere to be seen.

After thrashing about again for a while, I sat down on a stone. I gazed uphill, trying to make out the village or the pine tree. Utter silence. Not even birdsong or cockcrow. Not even a distant car on the road, wherever the road was. Humbled, I started slowly uphill, trying to find the path I had started on. If nothing else I could walk down the paved road, or hitchhike.

I made it to the village, and tried again to find the important left turn. Again I failed and retraced my steps. Finally, I realized that the left turn was closer than I thought, and led into the ravine by a stone stairway. It was part of that ancient network of limestone roads that crisscross the Mani and Crete. Down I went, through a lush green canyon filled with twittering birds, across fields of olives and wildflowers, and finally to a village I recognized, perched on the ridge behind Friend's house.

Once there, I opened a cold beer and sat for hours, writing the day's events into my notebook as the sun sank into the sea. Pleasantly footsore, I had moved for a few hours in a dream that was partly literary, an atmosphere of affection brought on by reading, enacted by walking—as if Greece allowed mind and body to meld, their old quarrels settled in momentary unity. Bruce was no longer alive to seek and enact this temporary faith, but I was. I felt refreshed and hopeful, even as I knew this was not and never could be my real home. Home was something I had to make and could not make alone, the way one makes a poem or a book.

Later that week, when I met Paddy by chance in the village post office, I thanked him for lunch and for taking me into the hills. But I never told him how lost I had been—how, for a few minutes anyway, I wondered if I would ever get back.

V

Learning By Default

Early experience, even undigested, leaves a
useful sediment for later.

—Kevin Andrews, *The Flight of Ikaros*

1

Again and again I come back to stories of choice and friendship. I was nagged in the early days about whether to become an expatriate like so many of my friends, among them the South African, Robert Crisp.

One day, when we had been in the village only a few weeks, I noticed the man with the silver beard and square jaw drinking *kokkinéli* at a taverna in the agora and introduced myself to him. Robert was happy to have the company. He was a writer, though he declared he was through with all ambition now. Among his books were a history of South Africa and two accounts of tank warfare in World War II, one of them notable for its admission of guilt in a friendly fire incident in North Africa. He lent me these, the poems of John Betjeman, and his ancient typewriter, claiming he had no use for it any more. From then on I hammered out my letters and stories on Robert's battered portable. The keys were sharp and ink-clotted, so they alternately punched o's in the page or filled them in with black blotches. My letters from Greece looked like a lunatic's musical scores.

After his experience in the war, including the British retreat from Greece via Monemvasia and later a serious head wound in a tank battle against Rommel, Robert worked as a journalist in London. He fell in love with a younger woman, left his wife, chased this siren to Greece, and was himself left for the translator and hellenist Philip Sherrard. Now he lived an impecunious existence in the tiniest of huts in the village of Stoupa. The hut was so small that he had to entertain guests outside, sitting in straight-backed chairs on what he called his lawn under the olive boughs. Robert was beginning to despair about money. Once he had even tried to hawk his war medals at the British Embassy, and he was deeply indignant at the empire's lack of interest. Before the war he had been a cricket star for South Africa, a record-holder of some sort, and he was known to block traffic on the road every now and then as he tried to explain the labyrinthine rules of that sport to any Maniots who would humor him. He came to our village often because the keepers of the one local hotel, a retired Colonel named Yannis and his Belgian wife, Simone, took him in, fed him a few good meals and let him use a shower.

Jonna and I were frequently invited to drinking parties with this crowd, knowing they were disapproved of by some villagers. But Robert was an enjoyable raconteur, fun to be around especially when he grew light-headed. He claimed he had cured himself of stomach cancer by taking his medicine with *kokkinéli*, and some sort of wine-into-blood miracle had indeed happened because his cancer had disappeared. At one of the hotel parties where we gathered for drinks and Simone's famous *moussaká*, we were joined by an elegant German woman named Taleta who summered in a refurbished stone house in Riglia, usually bringing a much younger man along as her chauffeur and companion. When we had all imbibed a lot of wine, Robert half jokingly proposed to Taleta. Her reply to him was wonderful: "No, my dear, we could never be a couple. You are a romantic and I am a realist."

"That sounds like a match made in heaven!"

"No, no, my dear. No, no." Taleta patted Robert's hurt expression , ruffled his silver hair, and said in her smoker's husky voice. "I've seen too much of the world. It would never work."

One of Robert's best friends was another Brit who had a house in the village of Nomitsí. His name was Tristram Popham, and he was the half-brother of Robert's old rival in love, Philip Sherrard. These expat circles were very small. A retired scientist, Tristram was living in one house while hoping to restore another, though a master builder had explained to him that a good earthquake could send the front wall into his neighbor's kitchen.

Tristram was a gentle soul who had apparently been jilted by his wife in England and had decided it was best to die in a foreign land. Though they had been years in Greece, neither Robert nor Tristram had mastered much of the language, and they were amazed at how quickly it came to younger people. Robert would have turned seventy that year, and I assume Tristram was in his sixties. Facing old age in uncertain circumstances, they both appreciated their friendships with the young.

It was at Tristram's in November that we spent a few days gathering olives, accompanied by another American named Catherine who wrote romance novels and read palms. We worked very hard for him, drinking a good deal of his local grocer's wine each night afterwards, and in exchange for our labors and companionship he gave us a long day's tour of the Deep Mani, the bleak southern half of the peninsula, in his Austin Mini. There we saw early churches that were left unlocked in those days before looters, including the Episcopi on the Stavri-Mezaros footpath with its extraordinary frescoes and the little bell hanging in a nearby olive tree. Now tourist buses park at the clustered towers of Vathia and invade the sunburnt villages by the sea, but the Deep Mani we saw was a spooky, primordial desert. It was a place where time seemed to have got sand in its gears and ground to a halt. The landscape gaped like an idiot from another age, stunned by anything that moved.

Our visit to that elegant early church came at the end of a long day in which we had gone all the way to Yerolimena, as far as the road would go, with stops at Vathia and the cape called Tigani because it was shaped like a frying pan. We could see that cape when we walked through olive groves to the church at Stavri. Afterwards, when we emerged from the trees, we sat on some stones by the empty road in dead silence, watching the olive harvest going on while the sun bled into Ionian mist.

What we saw that evening is recounted in a letter I sent to some friends of mine, returned to me recently as an aide-mémoire:

> The sun was setting and we saw people emerging from the olive groves at the end of a very arduous day. That is to say, the picking is not such hard work—they seem to take it slowly and they relax over their meal under the trees—but beginning and ending the day, carrying supplies out and returning home with huge bags of olives on their backs, looks very hard, especially

knowing it is all they have. The women do most of what is difficult. Mothers walking home with supplies for the meal strung in front and bags of olives behind, while their husbands merely lead the laden donkeys. As we sat by the road that evening a woman approached us who looked as though she had escaped from some monastery, a prisoner of mad monks. She had the wildest-looking eyes I had ever seen, but seemed to know the other women and to have just come from her own trees. She looked at us and said, "You speak English?" and when we said yes she asked, "Where you from?" We had begun to notice something fishy about her accent, but thought nothing of it and told her we were from New York. "No," she said. "I'm from Albany, can you believe it?"

"Are you Greek?"

"No way, are you kidding? I'm no Greek. I married a Greek, the S. O. B. I used to live in Jersey, Atlantic City, on the boardwalk. I married this guy and came over with him."

Basically, her story was this: her Greek husband had already been married in the old country. His first marriage was Orthodox, and his second was not, so, by Greek standards, he is not a bigamist and any children by his second wife are not hers to keep. The poor woman was living in Deep Mani . . . in order to stay near her children, trying to work out a way to get them to America. She could not entice her husband back to the States, of course, because as she said it, "He sets one foot in the States and I got him for bigamy."

Years later I found out that I had a friend in similar straits, despite whatever liberalization of marriage laws had come about with the PASOK government. But I have often been haunted by the ragged image of that woman in Deep Mani, a lost soul among the olive trees.[‡]

---

‡ Things are better now. In 2002 the interior ministry published a booklet demonstrating changes in Greek family law. These changes have generally sought to protect children and to give both parents equal rights in decisions made on their behalf.

2

Robert was stranded in Mani partly of his own volition, partly due to his perennially bad luck with money. Having confessed his friendly-fire accident in *Brazen Chariots*, his first book on tank warfare, he was one of those who looked askance at Paddy Leigh Fermor's wartime exploits, like the kidnapping of General Kreipe. When I pled Paddy's case over wine on Robert's "lawn," bumming cigarettes from Tristram and waxing poetic about the prose in *A Time of Gifts*, Robert finally confessed to a twinge of jealousy. His own literary gifts were far smaller and he knew it, but his principles as a soldier were offended by the "stunt" of the Kreipe kidnapping. Once, as a guest at Paddy and Joan's, he got drunk and gave Paddy a piece of his mind, and he was never invited back—or so the story went. I think he felt a bit sheepish about that. The enmity between him and Paddy was not a matter of class, as his friendship with Tristram, who was somehow related to Bells and Oliviers, demonstrated. And certainly Paddy never made anything of social class in *his* friendships or I wouldn't have been at his villa so much. To me it seemed that both Paddy and Robert were good company in their ways, but Paddy was lucky and Robert was unlucky. Paddy lived in the most gorgeous house anyone had ever seen, with a walled garden over the sea, while Robert tholed in a hut, depending on the kindness of friends and strangers. Paddy was a great prose stylist and Robert a genial hack.

I, meanwhile, was fascinated by the whole crowd—their breadth of experience, their *joie de vivre*, their expatiate lives. I wondered if I too should stay on in Greece, give America the shove. For much of that first year in Greece

I was convinced I would not return to my homeland anytime soon. I wanted to follow in my brother Doug's footsteps through Asia, but Greece had cast its Kalypso spell over me and I could well imagine spending years there, if not a whole lifetime.

For Jonna this would have been unthinkable. There were letters and phone calls from home. Her father's car dealership in Rochester, New York, was in trouble. His mechanics had gone on strike, souring what he thought of as a friendly relationship, and in a moment of boldness and anger he sold the business, putting the lot of them out of work. But now he was in middle age, drifting for the first time in his life, casting about for new opportunities, and Jonna was understandably worried about him. And there were other problems with her younger siblings. Her bonds to family were very strong.

But there it was, anyway. The choice. Where should we live? What should we do?

Most people live as if they never had a choice in the matter, as if family and country and the necessity of making a living spelled out their fate. In my twenties, foolishly or not, I was sure I would beat this system. I wrote to American friends about my desire to escape the routine economic traps.

By that time I had the film contract and had done the first, flimsy treatment for the script, convinced I could live by my pen. Even our Austrian friend, Wolfgang, the perpetual hippie, had received money for his Beat-influenced writings from some publisher in his homeland. Dana Gioia was working sixty-hour weeks in corporate America, doing his copious writing in late evening hours, training himself to live without sleep, while I was discussing the journals of Anaïs Nin with Jonna, thinking of Henry Miller and Lawrence Durrell and Paddy and Robert and other bohemians.

Henry Miller was an expatriate for a decade, mostly in France. His book about Greece, *The Colossus of Maroussi* (1941), was based on only a few months' acquaintance with the country. But Miller had the good fortune to know the poet George Seferis, the painter Nikos Ghikas, the soldier-scholar George Katsimbalis. He brought to his account an uncanny exuberance that transcends its more idiotic or romanticized passages. "I don't like Nauplia," he wrote. "I don't like provincial towns. I don't like jails, churches, fortresses, palaces, libraries, museums, or public statues to the dead." My first reaction to such a passage would have been disagreement—I *do* like the town of Nauplia, a lovely port with a little Venetian fortress in its harbor. But Miller's list carries me beyond my objection—I get caught up in his philosophy of individual liberty as well as his verbal energy. Here he is at Epidaurus, contemplating the impending war in Europe:

> What man wants is peace in order that he may live. Defeating our neighbor doesn't give peace any more than curing cancer brings health. Man doesn't begin to live through triumphing over his enemy, nor does he begin to acquire health through endless cures. The joy of life comes through peace, which is not static but dynamic. No man can really say he knows what joy is until he has experienced peace. And without joy there is no life, even if you have a dozen cars, six butlers, a castle, a private chapel and a bomb-proof vault. Our diseases are our attachments, be they habits, ideologies, ideals, principles, possessions, phobias, gods, cults, religions, what you please.

He was in love with the spareness of Greece and seemed not to see the dark side of poverty, the sexism and sclerotic moral codes of villagers. Perhaps he was thinking of the Bhagavad-Gita with its truths about our attachments and how they make us ill. But attachments also make us human, and if a kind of sickness is to go with our humanity, maybe that is not entirely bad. Hitler needed to be defeated, after all. And what's so bad about treating cancer? Miller never did go back to Greece after the war, nor did he ever see most of his Greek friends again. After my divorce from Jonna, I too thought I would never go back. But going back has enriched my life incalculably; getting beyond that first love to something more complex and less self-involved.

Still, there is truth in Miller's book, and some of the truth resides in its joy—the pleasure he takes at being there and seeing what he sees, tasting what he tastes, saying what he says. How appropriate that his meditation on peace arose from Epidaurus, where Asklepios was said to have been buried. There in the hills of the Argolid the ancients established a center of health based upon thaumaturgical methods. Patients would sacrifice to the deified healer and would stay on to sleep in the *abaton*, where their dreams would give them indications, interpreted by priests, about how to make themselves well. The Asklepion at Epidauros is not well preserved, unlike that at Pergamon in Turkey, where the sound of running water has curative power, floating one's dreams along on its subterranean current. But Epidaurus is still a peaceful place, and its theatre is one of the architectural marvels of the world. It does a writer good to think performances there would be associated with healing, as if drama arose from communal and medicinal impulses at the same time. As if poetry, music, dance, and performance were the ultimate acts of peace, leading a *polis* through the violent processes that could destroy it and toward some resolution that, at least temporarily, made sense of a fickle universe.

Twenty-odd years after I first read Miller, I took a group of students to Epidaurus, and they performed scenes from Euripides under the pine trees next to the theatre. The guard, a slight, graceful man named Yiorgos, brought one of his chairs under the trees for the American professor. Holding my elbow, he told me with pride that he had seen every production at the theatre since the 1950s. He had seen Callas. He had seen all the great directors. He quoted one of the choruses from *Medea* as if it were his national anthem.

3

My ambivalence about America in those years just after Viet Nam but long before our wars in Iraq was not a moral case. It was partly youthful confusion, partly a fear of the economic realities that would complicate my dream of being a writer. When I went back to Greece in 1997 I finally found and read a book that had been recommended to me sixteen years before, *The Flight of Ikaros*, by Kevin Andrews. First published in 1959 and frequently out of print, this book captures a young man's infatuation with Greece, then goes beyond mere infatuation in important ways.

Though he was half-English, Andrews referred to himself as an American. He arrived in Athens on a travelling fellowship in 1947 after combat service in the 10th Mountain Division during World War II. He studied at the American School of Archeology, but bristled at its pressure to conform to academic discipline and frequently took off on foot into the Peloponnesos.

What Andrews witnessed and described so well was a rural life that has all but disappeared. His first journeys were also made in a highly dangerous time, the last year or so of the Civil War, when the Greek army was combing the hills for Communist *andártes*. He would even meet a guerilla named Konstandí who had killed many compatriots and had fought in the terrible battle at Mistras in the hills above Sparta.

Flight of Ikaros conveys the pleasure of youthful journeys in the Peloponnesos:

Trips out of Athens by myself led to flowery fields that were becoming more and more familiar. All Greece was a friend now. Alone in a foreign land one tends to see one's surroundings in a direct and personal relation: granted, a limited view, but the raw exposure of a total solitude to absolute enveloping strangeness is a form of protection necessary under the circumstances. All the more so too if one happens to be untested, brimming with goodwill, and intellectually lazy, or if one distinctly prefers to learn by default: never by conscious, debilitating effort but by passive acceptance of whatsoever haphazard experience, as it happens on its own good time, not prematurely, not by dictation.

Such passages appeal to me still, describing an experience I have known—learning by default—and explaining in part why I too have resisted academic discipline and frequently tried to bite the hand that feeds me.

Eventually, Andrews stayed on in Greece, married a Greek woman and settled in Athens with his family. He wrote other books, none quite as gripping as *Flight of Ikaros*. This story manages to be personal and political at the same time. Andrews chronicles and quantifies the devastation of Greece in the 1940s. He not only gives vivid recreations of Civil War scenes in conversations with their participants, but provides a convincing historical explanation for the outbreak of the war after the Nazis retreated in 1944. Churchill, fearing Communist influence among the *andártes* of ELAS and EAM, tried to marginalize their role in postwar Greek government. Then soldiers in the British Expeditionary Force, attempting to disarm leftist guerillas, got caught up in a horrible battle in Athens. Two hundred seventy-three British soldiers and thousands of Greeks were killed, and the left was effectively pushed out of the West's influence, into the arms of Tito and the Communists. Churchill was surely correct to fear Stalin's influence in the region despite the guarantees of Yalta, but his military solution made Balkan Communism the only ally available to Greek leftists. With their meddling, Churchill, Stalin, Tito and eventually Truman helped drive a wedge between left and right in Greece, widening pre-existing differences and leading to a more ferocious Civil War that leaves bitter legacies to this day. Now, having seen Hungary and the Czech Republic in the 1990s, I know what a disaster it would have been for Greece to have become a Soviet satellite, if indeed that could have happened. Andrews's point is that extreme Greek leftists would not have become so powerful without the provocation of the West.

Andrews's politics were left wing, due at least partly to the fact that he lived in Athens during the time of the Junta (1967–74). My friend Nita Clothier, who had the good fortune to know Andrews, has sent me a xerox of "Athens by November Night," a memoir of protest and reprisal in 1973—it was reprinted in *Greece in the Dark*, published in Amsterdam in 1980 and now very difficult to find. This is a gripping account of three days in the city, beginning on November 15th. On his way to a movie, Andrews encountered a growing crowd of mostly student protestors at the Polytechnic. He spontaneously joined them until someone told him he had been spotted by police and ought to leave. Andrews came back the next day, and when snipers fired on the crowd on November 17th, killing an unknown number and wounding more than a thousand, he found himself lugging some of the wounded to safety. Covered with a stranger's blood, he relayed information about the fighting by telephone to the wife of a journalist. Later he stood in a mob facing a phalanx of troops, and was hit over the head with a club in the ensuing melée. One hand was broken as he tried to protect himself from the blows.

The protests were successfully beaten down, but at such cost that the Junta, weakened as well by the Cyprus situation, lasted less than one year more. Greece's strange terrorist group, November 17, responsible for a score of killings and plenty of bomb attacks, was named after this event witnessed by Andrews. For the next twenty-odd years, these terrorists targeted foreign military personnel or wealthy Greek businessmen considered dupes of foreign interests. The terrorists long ago lost most popular support in Greece, and it appears that they have been effectively neutralized.

What would Andrews have thought of such things? Despite his sympathy with some anti-Americanism and his intense pride at becoming a Greek citizen, he would surely have condemned the tactics of terrorists like any other rational person. In "Athens by November Night" it is clear that he was simply outraged at seeing innocent people attacked and cheered that some citizens had decided not to take it any more. At one point in the riots a stranger pointed out that he was a foreigner and could surely excuse himself from such dangerous participation. Andrews had forgotten. When one is embroiled in such events in a given place, he wrote, one is a citizen of that place.

Nita often took groups of students to Greece in the 1980s. They would stay at a pension called Claire's House in the Plaka, and she would invite Andrews to lecture to her group. She remembers he nearly always had one of his epileptic fits during these visits, and once he was unable to finish his lecture, and his brother, who had come along, had to do it for him. She also remembers that, after a meal of chicken, Andrews would gather up everyone's chicken bones and take them home with him.

There is possibly no writer about Greece I would more like to meet than Kevin Andrews. Alas, it will never happen. While swimming in the sea in 1989 he suffered another seizure and drowned.

4

At one point in *Flight of Ikaros* a Greek from the Peloponnesos tells Andrews about politics and village life:

> In this country nothing's illegal. Or everything is, depending where you stand . . . Do you know what it's like in a small village, when you go into a wine-shop or a café and look at the people all watching one another, each one knowing exactly what side the other belongs to, and everyone with a weapon in his house—some more weapons than others—and only waiting for the chance to use them? As soon as another war breaks out . . . Till then, however, they know I'm a Leftist, and I know well enough what they would do to me.

Not only are the divisions real between one village and another, one family or another, but the memory is long and there is no escaping it. Not even to this day. Friends writing about "my" village in Mani told me that they had to touch on the Civil War with the greatest circumspection and delicacy, especially if they wanted to go on living their lives in that village for at least part of the year.

In the winter of 1980–81 I found myself compromised by my friendship with the expatriate crowd who drank at the hotel. Yannis, who had the government contract to run the hotel at that time with his Belgian wife, Simone, was a retired officer in the Greek Air Force. He drank a lot in part to numb the pain from a back injury sustained in Africa. Had he fought in the Congo? I don't remember. I only recall that his doughy wife was kind to us and made a killer *moussaká*, and that Iannis poured strong drinks. He was a small, wiry man who affected an ascot and a pseudo-British manner, though I once saw him dance the *kalamatianó* when he was drunk.

One day I ran into Yannis in the agora, or main street of the village, and he invited me into a taverna for a brandy. It was cold and the wood stove heating the taverna made its windows steam so we couldn't see outside. We sat at a small table with glasses of Metaxas, and I was dimly aware that Yannis, who had his back to a wall, did not greet the three or four other men in the room, two of them hunched over backgammon, another watching us through bushy brows above a long beard.

I had a bit of Greek by that time, but Yannis spoke to me in his heavily accented English, telling me of his military service and perhaps stories of Africa that I no longer recall. What I do remember is that, almost without my perceiving it, his tone hardened. Maybe I had asked about the upcoming elections or about the European Economic Community, the merits of which Greeks debated even as they tried to bring their currency in line with its demands.

"Listen," Yannis said in a voice I can only call poisonous, "you don't know these people like I do. These people are incompetent. They will ruin Greece. And those that are not incompetent are worse. They are Communists of the most terrible kind."

I did not know enough Greek history to understand why, but I could feel the eyes of that bearded fellow watching our table, and I sensed that the backgammon game no longer held all the attention of the men in the corner. These men would not have known any English, but they knew Yannis.

"These are the people who would destroy Greece if we let them," Yannis said, using my politeness and his brandy to hold me there. "I have friends who would stop them. Karamanlis is too weak. He could have stopped them years ago—Andreas and his PASOK and the KKE, who are worse. Once we had strong men in power. I knew those men. I had friends who could steer this country on a better course. And I have friends now who are making plans. If those people steal the election with promises as they are trying to do, my friends will step in the save the country."

There we were, sipping brandy and talking English, watched by hawk eyes from two corners of the room, and I don't think I understood until later that the man who had bought me a drink and whose hospitality I had accepted numerous times and whose plump wife was the toast of the expatriate crowd was in fact a Fascist. Yannis had been a Colonel, just like Papadopoulos. He thought he could whip the country into shape and beat the opposition to a pulp in the process.

The Socialists of PASOK did win the election, of course, and in the years since have often been in power. And a new wave of Fascism never did rise up after the election of 1981, though the rantings of this ineffectual little drunk would not be the last I heard of such politics.

Later, when the campaigns were in full swing and the village agora was swept of multicolored leaflets strewn from passing trucks nearly every day, I tried to have a conversation about what was happening with two men seated in chairs outside a shop. In a rather naïve American way I cracked a joke about Greek elections producing a lot of garbage in the streets. One of these men, a fellow named Elias who was called a wise man and interpreter of dreams, snapped at me angrily:

"Don't say anything. You don't know what we have been through to have this election. You don't know what this election means to we Greeks!"

"Calm down," said the other. "Stay in your chair. He's just a boy, an American. How could he know?"

"Let him learn then," Elias said. "Let him learn who had to die for Greece to have this election, who went to prison. Who's rotting in prison now."

"He's just a boy, just a boy."

The ferocity of Elias had been like a slap across my face. I apologized and excused myself. But of course he was right, and it was dangerous for Jonna and me to go on being *ta paidiá*, "the children," no matter where we chose to live. It was high time we grew up.

5

Years later I would read much more about the Civil War and its aftermath. When I finally got around to Peter Levi's *The Hill of Kronos* (1981), in which the typical Greek travel idyll is rudely interrupted by the Junta, whose goons arrested Levi more than once, it was as if my earlier experience finally fell into place. I had walked through that village for more than a year, blissfully unaware who was a Fascist, who a Communist, a Royalist, a Socialist, a New Democrat. I had lived as if politics did not matter, which is the height of childishness.

There was a fascinating American named Jon Van Leuven who lived in Scandinavia, returning to Greece each year to work on his small house in Gournitsa, a nearly deserted village on a hilltop behind us and to the north which we had always called Aghia Sophia after its church. Jon had come to Greece out of his interest in archeology and had stayed on. We visited him at his house and he came to see us at Kalamitsi. It was there in the heat of summer, cicadas buzzing around us, that I told him I aspired to be a writer, and Jon—older, thin, bespectacled—insisted I should stay in Europe. "You can't be an artist in America," he said. There was some way in which our country nullified the arts, and in Jon's mind the multiple languages and cultures and perhaps the socialist tendencies of Europe made the arts both more possible and more important.

It was one of those moments of choice. Would I be an expatriate or would I go back? A film company dangled money before my eyes, and I took the bait. It was the promise of money more than a choice of America that compelled me.

Then it was just one damned thing after another until I was stuck there, poor and divorced and trying to make a career as an academic.

Greece wasn't entirely lost to me, though. I kept running into Greeks who were surprised that I spoke the language and gave me too generous compliments. Then: "Are you Greek?" Followed by: "You don't look Greek" or "You look Greek, you have Alexander's nose," or some such thing, as if anyone on earth knows what Alexander's nose looked like.

"No," I would say. "Only someone who loves Greece."

"German?"

"American."

"But you speak better than the Greeks."

"No, I make many mistakes."

"Greeks make mistakes too. It's a hard language. You speak very well."

"I am trying to learn better."

"Marry a Greek woman. That way you'll learn."

"But I have a wife in America."

"One here, one there—you should have both!"

It's a conversation I seem to have at least once a day. And though it is only joking politeness, I do feel slightly polygamous, one life in America, a counter-life for smaller periods of time among Aegean friends.

6

Late in our first year in the village my Aunt Barbara came to stay with us after leading a tour of weavers through northern villages. I took her to meet Paddy and Joan, who at the time had Stephen and Natasha Spender as guests. I remember Natasha's vivaciousness, Spender's relative dourness, my own usual attempts of show off by chattering away about everything I had read. I got Paddy warmed up with talk of Evelyn Waugh's *Sword of Honour* trilogy, so he would compare his own wartime experience to Waugh's. Perhaps Spender seemed so grumpy because Waugh had so despised his friend W. H. Auden. I don't know.

These were hot days in late summer when we had at our disposal both the hut in Kalamitsi and the house of Friend and Margarita, where Aunt Barbara could sleep in a comfortable water bed. Jonna and I moved into the big house to be with her, feeling a bit estranged from all its luxuries after months without electricity or running water.

When it came time for Barbara to fly out of Kalamata, I went north with her on the bus, then found a taxi to the little airport on the edge of town. The driver waited, and when Barbara had left he drove me back to the center of Kalamata near the old covered market. I knew I had missed the last bus into Mani and didn't have enough cash on me to pay for a car all the way home, forty-five kilometers. So I set out to walk in the late sun, climbing the curved road past the waterfront hotels.

I got a ride in the bed of a pick-up truck with some Gypsies part way up the hill until they turned off on a dirt track. Then I was on my own walking the narrow road as it wound above the city and the city disappeared and I seemed to have entered another time. Stone walls and fields of sun-reddened grass and the lengthening shadows of olive trees. Birdsong. Glimpses of the sea and the peninsula west where the town of Koroni lay.

I began to feel lighter on my feet, singing to myself as I cut across fields. Then I was walking down into the deep ravine with its haunted bridge, and night had fallen but I felt unafraid. Maybe I would walk all night and arrive at the village at morning, or maybe I would sleep in a field as I had done in Scotland in 1975. Maybe Jonna would be worried about me, or would wish me good riddance and go to bed happily alone. Weren't Wolfie and Isy due to visit us that night? She would have company then, even if I did not get back. I had not felt such freedom in years, but failed to imagine Jonna might want the same freedom, might feel suffocated by my dithering in search of life.

I crossed the bridge without a single accosting ghost—no victim lovers wearing nooses, no partisans dashed on the rocks below—and had started up the road on the other side when I heard the noise of an engine echoing off the cliffs. No, I wouldn't hitch, I would hoof it. But as the truck labored up behind me, I impulsively stuck out my thumb. The driver stopped, and I climbed into his cab. Between us on the seat were two Swedish girls with clipped blond hair, their backpacks behind us with his cargo. He asked me to translate for them, since all he knew was that they wanted a ride to some place in Mani.

They were very pretty girls with suntanned limbs and ready laughter. I learned they were looking for a place to camp, and suggested the beach north of our village. I don't remember more of our conversation, except that it came surprisingly easy to me, meeting these girls and having this talk.

So we chattered away as we descended the road to the village in darkness, and the driver left the two girls near the beach and I said goodnight and walked on to Friend's house and through the gate and up the jasmine-scented steps. I threw open the front door and walked in, and there was Jonna conversing with our guests, the bearded Wolfie and the flowery Isy, and I burst out, "I've just had the most marvelous walk, and I met these two beautiful Swedish girls!"

And the look on Jonna's face—glad to see me but puzzled. *Who are you? Who have I been married to all this time?* As Wolfie later put it, they had never seen me looking so happy, with such energy and joy. It was like a brand new person coming through the door and they at first didn't know what had so transformed me. Or as Jonna would later put it, what could it mean that I was so happy after being apart from her for the first time in months?

VI

Holding to Life

Suddenly you discover that you'll spend your entire life in disorder.
It's all that you have; you must learn to live with it.

—George Seferis, *A Poet's Journal*, trans. by Athan Anagnostopoulos

1

So the marriage failed and I fell to earth. Something had to wake me up, and this was a long, slow, excrutiating lesson in my own stupidity. Needing to find some work I could do, some way to get my footing in the world, I went to graduate school, eventually married Annie and got my first teaching job in northern Minnesota. My brain wired in a northwestern childhood to seek mountainous landscapes, I was at first bewildered by the flat open spaces around me. When the northern winters closed in on me and I suffered from cabin fever and despaired at another stack of freshman essays or new dictates from the bone-headed legislature, my image of escape took on the bright tints of the Aegean. I could almost smell heat radiating from white rocks above the briny waves. For years I had struggled to improve my Greek, though I never had the luxury of studying it in a classroom. My friendships with Greeks kept it from dying away. And for a decade or more the closest of these was with the poet Yiorgos Chouliaras. Another chance meeting. Another surprising bit of good luck.

Dana Gioia called me one night to tell me he had met someone in New York who approved of some translations I had done, especially of a short poem by Cavafy. This was Deborah Bowen, who organized an arts program at the Nicholas Roerich Museum on West 107th. Named for the Russian painter, the museum was small, filled with strange canvasses of snowy Tibetan scenes, often with a haloed saint in them. These were from Roerich's treks in quest of Shambhala or Shangri-La. Eventually I came to know the museum well. Dana told me that Deborah Bowen was planning a tribute to Cavafy, and that he had asked her whose translations of Cavafy she liked, and she had just noticed one of mine in a journal. This prompted Dana to tell her that he knew me.

And Deborah, in turn, knew a Greek poet looking for a translator, and it happened to be a time when I was casting about for someone new to translate. Within a week I had received some fascinating books: *I Alli Glóssa* (*The Other Tongue*) and *O Thisavrós ton Balkanión* (*The Treasure of the Balkans*), by Yiorgos Chouliaras. Many of the poems were difficult, and the author photos displayed Yiorgos's anarchic sense of humor. In one of them, three girls in St. John's Prep sweatshirts were jogging, while a bearded Greek smoking a cigarette mock-jogged behind them. The note underneath said he was born in Thessaloniki in 1951 and lived in New York, where he had studied the history of economics and politics. He had helped found the Greek journals *Tram* and *Chartis*, and had published several books.

I chose a few simpler poems, made English versions of them, and sent them to the author in New York. He wrote back quickly with copious notes in English. As a Press Attaché for the Greek government's office in Manhattan, Yiorgos spoke fluent English, but he wrote his poetry in Greek. What developed between us was a collaborative process of translation in which my sense of English idioms and rhythms proved helpful. We worked feverishly at these co-translations for two years, published dozens of them in journals here and abroad, then found ourselves so busy and caught up in other projects that we lost the momentum. While it lasted the process was intoxicating—a verbal vacation, a way of working at poetry that was utterly different from my own.

Yiorgos came of age in the time of the Junta, when as he once wrote, "All of Greece became a terrible poem." The regime pushed "anti-culture" and turned some artists into whores, others into political prisoners. The surrealism that had been so strong a part of Greek poetry for two generations was now especially a technique of literary survival. Opacity in writing meant that censors and secret police couldn't get it. Populist clarity would have played into the hands of tyrants.

Like others of his generation, Yiorgos felt an early attraction to American culture. He turned down an offer to attend Oxford University and went instead to Reed College in Oregon. After that he pursued graduate studies in New York, though he never finished his doctorate, and worked as a journalist. Several years after the socialist PASOK government came to power he took a position with the Greek Press Office in Manhattan.

When I first met Yiorgos Chouliaras he led a frenetic, culturally layered life. His flat in Astoria, where many Greeks lived in those days, meant that he could wake in a suburb of Athens, stop at a Greek café for breakfast, pick up the Greek papers as well as the *New York Times* on his way to the subway, and in forty minutes be at his office on Fifth Avenue. There among stacks of newspapers he would often spend much of his day on the telephone, interpreting America to Greeks and Greece to Americans, the cigarettes heaped higher and higher in his ashtray. Or he would find himself meeting groups of Greeks on tour in America, or living in the country as students or professionals. Yiorgos knew New York like a native. He knew the U. N. He knew the island, the best cafés and restaurants. He knew Brooklyn and Queens. And in every corner of that world he knew Greeks. He could live whole days among his compatriates and hardly speak a word of English, or he could listen to the Greeklish of immigrants, or get to know Turks in the city, away from the official animosities of their governments, or Americans of various stamps. As a poet and as a journalist he was connected to the arts world, constantly involved in readings, exhibits, installations, performances.

Often I found myself in a cab full of Greeks, speeding across the 59th Street Bridge into a nighttime Manhattan lit up like the Land of Oz. During these journeys Yiorgos would discourse in Greek and English upon the work we were doing. For him, experience was constantly being improvised. "But perhaps," he would say, "when we think we're inventing our future we are only inventing our past." And I would nod as if I had enough mental energy left to follow what he was saying.

He chain-smoked Rothmans cigarettes, and whenever I got together with Yiorgos I chain-smoked right along with him until my head swam and my lungs burned. When we worked on translations we would eventually end up sitting side by side at a desk or table, the Greek and English versions spread out between us, as we debated a word or decided whether to cut the most untranslatable passages in order to make a poem Englishable. He was perhaps too open-minded about these transgressions, but in truth Yiorgos's poetry is sometimes impossible to translate because it is utterly dependent on aspects of Greek for which there is nothing remotely equivalent in English.

To take a simple example, when Greek poets write alphabet poems, as Yiorgos did in his 1995 book *Grámma* (*Letter*), in which it is crucial certain words begin with certain letters, the translator's problem is that the Greek alphabet is not the same as the English one. You can get away with transposing some letters, but not all of them. Subtler problems arose with the idiomatic flavors of words, our sense that an English word like "smells" simply didn't convey the aromatic richness of *myroudiés*. So I would become a thesaurus, trying on different synonyms—aromas, fragrances—and we would puff thoughtfully over the page and now and then get up to empty the ashtray or make coffee or pour a couple of whiskeys.

I tried to get to New York at least once or twice a year. Either I would rent a room or I would stay at Yiorgos's. We worked at my place, his place, his office—anywhere we could find time and space. We faxed and phoned and sent heaps of manuscript and commentary back and forth.

My own poetry displayed obsessions with narrative, lucidity, a desire to write memorable lines and stanzas in what Yeats called "passionate normal speech." Yiorgos's was often surrealistic, cerebral, allusive, difficult. One of his very real contributions to Greek literature, it seems to me, is the way he sweeps his diaspora experience into his Greekness—refusing to distinguish Greek inside Greece from Greek outside, the esoteric from the exoteric. He has even said in lectures that Greek poetry might be predominantly a product of diaspora, from the Italian-speaking Dionysios Solomos, author of the Greek national anthem, to the exiled George Seferis to his own globalized generation. In a few poems, one can see the experience of exile quite simply put. Here, for example, is "Refugees":

On the back
of the photograph I write to remember
not where and when but who

I am not in this picture

They left us nothing
to take along
Only this photograph

If you turn it over you will see me

I am asked, Are you in the picture?
I don't know what to tell you

An apparently simple poem, until you notice that the speaker has disappeared into what he has written on the back of the picture; it illustrates a kind of mental bifurcation in which the loss of attachments becomes a loss even of a knowable self. Yiorgos had felt the mental instability of deracination, and at times seemed to rejoice in it. Nothing was anchored, nothing lasted longer than the punchline of a joke. Life was a matter of skating the distractions and tangents as smoothly as one could.

In another poem, "Occupied City," what begins like a straightforward political statement ends with an utterly incongruous bit of slapstick:

The headlights of the military vehicles
stain the white walls of the firing squads

I am pushed by photographers' flashes
deeper into the darkness of history

In the light of the kneeling black dresses
in the damp embrace of the earth

as bruised bodies are being washed

a bar of soap slides in its furrow, rolls over;
upon it one day
the regime will slip

It's the absoluteness of Chouliaras's irreverence, his refusal to take seriousness seriously, that makes some readers dismiss his work. Others simply find
much of it too difficult or too riddled with puns and jokes, too involved with
postmodern games. But he also has poems in which tenderness and lyricism
are admitted, and these too presented problems of translation, though fewer
than I found in his more cerebral sequences.

"September 1971" is dedicated to Dimitri Kalokyris, a poet and old friend
from Thessaloniki who had written to Yiorgos in America to tell him of
George Seferis's death. Seferis was a poet for whom Yiorgos had ambivalent
feelings. While his generation hardened itself against anything smacking
of populism, Seferis seemed to have participated in cultural nostalgia, his
poetry seeking a coherent Greek identity among the fragments of a lost world.
Generally, Yiorgos much preferred the unsentimental Cavafy, who had lived
in Alexandria until his death in 1933. But in this poem he briefly indulges
his own sense of exile and the way he shares with Seferis a search for Greek
identity. If American poets too often ask "Who am I?" Greeks are more
likely to question "Who are we? What does it mean to be Greek, no matter
what country we live in?" Yiorgos's poem alludes to Seferis's "The King of
Asine," which had taken a seemingly insignifcant fragment of Homer, the
name of a king in the Argolid, and turned it over and over, wondering what
it could mean. Here is the younger poet's response:

Summer incessantly flees from open windows
light burns
the room is flooded with butterflies

at such a time he too
was looking for the dead king's face
in a gold reflection

the boat was rocking
in the mind's furrows
and the field split in two
where the armored sun's bright thorns
rose up

the place smelled of basil
maybe this is the message
of the one we are looking for
in the stone, the birds, and the ship

Many names from those days
remain unchanged
but we, what do we know
Ασίνην τε;
a word in Seferis

It's a small thing, this homage, but here Yiorgos admitted his generation had not surpassed its elders. The poem is utterly literary, but even so it conveys a gentle modesty.

Several of Yiorgos's prose poems seem especially accessible to me. In some of these he is easier to follow despite his antipathy for punctuation, and on occasion I thought our English versions almost did him justice. One such case was his jazzy hymn to bread, part of an ambitious longer sequence:

bread, sweet bread, bitter bread, of society and of the confined, bread of my mother and my father, bread of the earth, a dried-up slice, with *klarína* or a saxophone only, bread of exile and of your homeland, bread of the hungry and the insatiable, bread of the fool and the unjust, syllabic bread, holy bread, of the dead and of the courageous, raisin bread, *chleba*, *nan*, bread shared four ways, consecrated bread, true bread, bread of fairy tales, white and black, moist bread and dry, wedding bread, unleavened bread, bread of the cook, hungry bread, of my sister, bread of angels, quotidian, bread from wheat and from corn, rice bread, musical notes of sliced bread, bread of food, bread with butter, bread and olives, bread and salt, bread of words, bread of good and bad poets, and of those who made their bread from words, ironic bread, bread of love and of the spasms of sharp little teeth in double-bedded sleep, greedy bread, moldy in the basket, bread of winter, bread full of summer, lips inflamed by bread, ah, betrayed bread, daily bread, of the useless baker of the demagogue, bread

Reading this, I think of the meals and the poems, the cigarettes and glasses of whiskey or wine, the hunger for an experience that was real. No matter how brainy these poems were, they arose from a spirit of love and friendship that moved me with a familiar touch.

2

Once Yiorgos came to Minnesota to give a joint reading with me. The Bosnian war was in full swing at the time. It was certainly on his mind when I picked him up at the Fargo airport and drove him across the Red River.

"So this river is the border between two states?"

"Yes. That was North Dakota, this is Minnesota."

Yiorgos thought for a moment, then mused. "Good place for a civil war."

The black comedy continued when he met my Croatian colleague, the writer Josip Novakovich. The two liked each other immediately, but once the subject of Serbia arose they were locked in argument over a table at Ralph's Corner Bar, and though both remained friends, only Yiorgos's determined flirtation with one of our female students distracted him from fisticuffs. The Balkans had come to Moorhead.

Among Yiorgos's friends in Astoria I especially remember the sculptor, Manolis, who once worked in Greek television and now lived as an exile in America, exhibiting his modernist work and mourning the loss of a younger woman he had loved. Manolis had a thick beard and mustache and long hair, like a cross between a hippie and an Orthodox priest. He was distracted by his work so he often forgot to eat and was pitifully thin. When we got together he would thoughtfully bite his pipe while Yiorgos and I chain-smoked and I tried to keep up with the Greek jokes filling the air. Trying to hear Manolis through all his facial hair was often a trial, even with the hearing aids I had started to wear.

By this time Yiorgos was courting a beautiful dancer, Vália Alexandrá-tou, who studied at the Martha Graham School and eventually became an accomplished choreographer. Valia was tall and thin, often wearing a black leotard, where Yiorgos was short and round, with flecks of gray in his trimmed black beard, his necktie pulled loose and his sleeves rolled up. She was grace and he was wit, and when they eventually married Manolis made a sculpture of two lovers in honor of their union. I had met one of Yiorgos's earlier wives who lived in Manhattan, but this marriage looked as if it would stick. Unfortunately, after he was transferred to Ottawa in the late 90s, Yiorgos and Valia drifted apart.

But in the days of their courtship and marriage I would visit New York and Valia would make up the sofa bed in their apartment. Yiorgos and I would work and smoke, work and smoke, and sometime late at night we would end up in a crowd of Greeks looking for a party at someone's home. I was like a mascot or hanger-on, my Greek not good enough to let me follow every conversational thread. Now and then Valia would cross the room to plant a kiss on my forehead, letting me know I was welcome anyway.

It could take hours for my Greek friends to decide where to eat. Once a tall, languorous fellow named Kostas, who was in love with a chatterbox named Fotini, told us of a good restaurant out on Long Island. It was owned by a Greek and served *garídes*, shrimp, and Kostas felt a keen hunger for shrimp that night. So we piled into cars and crossed Long Island like Xenophon's army in search of shrimp. Yiorgos and I were in the front seat of Manolis's ancient car, Valia with her friends in Kostas's jeep.

As he drove, Manolis peered desperately over the wheel through that forest of facial hair. I tried not to look at the roads as he swerved and dodged and rumbled. At last we were on the freeway and he relaxed into his old posture of mournful equanimity. Suddenly, out of nowhere in the Long Island night, Manolis broke into song:

Krátisa ti zoí mou krátisa ti zoí mou taxidévontas
anámesa sta kítrina déntra katá to pláyiasma tis vrohís. . . .

I've held onto my life held onto my life travelling
among the yellow trees under the driving rain. . . .

It was one of the haunting songs of Mikis Theodorakis. Every person in that
car joined in singing. The words were Seferis's, from his "Epiphany, 1937,"
the tune almost liturgical. But I felt that night, traveling through the dark
with these friends, that I was hearing the pure poetry of exile.

It occurs to me that I should get to the source of all this restlessness, the
trouble at the core. Now I must turn the page and try again. . . .

VII

THE END OF IMMORTALITY

1

In my early twenties, I was fairly certain I was immortal. Granted, my family was populated with mortals, some of whom had problems I could detail here if this were another sort of memoir. (In high school I considered Eugene O'Neill's *Long Day's Journey into Night*, with its drug addicts and late-night soliloquies, to be my family's story, my fate.) But I came from a clan of travelers, mountaineers and wanderers, and the idea of escape occurred naturally to me. Never letting anyone get too close, I left home at eighteen and too rarely went back.

At nineteen I took a year off from college, worked in Alaska for seven months, then spent another seven on the road in Britain, Ireland and the Continent. After the first five months in Alaska I wound up running the freezer crew on a cannery barge. It was a gutted World War II-vintage Liberty Ship, chained and cabled to shore amid the storm-pelted hills of Dutch Harbor, an Aleutian landscape of spectacular bleakness.

I remember standing on the upper deck in the dead of night while my crew unloaded pallets of frozen crab to a cargo ship that would carry it south to Bellingham, Washington, my home town. I wore a freezer suit, watch cap and heavy boots, and standing next to me in a down parka was my boss, a man twice my age. We neared the end of a forty-hour shift, but the electric forklift in the freezer had broken down, so there we waited, snowflakes slanting through worklights on the masts of both ships. I was a hard-working boy and this boss had taken a shine to me. That night he said, "You could run this place if you wanted to."

Perhaps he was right. I was only nineteen, but people thought I was smart. They called me Shakespeare because I was always reading or scribbling in a journal in down time. I was, though, a truly mixed up kid. Immortal, true enough, but not entirely well. A cynic about everything, especially the whole notion of marriage and family life, yet utterly alone and vulnerable, given to poetic stares and breaking into song when I thought no one could hear me. Nixon had resigned that summer, and when the news reached Dutch Harbor it only confirmed me in my cynicism. I had taken up with a cigar-smoking girlfriend whose family life was packed with suicides and other disasters. And there was some central core of arrogance within me. I had other options, and could go back to college. I wasn't fated to run a seafood processing operation a thousand miles from anywhere.

So I turned to this man, my boss, and let him have it. I gave him the plan—college, travel, then fame as a writer. Nobody could stop me.

He was too tough to show what he thought of my plan, though for a moment he looked like he'd eaten bad lettuce. We dropped the subject and stood there in silence till the work resumed.

2

A few months later I got out of a stranger's car somewhere in the Scottish border country, thanked the driver for the ride, slung my household on my back and started walking. It was a long walk: much of the time from January to July 1975 I was on the road, with brief residencies in London and Paris and Spain. A self-styled down-and-outer, nearly always alone, never letting friendships get below the surface, I loved the exhilaration of an empty road stretching ahead of me. Even snowfall and the prospect of sleeping in some ruined croft did not bother me. I had wool clothes and a down sleeping bag and was confident I could weather anything Scotland could throw at me.

Years later my father would describe how he came to London on a trip with Claire, who would become his second wife, and how I met them at the airport looking like a tramp, one sole flapping loose from a hiking boot, my old sweater drooping to my knees, my face all smile and wispy beard. I was strong from hiking hundreds of miles. If I was mortal, I hardly knew it.

My circumnavigation of Scotland involved a stay in Orkney, hitchhiking across the north coast and down through the Hebrides. Later that spring I went to Belfast in search of an American, a friend's friend who might show me around. I found his house in a Protestant neighborhood of neat brick houses just downhill from a Catholic one of bare larders and blocked-up windows. A British stockade stood at the border of the two neighborhoods, patrols leaving at regular intervals despite a recently declared cease-fire. Across from the stockade was a park, and after a long day there talking to children and pensioners, I learned that the American was away on the Continent for a month. The jovial old park keeper said he would take care of me.

When the sun set and it was time for him to close up, he gave me the last bit of food he had and locked me into his hut so I could have a safe night's sleep. He'd tell the other keeper to look out for me next day, he said. So there I was, reading *For Whom the Bell Tolls* by lamplight in a tiny space with a coal stove for warmth and a pot for tea, then trying to sleep in my bag on a thin foam pad stretched on the concrete floor. I imagined all sorts of dangers, but heard little of the world outside.

Next day another keeper unlocked the hut and let me out. People from the neighborhood brought me food, gave me advice. There had been a killing in the night not far away. Someone shot a man in the back of the head and left his young child there to witness it. The news made me disinclined to spend another night in the park. Finally I shared a cab into the city center with a few people who were running errands of one sort or another. They explained to the cabbie, who at one point talked us through a roadblock, that I was looking for an American and the American wasn't at home. The cabbie recognized the American's name and knew someone else who might have an idea what to do. On we went, through neighborhoods with low gray row houses and vacant streets.

The cabbie brought me to one house, got out with his engine still running and myself at his heels, and knocked on the door.

The door teetered and fell inward with a thud. A man inside the house who had been asleep hungover on the floor of his tiny parlor, said from his blankets, "Don't bother about the door, lads. Paras knocked it down in a search. I'm damned if I'll fix the hinges, they'll just knock it down again."

So the cabbie introduced me to this man, whose name I have lost, and left. I spent a whole day in that poor man's parlor. We watched cricket on his snowy TV screen, and now and then he explained a bit about the organization he worked for, along with the American. This organization took Protestant and Catholic children to summer camps on the Continent in the hopes that they would learn to like each other away from Ulster's animosities. The man lived on very little money. I walked out with him when he went to get cigarettes, the two of us talking the whole way to a corner shop and back. That afternoon he showed me his larder: an old oven that no longer worked in which he kept a loaf of bread, a bowl of eggs and a few strips of bacon in wax paper. He made me a meal, and he insisted on giving me the bacon. When I remember that gesture of hospitality more than a quarter century later, I feel moved and ashamed. Food never tasted so good, but my privations were temporary while his were a long-term condition.

Still, there was no point in sticking around. I thanked him, told him I'd leave, and he gave me directions to an hotel that wasn't too far away.

I was walking somewhere in Belfast with no map, no sense of the city's layout, carrying a mountaineering rucksack on my back and (this is perhaps a true indication of my oddness) a portable typewriter in a case. The previous day I had at least known where one neighborhood ended and another began, but now the row houses all looked alike. Perhaps I was momentarily lost when a gang of boys stopped me and shoved me up against a wall.

"Where you going?"

I told them.

"Where you from?"

"America."

"What's that you're carrying?"

"Clothes. Books."

"Books, he says."

"And a typewriter."

They were tough looking boys.

"What religion are you?"

I thought they were pulling my leg. It was such a stereotypical question.

"None," I said.

"You can't say that. Everybody's got a religion."

"I don't."

"What religion was yer father?"

"None. No religion."

Looking at their faces I sensed this encounter could challenge my immortality. Finally one of the boys said, "Leave him be. He's just a tourist. Let him go."

They were evidently keeping watch over some demarcation of turf that was invisible to me. My legs were jell-o when I walked away from them, and a passing car's backfire nearly stopped my heart.

I found a small hotel behind barbed wire and got myself a room and conversed that night with some very nice Scots who always took their holiday in Belfast. Because of the excellent prices, they said.

3

That spring of 1975, Saigon fell to the North Vietnamese, and I felt morbidly connected to history. I was just barely too young to have been drafted and, unlike my older brother, had only cursory experience of antiwar protests. Arguments in high school. Shouting matches with the Catholic doctor whose family took me in for two summers while I worked in the Skagit Valley pea harvest. A black armband to show solidarity with the moratorium after Kent State—that almost got me a black eye. But Doug had been tear-gassed in a Seattle protest. After college he had traveled through Southeast Asia on his own, smoked opium in a village on the Mekong River, witnessed rocket attacks in Phnom Penh. In my faulty logic, the least I could do was face some Ulster hoods eager to beat the tar out of me.

There were other adventures on my long hitchhiking tour, but I had decided to finish college, so I went back to America in July 1975 and accepted my mother's doting love for a month while I read very fat books and wrote stories. Then I returned to Colorado, feeling older and much more experienced than my peers.

In those days I still did some rock and mountain climbing, a perverse pursuit for me, since I must even then have suffered from vertigo. I can see myself quite clearly at the top of a climb, one of those sheer granite faces punctuated by scrub oak or saxifrage poking from crevices. Every night after a climb I had the same dream. The summit of that day's conquest appeared with perfect clarity, became palpable in my aching muscles and callused hands. There I was, right at the edge but anchored in like a man on belay, webbed and caribeenered. Then my anchor melted away. I saw myself drop over the edge and woke gripping the mattress of my dormitory bed.

Some two dozen climbs later I was fairly good at it, but after every single one I had the same dream. Finally I admitted I was spooked and stopped doing technical climbs. Walking up a fourteener was enough thrill for me, especially once I had fallen in love.

Sitting in a college dining hall, I spotted Jonna carrying her tray to a table. There was something willowy in the way she swung her slender hips the slightest bit as she rounded a table. She seemed intensely fragile, yet part of that beautiful, sophisticated world from which I was exiled, the world of people who always knew how to behave. It was a world of Easterners, mostly, and I was from the West. But I gathered my courage, joined her for breakfast, and was from that moment more interested in the adventure of sex than any other.

Doug kept climbing, though. When he returned from his travels around the world, having made it to high altitudes in the Himalayas, he was in his mid-twenties, interested in politics but hell bent on avoiding law school. He drifted for a few years, worked for a department store, then a paint company. Then he became a congressman's press officer and lived in Washington D. C., and after that a very successful campaign manager in Seattle city politics, along with doing work for the Puget Sound Council of Governments. People said he had a promising career.

One summer when we were together at the family home on Lake What-com near Bellingham, Doug joked despairingly about getting fat and grabbed a roll of his own midriff to show me. He worked long hours. It was hard to get enough exercise.

When Jonna and I were married and out of college in 1978, I worked in Rochester as a gardener and caretaker. Doug began to climb more seriously again. He married a woman who loved the outdoors as he did, and who had an interest in the law. But something was wrong about the marriage. Or about his career. Or about approaching thirty. He felt remorse for the way we had always fought as boys, and tried to make it up to me. We went out for a few beers at a waterfront tavern once, on one of my visits to the West

Coast, but found our conversation awkward, a few terse encouragements strung on a line of silence. There was real love between us, but also a residue of the wariness of brothers.

In the summer of 1979 I began my second year as a gardener on the estate in Irondequoit, next door to Jonna's parents. My younger brother, Don, was a photography student at the Rochester Institute of Technology, so he and I spent time together as allies, fellow Westerners in the foreign country of New York with its strange manners and extreme weather. I was healthy and in love with my wife and busy writing a novel about Alaska when I wasn't pruning or mowing, planting or weeding. Don, who had according to the Mason formula drifted for several years, had now discovered the talent that would lead to his career as a commercial photographer. He was also fascinated by adventure. He wanted to go climbing, and Doug had promised to take him on his first ascent of Mount Shuksan, a rugged, heavily glaciated peak near Bellingham.

They would be okay, I thought, though I had lost my own appetite for technical climbing. I remember going to a concert with Don in Rochester before he flew home, and talking about their plans. Then I don't remember anything else until a phone call in the middle of the night, August 26th, and how I stumbled into the living room of the little cottage I shared with Jonna, knocking over a lamp as I lunged for the phone.

It was my stepfather, Art, a man much loved for his jovial, loquacious ways. I was always glad to hear his voice, but tonight it sounded different. When I asked him how he was, he said, "Well . . . I'm not sure."

I had completely forgotten about the climb.

4

On Saturday the twenty-fifth, Don and Doug hiked into Lake Ann, a tarn fed by glaciers on Shuksan. It was sunny, and as they set up camp and practiced climbing some nearby boulders they talked about their route the next day, across the glaciers and into the network of rock chimneys that would lead them to a high snowfield and on toward the knife-tip of the summit. It was just like Doug to get himself injured before the climb. He took off his boots to wade in a stream near camp, and cut his foot on what must have been one of the few shards of broken glass for miles around. He was always more accident prone than the rest of us. I had broken a few bones, but Doug was always getting stitches, like the time he caught a ski pole in the back of the head—it was jokingly tossed by one of our racing buddies in dry-land training—and had to get himself sewed up before he went out that night on his first date. Now, when he and Don examined this new wound, they were sure he would not be able to climb on that foot.

The clouds drove in above them, obscuring the peak. My brothers huddled in their tent that night while a thunderstorm raged over the mountain and rain poured down. The climb would have to be scrubbed.

But when they awoke to a world remade next morning and looked up at the sunlit peak, their spirits rose. Doug tested his bandaged foot. He felt fine. They decided to go.

Carrying packs, gear, ice axes and a climbing rope, my brothers passed the stunted, mossy firs at timberline and ascended the damp trail to the glacier. They crossed on snow and ice to Fisher's Chimneys. I always liked chimney climbing, wedging my body, arms and legs inside narrow walls and inching upward. It felt more secure than face climbing, and I suppose my vertigo was less apt to kick in. So I imagine that portion of the climb being a pleasure for both of them, though these particular chimneys were more an alpine route over steep boulders than a shimmy inside walls. Doug at twenty-eight was getting slowly back into shape. It must have felt good to use his body and skill in this way. Perhaps he was able to forget the City Council campaign he managed. Maybe even the doubts he must have felt about his marriage vanished for a time. And Don, at twenty-one, must have been in heaven, getting his second taste of real climbing with his older brother—they had previously done the Coleman Glacier route up Mount Baker. This was the great older brother who had been a hero to us, who once owned a red sports car, then a jeep, who had lived and worked in Africa and traveled through Asia, sending letters home for two years from places we couldn't even pronounce, who held the attention of elders when he talked politics, whose girlfriends were gorgeous and who seemed so on top of things now, married and doing important work.

Both brothers photographed the climb. We have Don's photos, not Doug's, since his pack was never recovered. So I have shots of Doug from behind as he started up the chimney, which looks at first like a dark gray boulder field. Then what must have been the snowfield above the chimney, and one shot looking across pitted snow to a sunburst, the lead rope barely visible as it runs up toward the light. Maybe the sequence of shots is wrong, because I then have an earlier shot of the mountain with the two ice shelves of Curtis Glacier they had to cross. Then shots from the summit—snow and ice sweeping away in the brilliant summer air, Mount Baker in one direction, the Picket Range in another. One shot of Doug at the summit in short sleeves and sunglasses, his sandy hair disheveled by wind, his face in shadow as he turns toward the camera while a jagged sunlit snow ridge cuts the air behind him.

The view is so brilliant that I hardly notice clouds on the horizon. They look white and harmless in the photograph.

What joy my brothers must have felt. To have done the climb and done it together as brothers! Not the highest peak in the neighborhood, but the most beautiful, perhaps the most often-photographed mountain in all of North America, an image familiar even to climbers who have never heard its name. A constant presence in our childhood, it stands behind us in family portraits as well, all five of us together. My handsome father and beautiful mother with three tow-headed boys, ages two, four and eight or nine. In one particular photograph, Doug stands slightly apart from the rest of us on a rock that raises him almost to our mother's height, the perfect tip of Shuksan rising over his right shoulder, a universe of rock and ice below it.

It was on the descent that they got into trouble. Perhaps in an excited state from having summited, and moving quickly, they started down too far to "climber's right" of where they had gone up. At first it seemed easy, down-climbing face-in, sometimes facing out to walk, but soon the rocks dropped away at too steep a pitch.

Maybe, too, they saw the weather coming in. Maybe they judged that there wasn't enough time to ascend once more in search of the right route. They were not roped together at this point, and Doug decided to scout a way across the rock face into another chimney, or perhaps to a couloir they could use as a way down.

Doug had started the day in wool trousers, but now they were warm from exertion and he had changed to cut-off jeans. Still carrying his pack, he started across the exposed rock.

Then he slipped. We have always wondered whether it was that injured foot that made the difference, or whether his mind was on other problems.

Don heard him say, "Shit!" and saw him fall backwards.

He landed on his back on a rock shelf, then rolled off it and disappeared over the edge.

5

When I remember that Don was twenty-one years old and on his first significant climb, I am amazed at what he was able to do next. We have gone over these details more recently, and even to him they are like some barely remembered dream. I don't know how much time passed after Doug's fall, how often Don must have called our brother's name, knowing or half-knowing he was dead.

In the small falls I took when rock climbing, the first instant was a white whoosh in the brain without anything resembling thought. Only after the belay rope caught me and I hung there until the feeling came back to my hands did I absorb what had happened—alive and terrified. I don't think Doug could have felt much.

Don must already have been in shock. Driven by adrenaline, he made the traverse across that rock face to another chimney. There he met a third climber and told the fellow to head out and call for help. After that, he slid down on his boots and rear end, descending something like a thousand feet at high speed, ripping out the seat of his trousers in the process. At the bottom of this chute, using his ice axe, he leapt a moat where the glacier had melted back from the rock. He kept a cool enough head to know he must look for Doug, and when he landed on the glacier he ran about as best he could, trying to spot our brother, shouting at cliffs and crevasses.

Don stayed on the glacier, shouting and searching for hours. Clouds closed in around the mountain, just as they had the previous afternoon. By the time a rescue helicopter lifted Don from the glacier, another storm threatened.

From the helicopter they attempted to spot Doug's body. Eventually, the thunderstorm forced them from the peak. In what seemed like minutes the rock chimneys became gushing waterfalls.

Later Don told me that when the sheriff's car dropped him off at the lake house, hours after he and Doug were due for dinner, he heard someone in the house exclaiming, "They're here!" Then he had to go inside and tell them what had happened.

He knew Doug was dead, but tried to give our mother and Doug's wife some hope by telling them he might be able to survive the night on the mountain. He told them Doug was wearing his wool trousers.

When I got the phone call that night in Rochester, Art must also have guessed Doug was dead, but we all wanted to keep hoping and he let me hope that my brother was lying out there, perhaps badly injured but waiting for someone to find him. I spoke to that image in my mind all night, as if I could will my brother to live.

The next day I couldn't work in the garden, but paced up and down the shore of Lake Ontario, periodically checking in with my family by phone, trying to keep Doug alive in my brain. A continent away from my family and the mountains I loved, I felt more a foreigner than ever. My father, meanwhile, drove up from Seattle with Claire and stationed himself with Don at the rescuers' base camp, listening to reports on their radio. Late that day one of the search crews spotted Doug's body in such rugged terrain they were unable to get to it before dark. They could only confirm he was dead.

"We lost him," Art told me on the phone. My in-laws arranged for Jonna and me to fly west in the morning.

6

From a small commuter plane, heading north out of Seattle, I pointed out the mountains to Jonna. First Rainier, then Glacier Peak, Baker, and Shuksan's rock pyramid. My face already felt bruised and pummeled from sobbing, and I remember the look on my mother's face as the family met us on the tarmac at Bellingham. Doug's body had just been brought down from the mountain. My father said he would take me to see it.

He must have felt numbed as he drove to the mortician's. He had seen plenty of death in World War II, more when he practiced pediatrics before becoming a psychiatrist, but this was his oldest son. They had fought hard when my father left the family. Now Doug was dead and our father must have felt the Furies closing in on him. We tried to talk, but our words were strange, as if real feeling had been exhausted and now we had to manufacture it for each other's benefit.

"Once again," the mortician said, looking especially at me, "I don't advise viewing the body."

But I wanted to see.

He took us into a back room where the black body bag lay on a table. He unzipped the bag part way down so we could just see Doug's head and shoulders. Except for the large bruise under the skin of his forehead, he looked like he was taking a nap. His hands were held close to his face as someone sleeping might do, though of course that might have been a futile shielding gesture—estimates of his fall ranged from six hundred to a thousand feet. His eyes were only slightly open. Blood smeared one of his fingers. It was all so subtle. I had seen him fall asleep on the sofa at home looking almost exactly like that, a book fanned open beside him.

I was afraid to touch him. I was also aware of the twist in his body from a broken spine, and the fact that the mortician had elected not to show us everything.

"Good night, sweet prince," my father said.

7

Days later we took Doug's ashes into the mountains, spreading them in view of both Shuksan and Baker. As I sprinkled some into the heather and rock of the alpine meadow, they looked like tiny bits of pulverized bone. Something metal was mixed in with them: I was holding part of the zipper of my brother's cut-off jeans, a scarred little tab of brass. I looked at it, considered keeping it, then tossed it with the ashes to the wind.

We scattered more ashes on the slopes of ski runs we had known since childhood, then went back to the house and got drunk. There was a lot of sobbing. Jonna comforted me as I tried to sleep while my mother's animal cries came from the room below.

The next morning I went out to a car to retrieve a sweater and noticed we had left the plastic ash box in the trunk. There were still some unscattered ashes in it, and I felt a strange guilt at leaving them alone in the trunk all night. Pulling on my sweater, I walked slowly across the wet lawn, out by the big cedar tree with its rope swing hanging empty and unused. The great cascading greenery hung over a bare spot in the grass as if a storybook giant had slumped his shoulders and stood still for a thousand years, frozen except when wind nudged him from time to time. Not even winter storms off the lake could budge that tree, that shaggy trunk so unaware, so apparently unaware of its lighter branches lifted and swaying, turning and turning back. I stood there holding a mug of now-cold coffee and touched the worn knot of rope we used to swing on. It felt rough and I wanted that, I wanted something to feel rough. To feel anything at all. That day we held a small ceremony on the beach, burying the box with the last of Doug's ashes.

Going back to the shores of Lake Ontario, it was hard to see the purpose of anything. I seemed to spend months raking leaves. At the end of each day I saw my employer's lawn looking tidy and green, and the next morning it was covered again with the fallen. The work was discouraging. Nothing stayed in place in the garden, so there was no aspect of life in which things stood still. It was hard to learn how to live with this fact. The gray weather rolled in with waves from the lake, and I seemed to sleepwalk for months through my job, my marriage, my few connections to a world outside the intense privacy of grief. One day months after Doug's death I was walking in the hallway of our little cottage and bumped into my wife, who seemed to have been tip-toeing around me, or around the wall I had built up around myself. There we were in the narrow, wainscoted space. Our eyes met and I said to her, "I can't do this any more, can I?"

Jonna gave me a firm look. "No, you can't."

And that was the moment when I came back to life, or knew I should try to come back to life. Jonna's grandmother, a Christian Scientist, had said to me the night Doug's body was found, "You have to let him go," and I had refused all that time to follow her advice, as if it would betray my brother to do so. I kept old sweaters of his, old letters. I looked for him in dreams. But now I began to live with his absence.

A year later I went with Don and my father to the spot in the mountains where we had scattered most of my brother's remains. We walked in on the trail until it seemed the view of the two peaks was about what it had been, then sat down together on a gray stone outcrop, talking about Doug. Each of us had a feeling the mountain had claimed him like a debt to be paid. The way the storm had socked in, preventing searchers from finding him—it was as if the mountain were a god calling in the weather to shroud its latest victim. Of course we also feared that such thoughts were nonsense and Doug's death was a meaningless accident.

I talked about how I had met a family friend soon after it happened. This man was a chemical engineer, not given to sentimental spirituality. He told me what he thought had happened to my brother by waving a hand in the air: "Doug's energy went somewhere. There was that energy, and now here it is—it's part of this."

My father, Don and I sat on that alpine rock for half an hour, till one of us noticed something in little crevices under our hands. We bent and looked more closely. Indentations in the rock were filled with tiny fragments of bone. We picked them out with fingertips and held them in our palms, staring. Could these be Doug's ashes even a year later? There appeared to be no other explanation.

"This isn't him," my father finally said. "I don't know where he is, but this isn't Doug." And he waved a hand at the air, signifying where Doug had gone.

8

In the late 1990s my father descended into Alzheimer's disease. Once handsome and muscular, he became much shrunken, in mind and body rather like a young boy. When I visited him on the houseboat he shared with Claire, we looked at pictures, sometimes the same ones over and over, and sometimes he pointed to Doug. "That guy." He nodded, stabbing his forefinger at the picture, blinking back tears. Then he made a fist and held it over his heart.

Soon he did not even know who I was. Sitting next to my father, I had no doubt of our mortality. That youthful delusion of impregnability had left me many years ago. It's only a matter of time, and none of us knows how much of it we've got. Ever since Doug's fall, I've lived nearly every day with the presence of my death. I become short with people who waste my time. My father lived well when he could, tried to look squarely at life and not give in to mere conventionality. Separately, my mother fought through a terrible decade and a half after Doug's death and Art's later death of a heart attack, finally quelling her own demons and achieving some peace in old age. Two good people who lost a son—not such an uncommon story, after all.

Don became a commercial photographer and, ultimately, the most accomplished mountaineer in the family, having adventures I can barely imagine, climbing all over the world, refusing to be slowed down even by the onset of rheumatoid arthritis in his forties. Just when my mother had given up hope of having grandchildren, Don married Laura Domoto, and they now have two daughters, Cameron Aiko and Quinn Midori. Cameron was Doug's middle name, the same as our father's.

VIII

ANOTHER KIND OF GREECE

We are not in the same place after all.

—A. E. Stallings

1

As the years passed in Minnesota, I thought the Aegean was lost to me except through friendships, letters, books. But in 1996 I translated for a group of students and faculty traveling there, and those few weeks set my head spinning. The food, the light, the language coming slowly back to me—all of it quickened my pulse. The village where I had lived with Jonna was so near, yet I didn't dare go back, as if all that accumulated loss would bury me the moment I set eyes on Kalamitsi.

Then the Fulbright came my way and I knew going back was inevitable. I knew it was high time I learned about Greece unfiltered through my private grief.

My last days in Minnesota were spent shoveling heaps of snow in sub-zero temperatures. Annie had work of her own to do, so would join me in another month. I felt that lightness of irresponsibility again, wings on my boots.

Our friend Magda had arranged for me to stay with her parents and brother in Glyfada, the prosperous seaside suburb of Athens, at that time still the site of the airport. I had met the family in Athens the previous spring, and planned to stay with them three weeks or so, then move to Aegina in February, where I would rent one of Katerina Anghelaki-Rooke's bungalows.

I had also met Katerina once before—back when I lived in Rochester and had taken a night class from Al Poulin out at Brockport. Al's BOA Editions had just published *Beings and Things on Their Own*, a collection of Katerina's poems translated with Jackie Willcox, and he had brought the Greek poet to America to give readings. I remember two things: she was short and walked with a limp; and she was appalled when I spoke to her in Greek. To use bad grammar in Katerina's presence was like plunging a knife into her heart. It was like burning the Greek flag or pissing in the wine bottle. It was an insult above all others.

When I called her a decade later to ask about renting a bungalow she had mastered greater tolerance. Yes, I could have it at a good price for February and March, and after that we would see.

See what? I wondered. Was I being tested?

The Chalikias lived in a quiet neighborhood of concrete dwellings on the hillside above Glyfada. Their home was built on the family model common in Greece: business on the ground floor and upper floors for living. There were five stories. Above their business—laundering linens for restaurants—was a floor for storage, above that an apartment for Yannis and Penelope, or Popi for short. Above that was Alekos's flat—each of these had two bedrooms, a kitchen, bathroom and living room, the latter filled with family furniture and photographs. At the top of the building was Magda's smaller penthouse flat with a rooftop terrace overlooking the Saronic Gulf beyond other white family towers. Since Magda was at work far away in Minnesota, I used her flat.

They were a Corfu family who still prized their ancestral lands on the island and tried to visit them once a year. Yannis, who could be fierce or morose on occasion, then burst into rough gusts of laughter when you least expected it, was already nearly eighty when I met him, yet in superb health. Popi was a decade younger, still a beauty. They had raised their blond twins in Corfu and Glyfada. Magda had turned out to be a prodigy as well as an athletic beauty, and had left for graduate studies in Canada, followed by teaching in the States. She still sent money home, and had increasingly taken an active role in her family's affairs as their father's eccentricities threatened to run them aground.

A village man who fought in the resistance, Yannis lived in the city without for a moment really trusting its institutions and manners. In the village one never trusts officials, banks, policemen, or tax collectors. Yannis sometimes trusted near-strangers with a village connection or due to a tip from a relative, and ended up losing a lot of money in bad business deals. But when I first met him he seemed the epitome of the confident Greek *paterfamilias*, leading the family on shopping expeditions to the huge discount stores that imitated American chains, always seeking the best deals, whether for a new mop or a sack of groceries. These expeditions usually followed six hours of morning work in the laundry. Tourism was down and they were losing customers as restaurants tried to save money, so there was an unspoken dread or desperation in the work these days. After the midday meal and a siesta there would usually be an evening *volta* or stroll with their dog, Max, who resembled a droll black bear, and sometimes Yannis paid calls on his customers without ever telling the rest of us what he was doing, leaving us to wait for him in the street.

Alekos, Magda's twin brother, was a smart, sweet-tempered man whose ambitions had been thwarted several times, as much by his domineering father as anything else. After service in the army he ran a bar for a while. When not working for his parents he often waited tables in restaurants or clubs. He was briefly married to a young woman from Sparta, but it didn't work out, and he sometimes blamed the dullness and provinciality of Spartans for their problems. After the divorce, he fell into a trap that is sprung fairly often for young men in Greece. Out of duty to his parents he stayed at home, helping them run the business, but he was never entrusted with ownership of the business or even partnership, so he could never achieve independence.

I've seen other young Greek men get caught in this web, where Americans usually assume each generation has to make its own way, and I wonder if it doesn't have a source in the country's centuries of poverty. When children are the sole insurance policy for parents in old age, very complex ties of guilt and necessity accrue. If Alekos were given the business, his father would not be in control of his own old age, as if anyone ever controls that. Yannis's fundamental inability to trust his own family contrasted oddly with the trust he had placed in lousy business partners.

But all this analysis does nothing to convey the joy of my weeks with the Chalikias and the pleasure of every visit with them in subsequent years. They were generous people—their house was a Mecca for cats who knew they would be fed and cared for. Relatives from Corfu or America could often be found camped in one of the extra rooms or fitting sheets to a sofa. Popi always prepared the midday meal and presided over it while Yannis poured splendid wine he made from Santorini must. The wine was decanted into plastic water bottles from the barrels downstairs, and one seldom left the house after a visit without a litre of wine as a gift. I quickly learned that you could take Yannis a bottle of whiskey as a present, but you could never, ever, insult him by bringing anyone else's wine into his house.

After a meal, often of fish or lamb with salad, feta cheese, potatoes and bread, Popi always brought a bowl of fruit in season to the table. Oranges in winter, apples much of the year, or melon. She would quarter and peel apples and leave them in a tray for us to eat, so satisfying with the wine—a kind of gustatory counterpoint or sweet sharpness.

That winter there were also chestnuts roasted in the oven and peeled hot over one's dinner plate. Yannis taught me a children's rhyme to go with this dessert:

> *To kástano théli to krasí*
> *Kai to karídi méli*
> *Kai to korítsi théli fílima*
> *Vrádi kai mesiméri.*

> The chestnut wants some wine
> And the walnut honey
> And the young girl wants a kiss
> At evening and at noon.

When the fruit was peeled, Max was invited to join the family—he too liked apples. Occasionally a chair was captured by Attila—a cat with an attitude whose girlfriend, Grace, kept her distance. I ate a lot with these lovely people, but I also ate perhaps the healthiest food I have ever known. They wouldn't allow me to take them to a restaurant in recompense, so Alekos and I tried cooking them a Mexican dinner, using pita for tortillas. I also made a pork loin cooked in orange juice, a recipe I had learned in Oaxaca, but Popi saw at once that I had not reduced its sauce sufficiently. She took over and served the dish to us again for the evening meal, properly cooked, and I never challenged her culinary prowess again.

2

My first year in Greece was spent in a relatively backward, rural part of the country. Now, staying with city folk who had seen some of the world, I learned whole new aspects of Greek life. By then Greece had joined Europe, of course, and though it was still the poorest member of the Common Market, it was far more prosperous than I remembered. It was also a more liberal place. This was a family whose preferred form of exercise was swimming, and both Magda and Alekos had become devoted nudists. One of their circles of friends met every afternoon at the *limanáki*, a little bay off the road to Sounion. When I first knew him, Alekos was able to swim almost every afternoon, year round, and I took to joining him as often as I could. This hobby did not bother their parents in the least.

After the midday meal, while Yannis and Popi enjoyed a siesta, Alekos and I drove south about half an hour, parking on a bluff above the sea. We clambered down the rocky, scrub-lined path to the bay, and there we met the regulars, men and women of all shapes and ages, many of them baked nut-brown over every inch of their bodies, fearless of melanoma or the judgment of peeping toms on the road above. There were businessmen covered only with the newspapers they read while lying on the rocks, women who wore only sunglasses and tanning oil, occasional pale foreigners like myself. It was the most ordinary social gathering imaginable, except that no one wore any clothes.

The afternoon was spent reading, napping, talking of recent troubles like the flood in Korinth or the chaos in Albania. In particular there was

Katerina, not the poet of Aegina but a lively friend of Alekos and Magda who was always kind enough to engage me in conversation, always chattering away as she sought the warmest spaces on the slanting rocks. Slowly I learned not to focus so much on peoples' bodies, just to enjoy the sunlight, water and conversation.

This was January, mind you, when very few people swim in the Aegean despite *I Méres tis Alkyónis*, or the Halcyon Days. I love the myth, which Ovid beautifully told, and the fact that it so often points to an actual break in the winter weather. Daughter of the wind, Aeolus, and wife of King Ceyx of Trachis, Alkyone was said to love her husband so much that their happiness verged on impiety. Ceyx died when his ship was wrecked as he traveled to Delphi to consult the oracle. Alkyone grieved so inconsolably at her husband's death that the gods took pity on her and changed her into a kingfisher. In one version, Ceyx was changed to the same bird, while in another he became a sea mew. In any case there are fourteen days each winter when the seas calm and the weather warms so the kingfishers can nest on the waters. Whatever the explanation, the Halcyon Days are a very real phenomenon of the Aegean winter.

But calm winds and sunny weather do not always foretell a change of season, and the sea in winter is quite cold. The first few times I eased myself into the water its iciness seemed to cut my skin. I soon learned how to get past this initial shock and let the salty, buoying sea restore me. I started at five teeth-chattering minutes, emerging from the water numbed and reddened as if the brine had scoured my skin, but I came to love it and soon could stay in much longer. Nothing in my experience is quite so therapeutic as immersion in the sea. I heard from Annie about deep drifts of snow in Minnesota and how she had to shovel the roof, and here I was in January, basking by sunlit waves. "You are gonna make a very good skin," Alekos said, practicing his English. He rarely washed the salt off after these excursions, preferring to let the sea cure his hide.

Sometimes, too, we finished the day with a long walk in the hills—Alekos, Katerina and I—passing other perambulists or *hórta* gatherers, watching the sun set beyond Aegina from one of the dry, scrub-covered hilltops. One day, when Alekos and I had some responsibility at home and could not make the walk, Katerina shouted down the rocks at us, "I'll have to go alone, then. I'll meet an Albanian and he'll kill me!"

Albanians were blamed for anything, as Gypsies or Turks had been blamed in earlier days. Prisons had been opened north of the border, so any Albanians who came south were thought to be thieves or killers. Each night we saw horrible scenes on the television news—beatings of policemen, crowds of emaciated, rioting men. It was all too close for comfort. Some afternoons at the little bay our fellow nudists engaged in political debate. Not only the Balkans came up, but also the question of whether America was a materialist society, whether Clinton was immoral or just acting like a normal man, whether Italy would turn ultra-conservative. Or there were talks about vacations they might take, the schedules of ferries and prices of airline tickets—it was all so removed from the village I had known sixteen years earlier. Perhaps it was an indication of just how limited my understanding had been in those days.

Here was a country of worldly people who were far less puritanical than many Americans, who worked hard and took their relaxation when they could, who valued friends and family above all else, who respected education and eloquence, who were skeptical of government but aware of their precious freedoms, who knew about corruption but weren't entirely soured by it, who were polite about my Greek and didn't expect me to stand in for all American policies. I could not imagine our nudist Katerina wearing black for long if, God forbid, her husband were to die. She had to cook for him, sure enough, but she was otherwise far more liberated than women I had known in the village. After all, there she was, her huge breasts darker than the earth, her hair touched with henna, and she was able to talk back to any man in the bay on any subject that arose.

Greece had changed, but so had my ability to see and hear. To be sure, my congenital hearing loss got worse every year and caused me no end of embarrassment in English, let alone other languages, but I was no longer the boy using this country as a backdrop for my own spiritual vacation. I was coming to know the place, slowly and clumsily, but in an entirely new way.

Staying with a family as warm and complex as the Chalikias had opened up much more of the country than I had known existed.

After those nude afternoons, Alekos and I would often play skáki, chess, in his flat, leaning over the board with cigarettes. I spoke Greek, he practiced English, so our conversations would have seemed very strange to an outsider. "I'm going to make a very bad move on you," he would say.

And I: "*Prósexe, paidí mou.*"

"What you are going to get?"

"*I vassílissa den xérei pou einai.*"

"My queen? How you are going to get my queen?"

Now and then Popi would catch us smoking, which she had begged Alekos not to do. I protected him by saying I had been lost in thought and lighted two cigarettes by mistake. It was hard to resist smoking in Greece.

We had our differences, but they were rare. Once at the evening meal we were watching news of a minor incident on one of the islets off Turkey, and partly testing my Greek on a political subject, I ventured the very American opinion that the past was past and the two countries had better start anew and learn to live together. I had barely formed the words when Alekos and Yannis seemed to leap down my throat, brandishing knives and forks. No, I was wrong, I didn't know what I was talking about! The Turks will cut your throat if you let them! Alekos had read a lot of history, and he had his own list of legitimate gripes from the mistreatment of Asia Minor Greeks to Turkey's police state. Still, the savagery with which I was put in my place by my friends took me aback—another worrisome lesson about the Balkans.[§]

[§] For some Greeks these animosities no longer exist, but old hatreds die hard, as the world learns over and over again.

3

Sometimes, especially on rainy days, I stayed in Magda's flat and worked—reading in Greek and English, writing in my journal, using the laptop I had brought to print out drafts of poems. On those days I felt the glimmerings of recollection, my past in Greece filtered through the present, and began to think I might have a small book in me about the changes I had seen.

One day while I was hard at work, Yannis brought an electrician upstairs and stood by to supervise repairs of some switches. He noticed the bed covered with books, and I showed him the fat Greek dictionary given to me by Yiorgos Chouliaras.

Nodding his gray head gently, he took his time deciding that I needed correction. "You shouldn't read poetry with a dictionary," he said. "That's like reading a cold wall. Read to get the flavor of the words. Read with your heart."

He touched the center of his chest.

I told him he was right. I read Seferis first without knowing every word, to get the sound of it, then went back and looked up words for a fuller understanding—the same way I read poems in English. Then, to demonstrate that I was not a complete idiot, I recited lines I had memorized from Seferis's "Memory I." Yannis corrected my pronunciation of a verb in which I had misplaced the accent.

"Every poet must have a muse," Yannis said, but instead of hearing the word *moúsa* I heard *moúsi*—beard.

Every poet must have a beard?

"Oh no," I assured him. "Many poets are women. Katerina Anghelaki-Rooke, for example."

4

My Fulbright Fellowship demanded no steady responsibilities other than to work on my own writing and translation projects. I had also agreed to write a "Letter from Greece" for *The Hudson Review*, and filled my journal with notes. This was the first time I had ever had the opportunity to learn about Athens, for example, so I frequently took the bus into the city. Often I stopped at the Fulbright office on Vassilissis Sophias to say hello to Chip Ammerman, the genial director, and his charming staff, or perhaps to pick up my check and carry it to the Citibank in Kolonaki. Or I would walk through a neighborhood I hadn't yet explored, Pangrati or Kessariani, surprised by how many pockets of quiet one could find in a sprawling city of five million people. Or I would visit Katerina Anghelaki-Rooke at one of her regular cafes on the slopes of Lykavittos, or find myself attending a poetry reading. Among Greek intellectuals I discovered how truly impoverished a speaker of Greek I was. Fluent within a limited range, I could be quickly left in the conversational dust. How swiftly the wordplay and references would pass me by, how hard I found it to explain the sort of writing I did, the few books I had published. My tolerance for humiliation was tested, but that is the only way to learn. I had "known" Greece for nearly twenty years, mostly *in absentia*, but was only now beginning my real education.

Through Katerina I met writers, translators, professors, artists of all genres. And through Chip Ammerman I met Edmund Keeley, the novelist and translator, and more movers, shakers, patrons and matrons in Athenian cultural circles. The city's riches were now at least as apparent as its obvious frustrations—the smog, traffic and bureaucracy. Even before Athens began to spruce itself up for the 2004 Olympics it was a city in which one could find startling beauty and sophistication. Walking up Lykavittos on a winter night, one could see stars above the shadowy pines. Circling that scented hill, one passed through several neighborhoods, each with its different social class and appeal, though the cheaper cafes were obviously farther from the tourist centers and the chic streets of Kolonaki. I learned never to tell Yannis if I had had so much as a beer in Kolonaki, or he would lecture me about my foolish, spendthrift ways.

Riding a traffic-stalled Athens bus on a hot, smoggy day, one glimpsed the city's worst: the glum faces of people straining to get unscathed through their ordinary responsibilities, fighting crowds every step of the way. On those occasions I was happy to return to the quieter neighborhood of Yannis and Popi. But there were other days when discovering a new bus or train route or going to a concert or literary event made the city unexpectedly livable.

There were signs of Balkan and Slavic troubles everywhere: the Russian flea markets and immigrants, like the Serbian beggars one sometimes saw with post card ikons by their coin boxes to identify them as such, here for the pan-orthodox sympathy they encountered in Greece. One also saw Albanian street sweepers, Gypsy children peddling tissues or begging in the train to Piraeus. Athens was changing yet again, admitting more of the world and having to deal with attendant chaos, but it seemed a far richer, more exciting place than it had been in 1980.

One weekend I was flown to the Fulbright office in Thessaloniki, where I lectured about my poetic collaboration with Yiorgos Chouliaras. Alekos loaned me a coat and tie for the event so I would not seem disrespectful. In that northern city I also met Dimitris Kalokyris at the headquarters of the Cultural Capital of Europe, a refurbished mansion packed with computers manned (and womanned) by an army of attractive young people. Yiorgos had put me in touch with his old friend, who granted me an informal interview. A visual artist as well as a poet, sometimes called "the Borges of Greece" for his labyrinthine wit, Kalokyris was fashionably mustachioed, loquacious and friendly. He gave me one of his books with his wife's artwork on the cover. A deputy director of the festival, he was harried by the massive preparations to turn his native city into a "cultural capital." Efforts had been slowed by the usual corruption and infighting, and he no doubt hid his frustration behind his slightly distracted humor. But as we talked he focussed on his plans, including invitations to such well-known American poets as John Ashbery and Kenneth Koch. We talked of the old days with Yiorgos and his fondness for Katerina Anghelaki-Rooke, whose laugh he could imitate with gusto until it became a raucous bray. "Even in a crowd you can tell where she is," he said. "You only have to listen for her laugh."

Along with another artist who wore a red scarf against the cold and told me he too remembered Yiorgos from their school days, Dimitris gave me a ride back to the center of the city. The next night I lectured before more kindly and polite people, some of them professors who had had their own Fulbright experiences in America. If they expected an authoritative figure, they certainly did not find one in me. After my innocuous survey we gathered to cut the *vassilópita*, the cake eaten to mark the new year and bring luck to those assembled.

I had a day or two to explore the city on foot. More compact than Athens, Thessaloniki impressed me with its seaside tower and promenade, its old neighborhoods set back from the harbor. Perhaps there is more of the Slavic and Ottoman influence I remember from my travels through Epirus many years before. For such a small country Greece has so many places of such distinct character, each with its magnetic pull. Someone is always telling you that they have found the real Greece. They know the village you have to see, or the indispensable island. But to me it's all the real Greece—every stone, every face, every blaring horn or snatch of song or shout in the street, every traffic jam or snooty clerk, every spontaneous feast.

IX

In Katerina's Kitchen

Until the end of my story.
Until I understand what choice means.
Until I understand what end means.

—Katerina Anghelaki-Rooke,
translated by Jackie Willcox and the author

1

Packed and ready to leave for Aegina, I found it hard to say good-bye to the Chalikias, who had been so kind to me and would remain such great friends over the years. Yannis, suddenly tender, kissed me on both cheeks, saying *"Tha se thymómaste pánta"*—"We will remember you always." I was deeply touched by this, and felt that his words—even there in the suburbs—signified the timeless universality of journeys, the tenuousness of our lives and the importance of our connections to other people.

I met Katerina on the pier at Piraeus and we took the Flying Dolphin to Aegina, her childhood home. Dividing her time between a small Athens flat and the island house, Katerina was both cosmopolitan and quintessentially Greek, her father's side of the family having once watered its land from the Scamander in Asia Minor (the river Achilles turned red with Trojan blood), and her mother's deriving from Patras in the Peloponnesos, where Greek nationalists joined the rebellion against the Ottoman Empire in 1821. Katerina grew up in a highly cultured family, studied in Paris and Switzerland, lived in England, where she met Rodney Rooke, and taught in America. She learned Russian in childhood from her nanny, French and English at school and in her travels, and she was fluent enough in all three to make her living as a master translator. One small measure of how good she was at translating from English is this: not only did she successfully translate Dylan Thomas's lush *Under Milkwood* for the stage, but she was also undaunted by the word hoard of the Irish poet Seamus Heaney, a selection of whose poems she had just completed when we met in 1997. She was planning for his visit to Athens that spring, and had just changed gears to work from Lermontov's Russian, which she said was flying from her pen as though it had been written in Greek.

As the Flying Dolphin droned across the Saronic Gulf, she peered out a porthole and said, "There's my island, my lovely island!" Going back never ceased delighting her. This fierce poet and intellect could suddenly become a little girl, clapping her hands and swinging her legs with joy.

On Aegina we were met by Nikos and Ourania, who had a car. Her house was perhaps a kilometer from the pier, and Katerina's pronounced limp made walking distances a problem. Nikos, a tall man with a wacky sense of humor, had made money with his stylized paintings of nude women. He was now the proud owner of a video camera, which he kept running while he drove us past the waterfront cafes and pistachio carts of Aegina town. This was his Martin Scorsese phase, and over the next several months he would frequently film Katerina and me, claiming he would make a documentary about poets. What he caught on that first brief ride was a rather stiff, bearded, preoccupied American, and he would later show it to me as a demonstration of how far I had progressed under Katerina's tutelage. "See how uptight you are in the film? Now see what living here has done to you. Look at this relaxed fellow, here!"

Ourania was an astrologer. They planned to build a house in the hills, and in the meantime rented the larger of the two bungalows on Katerina's land.

The house itself was big and pink, standing at the edge of a walled pistachio plantation near the school. Katerina's father, a lawyer who worked for a British consortium, rebuilt it when she was a girl, and with its mastic tree shading the heavy front door and its thick walls keeping the rooms cool in summer and warm in winter, it was the dwelling place of Katerina's imaginative life, the setting of many of her poems and reveries. The bungalows were two small stone cottages, perhaps once stables or tool sheds. They had been simply refurbished. Mine, built into the wall at the edge of the road, became a sort of echo chamber whenever a horse and buggy clopped by on their way to the tourist waterfront; the ubiquitous mopeds whinged like chainsaws beyond the wall, the sound drilling into my skull. I placed my mattresses on the floor in front of the big window looking out on the garden, and the fagoméno trapézi or "eaten table" I used for both eating and writing stood before the other window, and a pair of glass doors opened onto a little trellised courtyard I shared with Nikos and Ourania. I heaped blankets on the bed and started a fire in the *tzáki* with a bit of the olive wood Katerina had ordered for winter, and quickly found that this smoky stone space was the perfect cold-weather nest for a scribbler.

Despite the gentility of her upbringing and the rigor of her intellect, Katerina was a Rabelaisian spirit. Her godfather was the novelist and poet Nikos Kazantzakis, author of *Zorba the Greek*, and I couldn't help thinking she had absorbed a bit of Zorba's paradoxical soul along with the souls of every writer she ever translated and every lover she ever took to her bed. Her energy belied the fact that she almost failed to survive her childhood. After a terrible infection in infancy, she underwent surgeries on several limbs. In fact, the first time I saw her limping toward me on an Athens street, years after our short meeting in Upstate New York, I thought she might be a dwarf. But within minutes the force of her character had simply swept away all concern for her health. She was one of the most vital human beings I had ever known.

Vitality and pain—I wondered if there was something essentially Greek in the mixture. Is the flatness of some American character related to a denial of pain? Is the constant presence of pain partly responsible for Katerina's loquaciousness, humor, and poetry? She too had thought much upon these questions. In a 1993 essay called "Kazantzakis's *Buddha*: Phantasmagoria and Struggle," she wrote the following meditation on human pain:

> This pain softens only with time, cannot be shared even in love, and is the result either of the harsh reality of human society or of the inner hell of attachment; it may even appear to be the work of nature's destructive power. Human pain is the point where all the disciplines of the mind, philosophy, religion and art meet. Art does not seem to try to find solutions but aims to transfer the problem in all its poignancy to another timeless sphere. It is obvious that if one is to take away from painful human situations the element of time, pain is abolished automatically. Art indirectly shows us a method of overcoming time and pain and, through the process of creation,

of translating the ephemeral into the eternal. While a poem or a cantata bear witness to the pain which incited them, art in its infinite time has already exhausted that pain, and the cicada shines in the transparency of its death, a bright carcass on a branch.

I was learning from her about things I had shut away, as if afraid anything I might actually feel were frightening or dangerous. Conversations with Katerina might be funny, but they were never frivolous. From my first night on Aegina, while the fire warmed the stone walls of my cottage and I joined Katerina in her kitchen for a bit of leftover *pastítsio*, I realized that good fortune had led me to the perfect teacher, a woman of undivided complexities and powerful convictions. A great soul.

Katerina, 2001
PHOTO BY DAVID MASON

2

That kitchen! You stepped through the front door into the darkened hall at the foot of the stairs. On the right was her library with a dusty, untuned piano. On the left a blanket hung in the entryway to the kitchen to keep out the cold. So you swept the blanket aside and entered a large-ish room with windows on two sides of its dense walls, a lit fire in the corner *tzáki*, a sofa and low table heaped with newspapers, another table for eating, a counter and sink where old food floated in the last heap of unwashed dishes, a stove slick with old cooking oil, a fridge with a hulking TV on top. And there so many hours passed in winter. Warm, well-lighted, a place of food and conversation. Katerina tried to come to Aegina every weekend, often with Rodney on his days off from work at the British Library. For the time being Katerina, worried about her health, was not drinking alcohol, so I took my own bottle with me and refilled my little glass as we ate and spoke or watched her television or, when Rodney was present, ate and spoke and watched the telly with Rodney.

Such polyglot wordplay crossed their kitchen table. I was a spectator at a verbal tennis match, trying to catch all the jokes whizzing by. Nothing delighted Katerina more than some subtle play on words, and Rodney's Greek was splendid enough to delight her. I was especially partial to the *paroimíes* or folk sayings she taught me, like this one explaining the way people dodge responsibility: *Exo ap' to choró, pollá tragoúdia léne*—"Outside of the dance, they sing a lot of songs." Or another which she called one of the most beautiful of all Greek sayings: *O lógos sou me chórtase kai to psomí sou fáto*—"Your word so fills me up that you can eat (or keep) your bread."

As we spoke of her work on Heaney, it occurred to me that Greece shared many attributes with Ireland, where I had also spent much time. Both countries have long histories and legacies of outside domination. Both countries—at least compared to the U. S.—prize learning and poetry. The Irish had their hedge schools, the Greeks *to kryfó scholeió*, the "hidden school" depicted on the new two-hundred drachma note at that time, where you could see a bearded Orthodox priest giving lessons to Greek children during the Turkish occupation. Because of Greece's precarious political history, people tended to be readers of newspapers and addicts of television news. As in Ireland, there was a rich tradition of verbal improvisation. Katerina spoke of translations of Emily Dickinson into Greek and wondered at Hamlet's line "The rest is silence." There was an English language tradition in which the best could not be said because it belonged only to God. Perhaps this was Protestantism at work. But in the Greek tradition, she asserted, the world was spoken into being. The *word* was original creation. That phrase *fagoméno trapézi*, "eaten table," with which she had described her own writing table in a poem—I asked her if I could translate it as "gnawed," having tried "battered" and "weathered," and she tested the word with and without a hard 'g,' then said in English, "Why not? It's a free country."

Once I apologized for my "village Greek" and she turned on me:

"Village Greek? Don't flatter yourself. Your Greek is not village Greek. Village Greek is a thing of poetry, a thing of such beauty and invention, such expression. Your Greek is just school book Greek. It isn't alive. It's idiot Greek. It's for tourists."

I was stunned. I had been coddled by Greeks who were grateful to find anyone speaking their language at any level, and now I stood in the presence of someone for whom language was blood, language was living and dying. Speaking Greek with Katerina was like facing a well-fortified army while stark naked in No Man's Land. One fairly cringed at the prospect of her withering fire.

She was especially appalled at my small cache of swear words, so there were baroque lectures on Greek obscenity while she wielded a spatula at her sputtering stove. She was frying little knobs of fish for a dinner, wheeling now and then to tell me a joke she had heard in New York or London or Athens. There was much to be said about *malakía*, of course, the world's masturbatoriness, which went far beyond mere *omphaloskopía* or naval gazing. And one had to understand the lore of the *poústis*, the queen or queer, and the *gómena*, which could be a whore, a paramour, etc. The latter might have come from English—the whores of Piraeus learning to greet American sailors in the time of the Truman Doctrine with "Go men?" or "Go with men." Maybe it was related to *góissa*, or witch. There was also the *roufiános*, or ruffian or pimp, and of course the *skrófa* or slut. Furthermore, it was important to note the difference on the tongue between the formal *stíthia*, breasts, and the earthier *viziá*, tits. A true vocabulary pertaining to genitalia would of course take into account both ancient and modern usages, from Aristophanes to the latest dirty joke.

Thoughts of love could also bring out her tenderness as she discoursed upon her past affairs or the love lives of her many friends all over the world. She could converse with a film on TV, shouting at the idiocy of some character on *Santa Barbara*, her favorite soap opera, then flip the cod in the spattering oil, wheel on her rapt student and offer a perfectly turned verbal disquisition on the etymology of *moúni*, cunt, or *andartomoúna*, rebel cunt.

She sought language where it lived: in the best books, the streets, the conversation of friends. Sometimes the most beautiful images would emerge in her conversation; I especially remember her saying that a good poem should read as if it were a bird precisely at the moment it lifted off the earth.

Katerina's genius for friendship could be seen on her birthday in February, when dozens of people gathered at the house in Aegina to wish her well. That particular year she used the occasion to start drinking again. I had come into her kitchen about noon to ask if I could help with preparations, and Katerina, at loose ends while friends had begun to prepare food at her stove, said one word to me: "*Ouzo.*"

I lifted the bottle from the kitchen table.

"Wait." She stood a tall glass on the table, then filled it to the brim with ice cubes. "Pour."

I poured a cautious inch.

"Pour."

I added a dollop.

"I said pour!"

I filled her glass to the brim. Katerina downed half with alarming speed, then pounded the glass to the table. "More!"

And so the day went.

I met a number of writers and critics in Katerina's garden that day, among them Dinos Siotis and his American wife, Barbara. Dinos had joined the Greek Press Service while a student in America. He had raised a thousand dollars in support of PASOK and was rewarded with a job. He was also a poet and publisher, whose Wire Press had published a journal called *The Aegean Review* in which a story of mine appeared, and were now producing the glossy *Révmata*, or *Currents* while he was based in Athens—later he moved to the press office in Boston. Siotis's magazines, now including *Mondo Greco*, have always sought to combat the parochialism of some Greek publishing by including work of international interest, and when I first met him his *Révmata* was sometimes criticized for its fashionable American influences. I found him a witty man with a refreshing appetite for pop culture. After the party that night, we sat in Katerina's kitchen, watching a surreal television program that tried to match people sitting on a stage with callers from around the country. The program's naturally funny star, Annita Pania, was then winning the ratings war among popular blondes on TV. In the background, young men lifted weights to demonstrate their prowess to female viewers, or they showed off their singing and dancing. Katerina and Dinos laughed at the bad Greek spoken on the program, often mixed with English, and wondered aloud whether the language could survive this onslaught. Later, subdued by ouzo and the spectacle on TV, Katerina said it made her feel like wrapping herself in the flag and jumping off the Acropolis.

3

When I first left the village in Mani in 1981, Pipitsa, the mother of our teacher Aleka, came by to say farewell. We had eaten meals at her home and befriended her children. Now that we were leaving, she said, "*Tha mas xechásete*"—"You will forget us." I promised her that I never would, and hardly a day of my life had passed when I had not thought of her and others in the village.

When Annie escaped the snows of Minnesota and joined me in February, we rented a purple bug of a car and sped through Athens traffic out to the Pelonponnesos. I knew I'd be taking her back to the village but again hardly dared to bring it up in conversation. Split between two lives, like two marriages—what if the whole thing proved a disaster? Annie wondered what I was up to in my bungalow life, but I had no means of sharing it with her. It was still so unformed in my own mind, like a draft of some manuscript I was unready to make public—the book that would connect it all, or connect me to the lost world of some remembered happiness. She knew, of course, how hard it was to bury her own past—Scotland, her first marriage, her lovers—and perhaps because of this she was patient with my own quest.

We headed first for Sparta, a town I had not seen since 1980. Seferis had been there in 1951, recording in his journal: "Wide streets. Sparta makes you think of a child wearing his father's jacket. The hotel is called the Menelaion; at night its walls sweat snores." We too found it a sleepy town, devoid of tourists that time of year, and we were preoccupied with being together after nearly six weeks apart.

The countryside bustled with the last of the olive harvest. Now the oranges were ripe, and everywhere were trucks loaded with crates of fruit. Smoke rose from small fires made of brush pruned from the trees.

The ruined Byzantine city of Mistras seemed unchanged from my first glimpse of it with Jonna those years before. Again the sky was overcast. Smoke rose from the valley below. The almond trees were in bloom, and each breeze sent snow-showers of white blossoms into the wet grass. Wandering hand in hand through broken walls and churches, we found one of the last nuns there leading her three goats. Seferis again: "The Pantanassa, a nunnery; eight nuns, they told us." Now there were only three, just like the goats.

From the fortress above the city I tried to imagine the terrible battle fought there in the Civil War. But at one point real snow fell, flakes drifting from the lofty crags of the Taygetus and commingling with blossoms from the almond trees. It was utterly peaceful, utterly quiet.

I had always wanted to see the medieval coastal town of Monemvasia, where the British retreated in World War II and where Robert Crisp had returned to live before he moved to Mani. So Annie and I spent a night in a stone hotel inside those walls, mildly disappointed by the yuppification visible in narrow streets, the expense of the cafes. We found the family home of Yannis Ritsos with a bust of the poet in front, the yard looking unkempt and overgrown. Next morning we lingered by the sea outside the walls, then got back on the road in our purple car.

How honest I was with Annie about what we were doing there? I enjoyed the sights, of course, and Annie's fresh way of looking at the world, always more observant than I've ever been. But I had an agenda I could hardly express. More than anything, I wanted to see Kalamitsi, the little house in the bay. This desire felt somehow disloyal. I couldn't talk about it. The whole scheme smacked of madness or sentimentality or both—going back to the village, finding out what was lost. I felt it like a lump in my chest, anxiety and dread and joy all bound up together, and it seemed to have nothing to do with Annie or the life we were making together

We paused at Gytheion for a lunch of fish and wine, looking out on Kranaï, the pine-covered islet in the bay where Paris and Helen spent their first night as runaway lovers. Then we crossed the Mani at mid-peninsula to Areopolis and started north on the road along the Messinian Gulf. We had plenty of time, but I couldn't bring myself to stop the car. I drove as quickly as the winding coastal road would allow, growing tense with excitement as sights became more and more familiar. It had rained for days, but snatches of sunlight flared in the high grass and the terraced olive groves. The west side of the Taygetus now rose higher and higher on our right, up into mist and cloud.

Mani had been discovered by many more foreigners since I first lived there: more houses, more signs for hotels and restaurants in English, more cars on the road even in winter. But an excitement I could barely contain rose inside me. I recognized names of villages, saw places I had walked or hitchhiked when young, where I learned the words to Greek songs or met the clamjaphry of foreigners who lived there.

Before I knew it we were starting down the hill, past the old hotel and into the village by the sea.

We went first to Lela's taverna, built into an old house on the rocks above the water with a vine-covered terrace for warm weather dining. It was quiet that time of year. When I went inside I recognized Petros, Lela's husband, immediately. He sat alone in the taverna, the same lean face and mustache under his black beret.

"Petros," I said, "do you remember me?"

He smiled in a friendly way, but his eyes showed no recognition, even though he had once taught me all about growing vegetables. I spoke to him in my fickle Greek that was always coming and going: "Petros, my name is David. I lived here many years ago. You worked for Kyrie Michali then, in the garden. You taught me to plant vegetables."

Nothing. Perfectly friendly, but no sign of familiarity.

A goiter bulged from his throat, an air of feebleness about him that had not been there before. Then I heard sounds from the kitchen and called Lela's name.

She entered, wiping her bony hands on an apron. She was still lean from work and sleepless nights, no matter how prosperous the taverna had made her family. She had the same sharp features, lines a bit more deeply etched, the same observant eyes. Again I went through the ritual. "Do you remember me? I lived out by Fermors in Kalamitsi, the little bay. You cooked for Mister and Missus and Petros worked in the garden. I was a friend of Anna's, and also the Americans, Friend and Margarita."

Lela brightened. Whether she knew me or not, she was too polite to say so. She welcomed me with the traditional kisses. I introduced Annie to her as Anna, which was also Jonna's name in Greek unless they called her Ioanna. I asked about that other Anna, who with Theodoros had taken such good care of us in the old days. "*Péthane O Theódoros,*" Lela said. "Theodoros died eight weeks ago. Anna has gone to Athens to Voula's, her sister's."

And Friend and Margarita?

Friend was there, writing a book they said. Margarita was changed and did not come to the village so often. But their daughter, Lisa, was married to the President of the village.

I had met Lisa when she was a teenager in Buffalo. She had married Yiorgos, the shy electrician from Petrovouni. One long ago summer I noticed the two of them courting in secret. Now Yiorgos, as President, had combined the olive oil operations, moving them from the old factory by the sea to his childhood village in the hills. Petrovouni was now accessible by a road wide enough for cars.

After arranging to rent a room from Lela, we left her busy at kitchen work and we explored the village. There were shops along the road—more now than in the old days—and the principle grocery stores were now large markets side by side, north of the church. There were new hotels and guest houses, signs of a thriving tourist trade. In the old days almost the only house made of concrete was Friend's, but now his was more or less decorously hidden with plantings while other, more naked obscenities had sprung up here and there among the beautiful older houses of stone with their red tile roofs.

We sat at a new *zacharoplasteíon* and ordered coffee. For the time being the rain held off, and we soon found ourselves in conversation with an odd English couple. The man was swarthy and cheerfully crude, like Liza Doolittle's father, while his wife had the delicate plumpness of a Barbara Pym character. They were delighted to tell us just how horrible it was, building a house in village X to the south, how untrustworthy and dirty the workers were. These two were like throwbacks to some colonial fantasy—the revenge of the middle class. When I told them why we had come to the village they were decidedly unimpressed. The woman shook her head in a patronizing—or is it matronizing?—manner: "It's always a mistake, you know. To go back. You never, ever do it."

I began to feel seriously depressed.

Then the rains came with fresh ferocity, clattering on tile rooftops and gushing in gutters. It was a mess.

4

Friend had temporarily left the village on an errand, but that night Lisa visited us while Yiorgos watched their children, Kelly and Kosta. She remembered me well and wanted to meet Annie. She also desperately wanted to talk with Americans who were closer to her age.

Born in Crete, Lisa was adopted by Friend and Margarita back in the sixties when they first lived in the village. They had come for two years while Friend contemplated an anthropological study of the community. Though they had one son, they believed they could not have another child. No sooner had they adopted Lisa, however, than Margarita became pregnant again. She gave birth to their second son by lamplight with the help of a midwife, which made her a sort of honorary village woman. In her old age Margarita had seen enough; Greece had lost its allure for her. I hoped to find out why.

Perhaps what Lisa told us was part of it. Raised in Buffalo, married to a Greek and living in this parochial setting, she had been walking a social tightrope for years. She even spoke Greek with a New York accent, as if determined not to lose that part of her identity. What poured out of her that night was a monologue on the roughness and violence of village life. There were hints that something was wrong in her marriage, but she was not comfortable enough with us to say more. She did say that her American upbringing was not good training for the job of a wife and mother in Mani. While her husband's parents lived she was expected to slave for her mother-in-law. But when they died she was suddenly expected to take charge while her husband fell to pieces. She had to wash the corpses, dress them, bind them, prepare them for the grave—and she had never so much as seen a dead person before.

Poor Lisa was thrust into a position in which she could do nothing right. She would always be the foreigner, the outsider or the whore who had stolen the affections of a handsome local boy, a real *palikári*.

I wanted to hear more, but for the rest of that visit I saw Lisa only in the presence of her father or husband. Her story would come later, in bursts. Meanwhile, I began to sense a tale taking shape. Maybe it wasn't such a mistake to come back to the village after all.

For breakfast Lela served us toast and coffee in a hurry, saying, "Today a good man died." She had been up all night at the vigil in the man's house. Villagers have always handled such notable happenings themselves, because in the past they could not depend on help from the outside world. The man's name was Anastasi, and he was much loved, and I dimly remembered him. I made up my mind to attend his funeral that afternoon.

But first Annie and I took a drive down the coast. It is a luxury to have a car on such journeys and we both felt the need to make use of it. And I wanted to show her another kind of village, further from the sea.

South of Stoupa we turned off the main road and climbed toward the mountains. In the old days one had to park at Riglia and walk up to Ano, or Upper Riglia, but now a narrow concrete track led to the upper village's square, where I parked our little rental car. The rain came down so fiercely that to spend any time at all in it was like taking a cold shower in one's clothes. Nevertheless, we hunched together under an umbrella and dashed up the path with its leaping raindrops between gray stone walls of old houses that seemed deserted.

I knew where I was going. First the tiny chapel, now locked up, next to what had been a stable, then through the wooden door in a courtyard wall to Wolfie and Isy's house.

There was no one there.

I called out a few times. Carpenters' tools lay at the door atop some steps. The house was being fixed up, no doubt by foreigners—perhaps it was Wolfie's ex-wife, the bitch, who had owned the place with him.

Of course he wouldn't be there, but I felt driven to look anyway. No word from either of them since just after they left for Indonesia so many years ago. I left a note explaining who I was, telling how I could be reached if anyone had news of my friends.

Back in the *plateia*, before getting into our car, I noticed an old man watching from the doorway of the *kafeneion*. I told him that I was in the village many years ago and that I had friends, Wolfgang and Isabella from Austria, who lived near the little church.

The old man nodded. He remembered them. "They left," he said.

No one ever responded to my note.

5

We missed Anastasis' funeral. Partly it was our drive in the hills. Partly the rain the kept us indoors. That day I sought out Pipitsa, Aleka's mother. She invited me into her home and served me Greek coffee and sweets, but confessed frankly that she didn't remember me at all. She was a hard-working woman, tough as nails. I told her about Aleka's lessons, about having dinner at her house when she served us her youngest daughter's pet rabbit in a lovely *stifádo*, or stew. Aleka was married to a policeman in Athens now, she said, and the little one was a university graduate student in England, where her brother was a professor. As she spoke Pipitsa was perfectly polite, but honestly couldn't remember ever having seen me before.

"Sorry," she said. There were so many foreigners these days. You couldn't tell them apart.

That afternoon the rain let up, and while Annie went exploring with her camera and tripod, I took a walk to Kalamitsi. When I got to the bend in the road south of the village and recognized the little bay below the bluff, I looked about for the old footpath. Lela or Petros had told me it was overgrown now.

But it wasn't. I bent the wet grass that obscured it, and there was the narrow track of dirt and rock, like something made by goats skirting the bay. I walked down along the rim of the bluff and into the olive groves beyond, my jeans quickly soaked by the long wet stems and brambles. I could smell the earth, the grass, weeds and early wildflowers after the rain, and every step brought me trembling closer to the little house.

Sixteen years. There were a few new houses in the olive groves—guest houses, I supposed, but the walled land where Jonna and I had lived for five months was overgrown. The old owner, my nemesis Barba Yiorgi, was long dead. His American granddaughter owned the land now, but lived on Crete—or so I had been told. The iron gate in the wall was locked. At first this deterred me. I looked at the tiny stone hut with its aged tile roof. The paint and whitewash I had given it were faded away. Hard to believe I had passed such happy hours there.

Wedging one foot against the lock halfway up the gate, I reached up and pulled myself over it, landing on the other side. No one had noticed me. I was trespassing. But the groves appeared to be empty, and the land inside the walls was obscured by growth, wild onions as tall as a man and other weeds that would have driven Barba Yiorgi into a rage.

I looked at the little house, the shut window where we had stood our pot of basil, the wooden door. In the old days we had kept the door open and hung a blanket in its place to keep out bugs but let in air. Now the door was locked, so I walked the land, looking for signs of my former life. The old pig sty, my source of dry manure for the garden, had been knocked down. But there was still a wild, improbable stand of bananas where I had once hung a hammock, and the cypress and olive trees stood where I remembered them. I picked my way down the rocks at the edge of the sea, where Jonna and I had so often gone swimming with Wolfie and Isy.

They were all lost. I stood there, looking at the sea, or rather looking into it because even in this flat light I could see the bottom, then at the rocks that had once seemed our own private rocks, and the distant island. It wasn't self-pity I felt, but a sudden onrush of past time. The years of this place were folded and put away where I could never find them. I was trembling as I climbed back up and sat on the little plank bench we had used so often in the shade of a great evergreen.

Leaving the land, I followed the path around to where the spring had been—our source of water. Many years ago, someone had cut a bowl in the rock where the water gathered, beautifully clear, before it spilled into the cistern below. It was covered with brambles now, and no one walking by would know they were passing the greatest gift to the human species, a freshwater spring. The old cistern in the shade of a great, chaotic fig tree no longer fed anyone's garden. A thicker mat of slime coated the water.

Kalamitsi

A path I had not walked for sixteen years,
now almost hidden under rain-soaked grass
so even the locals told me it was gone,
but two steps down where it rounded the bay
and I was back. My heart beat all the faster.

Though half the olive trees had been cut down
the stone wall stood, the gate, the little house
looking as if no one ever lived there,
the cool spring where I dipped a pot for water
hidden by bramble mounds, the cistern greening.

I stiffly climbed the gate (now chained and locked)
and walked the point of land and knew each tree—
nothing but private memories, after all.
It wasn't the loss of time or friends that moved me
but the small survivals I was here to mark.

I had come through to see this much again,
and that plank bench under a cypress tree
where I had placed it all those years ago
to soak up shade on summer afternoons—
only a small plank bench, but quite enough.

6

Friend was back, and that night we took him and Lisa to dinner at a new taverna. Nearing eighty, he was still spry and clear-headed. He had quit smoking some time ago, but chewed nicotine gum like a bandit. We were glad to see each other, and Annie had to be patient as the rest of us chattered about changes in the village. They told me I had to meet Marikaty. Wonderful woman. Athanaseas family.

I liked the name—Deathless. And soon enough I would meet Marikaty and her mother and daughters. This was the year of the Hale-Bopp comet, the year of miracles, and that night Friend said that I was welcome to have his house for April and May. He had to go Stateside. No one had dibs on it. Yes, I said, then and there. Yes, that would be perfect. Annie would rejoin me in time for Easter. I would live with my second wife in the same house I had enjoyed with my first.

We stayed three days in the village, and by the time we returned to Aegina we had seen the Leigh Fermors several times and met Lisa's talkative children. At our last lunch with Paddy and Joan at Lela's we were given the unfinished third bottle of wine for the road, and we set off in our purple car, climbing the switchbacks toward Kalamata. I couldn't contain myself; I had to stop the car and look back on the village by the sea, the terraced olives and crags of Taygetus. Everything was so much better now, knowing we'd be back, knowing this wasn't the last time.

7

When Annie returned to the blizzards, I hunkered down in the Aegina bungalow for a rainy March of reading and writing.

Acrostic from Aegina

Anemones you brought back from the path
Nod in a glass beside our rumpled bed.
Now you are far away. In the aftermath
Even these flowers arouse my sleepy head.

Love, when I think of the ready look in your eyes,
Erotas that would make these stone walls blush
Nerves me to write away the morning's hush.
Nadir of longing, and the red anemones
Over the lucent rim. My poor designs,
X-rated praise I've hidden between these lines.

She never minded what I had written about Jonna, but was shy about having this poem to her read in public, shy of being praised in any terms, let alone these. I wrote a lot of poetry that winter.

There was much to be learned. I read the translated stories of Alexandros Papadiamantis, some of Vassilis Vassilikos. I struggled with grammar and tried translations, raiding Katerina's library for the poems of Jenny Mastoraki,

Eleni Vakalo, Anastasis Vistonitis, Galatea Sarandi, Antonis Sourounis, Alexis Panselinos. I found the new Kedros series of Greek fiction in translations, including *The Mission Box* by Aris Alexandratou, and a novella called *Her Night on Red*, by Kostis Gimosoulis.

The latter was translated by Philip Ramp, an American writer who had lived with his wife, Sarah, on Aegina for many years. Making his living as a translator, Philipo, as he was known in the tavernas of Aegina town, was starved for literary conversation with a fellow American. We got together often. Drank together. Drove the island together in a car I had rented for a day with Fulbright money. I was living so cheaply, rarely eating meat and sometimes getting free food and lodging from friends, paying Katerina plenty by Greek standards, *típota* by American, so I was more or less loaded with dough and could often stand my friends a round.

On our trans-island drive, Sarah told me how they had first met Katerina in the Plaka in the sixties. They heard the music of the *zembétiko* from one of the tavernas and saw a young woman there, dancing alone despite her bad leg, a cigarette dangling from her lips.

Sarah and Philip were new to Greece and asked if that wasn't a dance that only men performed.

Yes it was, they were told, but this was a special woman, Katerina Anghelaki. A poet.

So Philip's strongest literary friendship began. Sarah had convinced herself that Katerina didn't like her any more, and when I saw Katerina I heard it was Sarah who didn't like *her*. So each was convinced of the other's antipathy, and they avoided each other. I sidestepped these conflicts whenever possible—sometimes by staying alone in my bungalow, feeding on bread and lentil soup, a dish I was expert at cooking on the little two-burner stove in my kitchen. I did laundry in a plastic tub and hung my clothes among the bare pistachio trees. I read and wrote, read and wrote. Now and then I hung out with Nikos and Ourania.

One night in Athens the three of us went to hear Katerina perform at a tribute in memory of Odysseus Elytis, who had died the previous year. The room was jammed, so I sat on the floor with a crowd of other people. Dora

Bakopoulou played piano, and the cream of Greek poetry were all there, looking rather like a convention of hermits, and Katerina's passionate but controlled reading blew all the men off the stage.

Afterward I stayed with her and Rodney in their apartment behind Lykavittos, slept on the sofa after wine and TV, and negotiated the undergarments hung up to dry as I used their bathroom in the morning. Their city apartment was like a temporary base, though much of their time was spent there due to Rodney's job and Katerina's literary life. The muchness of Aegina compensated for their cramped life in the town.

Apókreos, the carnival before Lent, began on March 2. That day on Aegina there was so much wind and rain that I could hardly hear the church bells ringing for prayers. I was in a monkish more than a carnivalesque spirit, and mostly stayed indoors at the gnawed table.

At one point I walked out to a card phone and called Annie. Her voice sounded so sweet and lovely that I ached for her company. She was worried about all the snow in the Red River Valley, with talk of possible record flooding. It sounded dismal there but she was in good spirits, documenting the impending disaster on film. What is important in a place? Annie was there for the deep bonding of a community in disaster. I was far away, trying to realize the real Greece while piecing a private narrative. Was it necessity or pure selfishness?

I called Yiorgos Chouliaras in New York, and we complained about never being able to see each other any more. "We are always doing other people's work and we never do what is really important," he said.

Now I leaf through pages of x'd out poems in my journal, vocabulary lists, rough translations, notes from reading, overheard statements, and land on the entry for March 8 when I watched *Stella*, the great Melina Mercouri movie, on TV with Katerina and Rodney. Katerina sang all the songs in the movie while Rodney, in mock irritability, yelled "Shaddup!" We were all drinking heavily that night. Moods and tones shifted like water. Katerina showed me a photo of herself as a teenaged girl dressed in the costume of a harem concubine, complete with veil.

"Are you trying to tell me something?"

She batted her eyelashes at me. "What would you like to hear?"

Carnival put people in flirtatious moods. Two days later, Nikos and Ourania returned from Patras with hours of video taken at the festivities there, so we gathered in their bungalow and watched the dancing and mating rituals in the streets. Then we moved to eat and talk in Katerina's kitchen, where the conversation turned to mythology and our intuitive sense of another world that somehow mirrors or focuses this one. As if we were not individual people but expressions of passions deeper than ourselves, nameless forces that mythology tries to place. So that was carnival—a chance to let these theatrical spirits loose in anonymous encounters. By showing me the photo of herself as a harem girl, Katerina was trying to let me know that she, too, had had that life of being swept away.

We were joined by the wild white cat she called *Skatoúli*, Little Shit, because he was always covered in dung from the ratty places he slept in. With Little Shit I was always torn between the desire to let him indoors, and concern for the sanitation of my living quarters. On this night he had been washed by the rain and we let him curl up and purr by the fire.

That same night I wrote in my journal: "The strange inwardness—when there is bad weather in Greece everyone looks like they've had a death threat."

8

As always, TV was a good way to learn vocabulary. I was invited to watch even when Katerina and Rodney were not at home. So some nights I took my evening meal to the big house and ate while watching the news. Or I would watch American movies in which violent heroes said "Fuck you" to the villains and the Greek subtitles offered as translation "Go to the Devil!" I also became a fan of the pantomime comedy, *Mr. Bean*, a favorite of Katerina and Rodney's. When the three of us watched *Bean* together—Greek poet, English librarian, American scribbler—we laughed till we cried.

Newspapers were another way to learn. One of the world's big news stories that year concerned *klonopoíisi*, cloning, a word combining *klonos*—twig or offshoot—with *poíisi*, which can mean poetry, making, construction, fabrication, etc. A headline in *To Vima* read: <<*Klonismós*>> *tis politikís! Ta próvata, o laós, ta tzákia kai to méllon* (Cloning of politics! The sheep, the people, the political dynasties and the future). There was, Katerina explained, an additional pun on the spelling of *Klonismós*, suggesting a shaky foundation. Below it were two photos, one of Dolly the lamb, another of Kostas Karamanlis, nephew and namesake of the famous conservative leader, now the head of the New Democracy party.

There was the motto on some currency: "*Opoios Elefthera Syllogatai Syllogatai Kala*"—Whoever Reasons Freely Reasons Well. This on the same note that depicted the hidden school which had reminded me of Ireland.

When we spoke of Ireland, her work on Seamus Heaney's poems came up as well. When her publisher, Kastaniotis, brought out her selection of

Heaney's poems, I found the book an excellent tool for study because I knew the originals well. In fact, the first poetry book I ever bought on my own was Heaney's *North*. Something in the verbal texture and public stance of those poems attracted me immediately, and Heaney had been yet another literary hero of mine since college. Katerina called her translation *Ta poiímata tou váltou* (Poems of the marsh or swamp), and she had fascinating things to say about the difficulty of translating Heaney's bog into Greek. One of her two prefaces was called "In the marshland of translation"—a place with which I, too, had become familiar.

Her own new book of poems that year was *Oraía éremos i sárka* (The flesh is a beautiful desert), a title reflecting Katerina's sensuality as well as her grief at her own losses. Years later, having lunch with Katerina in Athens, I would find myself listening once again to her ruminations on her love life. As a poet she wondered what her life would have been like if she had married a compatriot. "But can you imagine?" she said, her voice refusing anything remotely like self-pity. "Can you *imagine* any Greek boy taking a girl who *limps* to meet *the mother*? It's inconceivable!"

Her marriage to Rodney was cemented by compassion and language-love. At times their conversations were almost violently playful—like two cats going at each other. I remember conversing in her kitchen about the full flavors of Aegean fruits and vegetables, as opposed to the tasteless pulp Americans buy in supermarkets. I sang hymns, as it were, to Merlin oranges, and especially to the tomatoes of late summer.

"Ah, but they used to be so much better," Katerina said. "When I was a girl, I remember walking in the front door there and smelling a fresh tomato on the kitchen table!"

"That's because it was rotten," Rodney muttered without raising his eyes from the newspaper.

"What?"

"I said that's because it was rotten!" he growled in his native Liverpudlian.

"Bah," said Katerina. "You English have to take everything down to your level."

"Because that's where it really is."

Katerina pouted like an injured child.

9

Journal entries. Aegina:

20 March 1997:
Today a high wind from the south and very few ships sailing. Newspaper racks indoors at the shops. I tried negotiating my residence permit with the tourist police and have arranged to come back next Wednesday, after the celebrations of 25 March. A rather lonely day today, though Nikos and Ourania are just back on the slow boat (the only one to make the trip today). Ourania's glasses were stolen by someone on the boat, so now she has to wear her dark glasses to read and work. She tried to find the English word for how she felt and I helped—it was "furious."

Later:

My new command to Katerina: "*Fáto!*"—Eat that! When she's in a bibulous mood she forgets she needs nourishment.

1 April 97:
When Katerina is "on" it is such a privilege to know her. Watching a documentary about Melina Mercouri, she tells me about knowing Melina and Jules Dassin in Paris. "I grew up in the most privileged epoch of Greece for many years to come. Hadjidakis, Theodorakis, Elytis, Seferis, Gatsos,

Melina—all at the same time!" The creation of permanent songs, and a singer of extraordinary husky vitality to express them.

Melina in Dassin's *Phaedra*, scene in the British Museum when she says to Anthony Perkins, "I need some air."

Nights when you don't want to sleep, there are so many songs you want to learn.

Later:

The first big storm, thunder, lightning and heavy rain, and now I know that this little bungalow leaks. Water runs down the stone wall just inside the bathroom, plunks from the ceiling onto the desk. I've been moving my papers about to keep them dry. Strange, how I sometimes feel cheerful in a storm, especially if I am inside, dry, and can make myself a hot drink. The truest comforts are the rudimentary ones, if you have the time and the inclination to enjoy them.

10

In March the pelicans had returned to Aegina. They nested on the roof of the old jail, which was then a refuge for homeless animals, or landed in the pistachio groves. I took long walks in good weather, and on days of hard rain made my way from doorway to doorway in the town, buying my few supplies. I began to strategize for my return to the village, deciding that I would haul my gear (including the laptop) south in a rental car, then return the car to the agency in Glyfada and take a bus back to Mani. I could see the Chalikias in the process.

Katerina did not understand the pull of the Mani for me. I tried to explain that this was merely my attempt to close a circle, as it were, but I didn't really know that. Perhaps I also felt that I had to get away from her censorious criticism of my Greek language abilities, which sometimes left me so shattered I could hardly speak in her presence. I had to get off on my own in order to find my tongue again, and even an approximation of fluency.

Perhaps, too, this would be the angle taken in the article I was writing for *The Hudson Review*—going back to the village, recapturing fragments of lost time.

Anyway, I would be back. And I would be temporarily replaced in the little bungalow by her good friend, Jackie Willcox, who had come to visit from England. On my last night in Aegina Jackie and I took Katerina to dinner and had a night of the most beautiful, somewhat drunken communion, and in the morning I left early for the Flying Dolphin without saying a proper good-bye.

X

BACK IN THE VILLAGE

I stood with constricted heart looking
at my own past.

—Dilys Powell, *An Affair of the Heart*

1

During the last of the heavy spring rains I arrived at Friend's house, opening jalousies to let in the uncertain light. Before settling in there was one visit I had to make. I had to see Anna, who had mothered us so well in our first year in the village. By now she had returned from her sister's. I could have looked her up in Athens, but somehow never got around to it, as if only the village was the proper setting for our reunion. I had written a few letters to her over the years, but had never received a reply.

At an early evening hour I walked down the agora and knocked on Anna's door. She was knitting. Still wearing black, but with a gray vest. Still thick featured and mustached, her hair a bit saltier, dark circles under her eyes.

"Anna," I said, "do you remember me?"

She paused. "David?"

Then she swung open the door, swept me in and sat me down in the parlor where I had spent so many hours in my previous life. As always, she offered me tea with brandy and a sweet. I extended condolences for Theodoros's death, complimented the addition they had made to the house so they could rent rooms to tourists. We talked briefly of Friend and Margarita, Lisa and her two children.

This was better, I thought. At least she hadn't forgotten me.

At length I began to explain my *megáli istoría*, my long story about the years away and why I had not come back to the village until now.

Anna listened closely, and when I came to the divorce a very strange thing happened. Anna decided she had to take sides in the matter. Though she had been infinitely closer to Jonna in the old days, calling her "doll" or "beautiful child," teaching her knitting, embroidering, crocheting, she was now suddenly on my side, even though I presented the divorce as a simple story without such antagonisms—wary of making myself out to be a victim or a saint.

"I'll tell you what I remember of her," she said. "She had something— something like *egoismós* about her." Egotism. Self-interest. It was a dramatic gesture for my benefit, but I was startled by it nonetheless. If she could say this about Jonna, who had shown nothing of the sort when we lived in Greece, what on earth would she say about others when the opportunity arose? What might she say about me?

Eventually I assured her that Jonna still loved her, and by the end of our meeting Anna instructed me to return her love, adding that she was looking forward to meeting my new wife as well.

But the whole conversation was a sequence of gestures without a genuine touch. Something was harder, tougher, in our old friend. And maybe at long last I had outgrown *ta paidiá*.

2

By the next afternoon the skies had cleared. From then on, each night I could clearly see the upended broom of the comet suspended in the sky. At night there was less traffic on the road, so the village stilled to faint rustlings and muffled conversations. Birdsong died out and one saw fluttering bats against the darkening sea and the cypresses. This was the period in which Paddy drove me into the hills to show me where they had buried Chatwin's ashes. These were also the days of catching up on the news about old friends. Robert Crisp had died—felled by the very cancer he had kept at bay with his prescription of red wine. Tristram was dead. Yannis the fascist was dead. His wife, Simone, had sold the new hotel by the beach and nobody seemed to know where she had gone.

From Lisa I heard about the village idiot who always stood at particular spots for specific times of the year, true to some private association. And Jimmy the Australian who, since his break-up with American Christina, was more and more isolated from everyone in the village except his own father. And Stratis the fisherman, whom I knew before Eleftheria left him, still a big child, happy, singing at the top of his voice. The core of life in the village went on almost unchanged, as if in some way uncorrupted by the wealth tourism had brought. As if the real lives of villagers were always held apart from the life they projected to strangers.

Troubling news arrived from home. The Red River was flooding. People I knew were out sandbagging on the dikes. Annie helped friends and strangers any way she could, no longer merely documenting the rising waters. She was involved. It was so much like her to take friends and neighbors seriously, so much like me to be pursuing a mad desire to know the village again. Some of our friends would lose their homes. Eventually, sixty thousand homes would be evacuated in cities, towns and farms. In a bizarre turn of events, much of downtown Grand Forks would catch fire and burn above its flooded streets.

So much suffering at home had brought communities together as never before, yet there I was in the village, thousands of miles away. Swallows swooped over rooftops, behind them the sun-burnished sea. Days passed like worry beads rolled in the fingers of an absent-minded codger. At night the fanning comet in a field of stars.

3

Annie rejoined me in time for Holy Week, but she was like someone looking back to another life. She was traumatized by the floods and felt guilty for leaving our friends in trouble. She was full of stories about flooded basements, ruined libraries, the slow accumulating shock brought on by unstoppable events. The community had come together, and people experienced a sort of adrenaline rush even in the face of massive devastation. Because of its dikes, our town was relatively unscathed compared to Fargo, Grand Forks and many smaller communities. But it had taken huge efforts on the part of everyone, aided by troops brought in to sandbag or patrol for looters or rescue victims from the roofs of houses. But all I could think of was how good she looked, stepping off the commuter plane in Kalamata, long-limbed and smiling.

As always in Holy Week, all of Greece picked up and moved. Athens emptied to outlying villages and islands, and the villages became sudden metropolises, extended families crammed into ancestral houses, dozens of unfamiliar children racing about the squares and lanes. Somehow the distant disaster in America, the closer preparations for resurrection and the comet suspended in the heavens all seemed portents—but of what? When he had all of his wits, my father had preached awareness. Be here now. Take it all in. Hold the wine glass at your lips a moment longer and let the dry, sunny flavor linger on your tongue.

We were well-fixed in the home of Friend and Margarita with its marble-chip floors, white marble counters and tables, its sheepskin rugs, its modern appliances and its enormous waterbed where we could rub our feet together under the covers and press our bodies together. The house might be an architectural nightmare on the outside, but its homely façade was well disguised by heaps of blooming foliage and an overflowing garden.

It was Marikaty who gave me a ride to the Kalamata airport and brought us home to the village. She was a dark-haired, gentle woman with a kind of placid humor and indispensable wisdom. With her business partner, Stratis, she owned one of the newer and more sophisticated shops in the village. But really Marikaty was a cultural facilitator both in her Athens life and her village life. She connected people, especially in the arts. She made things happen. Like Katerina she had a genius for friendship.

She lived in the house built by her mother's family, and her elegant mother, Electra, still lived with her. Electra had married into a military family and moved away to Athens and Thessaloniki, returning to the village during the German Occupation while her husband fought. Marikaty had grown up with a sense of social position and had even gone to college in America. Her English was excellent, and she was habitually generous to anyone willing to speak Greek. A divorcée, she was once married to a poet with whom she had two extraordinarily beautiful daughters, Electra and Alexandra, both now grown up but home for Easter with a school friend.

Marikaty gave our stay in the village new purpose and shape. She was writing a book on the Outer Mani in collaboration with Friend, to be published in both Greek and English. More than a guidebook, this volume would be steeped in the region's oral history. It would also be illustrated with photographs, so Annie took on the work, which gave her an additional reason for poking about in the hills. Luckily she had brought some of her equipment along.

As Easter week progressed, the air was more often punctuated and perfumed by explosions of firecrackers and home-made bombs, reminding me how it had been sixteen years before. These explosions could be dangerous, one villager missing much of his face due to some misadventure with dynamite. Explosives were plentiful, not only for the now outlawed practice of dynamiting fish, but also for blasting the road to Petrovouni on the bluff above. That village had an old hollow olive tree where sticks of dynamite were set off, sending a magnificent roar over the rooftops below. And in our village one used to see boys tossing firecrackers under the skirts of women, laughing bizarrely as grandmothers hopped at the detonations, screeching and trailing smoke.

On *Megáli Paraskeví* or Good Friday for the ritual of the *epitáfios*, the bier of Christ, decorated with flowers and lighted candles, was born out from the church and through the village, first in the back lanes among the olive trees. The village's lights were all turned off so the procession—the priest, the girls singing mournful songs and anyone else who chose to follow—wound through a village lighted only by bonfires casting spectral shadows from the trees. As we turned north and proceeded through the agora, the only light came from beeswax candles in our hands, candles on the balconies of houses, and the fires. The air was full of smoke and the acrid smell of gunpowder.

That was an Easter the like of which I had never seen in America, though my family were not church goers. The Greek Easter as I first saw it took me back to a smoky, almost cave-dwelling world of earth cults and Dionysian gore. The dead king who would bring resurrection of crops, the slaughtered lamb whose entrails and head helped break the Lenten fast, and whose body made the Sunday supper.

Annie would see an Easter unlike any she had seen before.

On Holy Friday we went with Marikaty into the medieval part of the village, which had been little more than ruined towers when I first knew it, and a walled compound near the old church, its bell tower deeply grooved where the bell rope had abraded the stone for centuries. Now several of the old towers were being refurbished. One of these was owned by Marikaty's partner, Stratis, who also came from an old village family. A lean, elegant figure, he greeted us warmly, and despite suffering from an illness he declined to name, invited us into a tastefully furnished *salóni*. Over coffee I asked Stratis how it came about that the Resurrection should be celebrated with the anarchy of gunpowder.

Ah, but these explosions had nothing to do with Christ, Stratis told us. They dated back to the time of Turkish domination in Greece: "A way of saying, 'Look, we are alive. We are here. There is no way you can finish us.'"

4

That night the newer church filled with families, children coming and going. The priest sprinkled holy water on a wee girl who wailed when it got in her eye. Some came to kiss the ikon, touching it lingeringly with their lips. Some lifted babies to kiss the saint. Some kissed the air above the ikon as if concerned for its sanitation.

Now the parade of the *epitáfios* was slightly less magical due to the presence of electric lights and the absence of bonfires. The procession paused at each house it passed, where candles were lit from those born out of the church. There were also rows of brightly-colored paper lanterns set on the ground or strung before doorways. Families expanded. Some people greeted old school chums from the days before they scattered to the cities. Not as many bombs went off or were thrown under ladies' skirts, and no dynamite roared from Petrovouni. Still, I was moved by the procession, the dramatic re-enactment of the funeral of a young God.

On Holy Saturday I showed Annie the old limestone road that angled up the hill to the villages above, and told her how we used to see a blue-robed priest descending it on mule-back like a figure out of Chaucer. I still remember that old priest from Gournitsa with his white beard, sweat-stained robe and agitated way of speaking. At our first encounter he greeted me with "*Yermaní?* German?"

"*Ochi. Amerikanós eimai.* I'm an American."

"Bravo!" He leapt from his mule and took my hand. "*Yermaní—kakó!* Bad! *Ameriki* good people! Russía—*kakó! Kakó!*" He made guns with his fingers.

"Bombombombomb! *Kakó*! Murder! Death! All kill! All *Kommunistikí*! Bombombomb!"

And that road—now you would have to know where to look for its meticulous stonework in the scrub, just wide enough for a cart. We walked slowly up to the base of Petrovouni, then through the moist gully with its walled garden and goat pens, its polled mulberry trees and lush birdsong. Then on into the olive groves and a silence of stunning depth and duration. On a hot day the leafy circle of shade under an olive tree was as welcome as a pool of water.

We returned by way of the village itself, and in the little *plateia* encountered a man I did not know by name who was skinning a slaughtered goat he had hung up in a mulberry tree. Goats were more plentiful than lambs in Mani. He was preparing to break the fast that night and in the morning would roast the rest of the animal on a spit for Easter Sunday. I conversed with him briefly—he knew Friend, of course—and Annie photographed him as he knifed the skin from the flesh as easily as one might pull off a wet sock.

All day we greeted people with "*Kalí Anástasi*—Good Resurrection," as lovely a phrase as any I know. And that night we broke the fast with Marikaty, her mother and daughters, eating the soup made from the lamb's entrails she had bought in Kalamata. Home from church, her daughter Electra had made a sooty cross on their lintel with her long candle.

As Annie and I walked home in the dark we saw boys throwing firecrackers at each other or at strangers. Sometimes we felt the powerful concussions of these explosions.

But Sunday was peaceful. Sounds of music and smells of feasting drifted from houses throughout the village with chatter and less frequent blasts. I was reading some of what Friend had written for the book, and noticed the caution with which he approached the subject of the Civil War. In the hills outside the village there had been *andártes* of the left and the right. At that point in his writing Friend was deliberately vague about alliances, choosing not to name names, but concluding that "many villagers will die with scars on their souls from those years."

I was also reading historian Mark Mazower on the German Occupation, the reprisals, etc. How the gravestones of Ottoman Jews were used as building materials in Salonica. How the S.S. Chief Walter Blume devised a "Chaos Theory" by which, as the Germans retreated, they should execute all Greek political leaders, rendering the country incapable of civil control.

"Blood brings blood and more blood," Seferis had written of the forties in Greece. Countries do not easily recover from such things.

5

With Marikaty we hiked in the hills near the village of Exochori, and she
showed us the fields called *kaló* because of their good soil. On another day
we drove to the village of Saidona, which had resisted the Italians and had
been leveled in retribution, whereas the seaside village of Selinitsa, which we
called Ayios Nikolaos, had been a center of the right wing X's (*Chítes*) and
still had an ugly fascist bunker facing the mountains—the enemy within. In
our village an olive tree of special import grew in the *plateía*. Whenever it got
about that someone had been betrayed in wartime, people would whisper,
"The olive tree must have told."

The excuse of the book made us travel with greater determination. Marikaty had a scholarly background, and had published a volume on the ancient
Greeks. She told us that Pausanias had mentioned our village and a temple
to the Nereids there. She told us of the little offshore island, Meropi, with its
remnant of Venetian walls. I used to swim out there as a young man, but in
my laziness had never learned anything about it. She showed us the monastery of Panayeia Faneromeni—the Virgin Revealed—separated by a ravine
from Gournitsa, the village where John Van Leuven spent his summers. In
the village of Platsa we saw a christening, and when it was over we lingered
in the church of Ayios Nikolaos to examine its remarkable frescoes. In one,
three women lay in bed, their father beside them discovering Saint Nicholas
climbing in at a window with a bag of money. Marikaty explained that this
father was going to force his daughters into prostitution, but the saint saved
them from shame by leaving money each night. The suspicious father kept

watch, and in this scene was discovering the source of his good fortune in the white-bearded saint. The Twelfth Century iconography on display in Mani was less canonical and wooden than some Orthodox painting; I could not help thinking that such technical mastery and humanity somehow fed into the Renaissance of the West.

At Nomitsi, where Tristram Popham had lived, we got Kyrios Petros at the taverna to bring the key to Ayios Yiorgos, a church with more fine frescoes, especially a Tree of Life with Christ sprouting out of the trunk.

The quiet of these villages was interrupted only by the drone of bees and volubility of birds.

One day back in the mountain village of Saidona, climbing an overgrown hillside and looking out over dazzling blue depths, we met an Albanian who had lived four years in Thessaloniki, then one month in this village about as far from his homeland as it was possible to get in mainland Greece. I found that we could converse well in Greek. He was working for an old woman who asked me if I was Italian. Remembering the Occupation and why some nearby houses were still in ruins, I said, "No—American."

"You're a good child." She pried more of my story from me, then spoke to the Albanian as he swept her terrace. "This American is a professor. He has brains."

"Yes," said the Albanian, "I only work with my hands."

I said that I knew what it was to work with one's hands. "I was a gardener for years."

They were unimpressed. It was much better to be a professor.

To walk in that landscape was to walk through time. Maybe any landscape is that way.

Agnostos Topos

We had walked a whole day on high ridges
somewhere between the heat-struck sea and peaks,
each breath a desert in a traveler's lungs,
salt-stung, dusty, like summer's rasping grass

and the roughness of stone. Biblical thorns
penned us, while the stunted ilex trees
shadowed the path. It seemed from these dour fields
we could not emerge on anything like a road.

A landscape no one had commodified
or fenced. If there were gardens here
the poverty of soil defeated them.
If there were homes beyond some goatherd's hut
the gravity of ages pulled them down.
No sound but cicadas like high-pitched drills
ringing till red sunlight hissed into the sea.

And that was when, our shins scratched and throats parched,
we stumbled into a village on the shore
where people, stupefied by days upon days
that were the same, told us what to call this place.
The distance to a road? *Two cigarettes*,
said the old man who sat webbing his net.

Now the road cuts down from the cliffs above.
I've been back, bought wine from the old man's son
who keeps his car parked in an olive's shade.
It's better, of course, that one can come and go.
One needn't stare a lifetime at hot cliffs,
thinking them impassable except to goats
and men whose speech and features grew like thorns.

The old man's dead. The friends I traveled with
are long since out of touch, and I'll admit
I've lost much of a young man's nimbleness.
I call these passing years *agnostos topos*,
unknown country, a place of panting lizards.

Yet how like home it seemed when I walked down
out of the unfenced hills, thirsty, footsore,
with words of greeting for the fisherman.

6

Trying to connect the disparate parts of my life, I took Annie to meet our Anna in the village. She sat us in her sunny kitchen and gossiped away cheerfully. But just as suddenly Anna's face darkened as she told us the latest news from the television. A young Greek had died of a drug overdose on one of the islands. It was too common now. *Ta fármaka*. Drugs. And of course the drug dealers were all Albanians who escaped their country in gangs. For all I know, she was right, though as I write this I recall more recent stories about the capture of decidedly Greek drug dealers. It was the knee-jerk xenophobia that bothered me, the immediate assumption that bad things should be blamed on any non-Greeks who happened to be handy. Before I could answer Anna with some banal palliative, she shocked me by saying, "It's PASOK. It's socialism. We've had enough of socialism in Greece. Enough of democracy. The children are dying. *Théloume fasismó*. We want fascism now."

I said nothing, or nothing that I recall, but that remark utterly flattened the affection I had felt for her. Maybe the whole friendship had been a lie, possible only because of my naivety. Maybe she had always been a fascist and I simply had not understood. Now the air between us was full of poison. I only saw Anna one more time, the day I left the village. I have been back to Mani since that year, but have not been able to bring myself to knock on her door.

7

The village of Kastania, not far from Saidona and situated in the shade of great slabs of mountain rock, was one of the loveliest I had ever seen. I tried not to think of its political history, which had in the past been right wing. Annie and I went there with Marikaty, then on our own in a rental car, assigned to photograph its three churches. We walked up the steep slopes of the village, nearly wading in spring snowmelt that gushed from its overflowing fountain and down through the lanes. It was the clearest, freshest water in the world, and in the heat of spring it might have been pure silver, it was so precious.

After photographing the most accessible churches, we wandered into the graveyard at the village's north end. Annie and I always spent many hours in graveyards, lured by storytelling told by headstones and the lay of the land. For her it was partly an immigrant's experience, knowing so many of her relatives only by their tombstones or the lack of them, but it was also her journalist's nose for a story and her curiosity about other people. I followed Annie, learning by her look.

There we were among the dead of Kastania, gazing over the rooftops nestled below and across from us, when we noticed a third church above the village that had not been visible to us before. "Better get that one too," Annie said, shouldering her bag.

So we strolled down into the little maze of lanes and wandered about, looking for a way to the church. At last we found a wooden gate in a wall that seemed in about the right place, but we couldn't be sure this wasn't someone's private land.

Just then a thin, elderly but vigorous man came up the lane from his house. He remembered us from a previous visit with Marikaty, and yes, this was the way to the church, through his goat pen.

His name was Nikos and he was a goatherd. His flock was on the mountain now for the summer, tended by a boy until he and his wife could join them. But he was happy to lead us through his pens where a few kids still suckled and scampered, and up to the church with a rather plain interior, which Annie frugally photographed so as not to appear uninterested.

There was a little dirt yard by the stables where Nikos set us down on two stumps and offered us his hospitality. His wife was making *mizíthra*, fresh goat cheese with a mild flavor, and they insisted on feeding us bowls of the warm, yogurty cheese which had not yet been hung up in cloth and had the water squeezed from it. His wife, dressed more or less in rags and a headscarf for her work, gave us rusks and glasses of fresh spring water.

"Well," said Nikos, touching my arm, "did you steal your wife or did she steal you?"

"She stole my heart," I said.

Nikos pointed to his wife, who stood shyly apart. "I stole her."

"From her father?"

"Yes!" He cackled, slapping his knee. "Love and health—that's everything in life!"

We talked of America, where he had relatives, but here we were sitting under fresh goat skins that hung on a limb, no doubt left over from the Paschal feast, eating *mizíthra* and drinking mountain water, and I thought of the swineherd in Homer, and how this village hospitality could have been duplicated nearly three thousand years before. Of course Greece is more, much more, than the literary images it evokes, but for a man inclined to such connections it was a deeply gratifying moment.

Nikos was one of twelve brothers. Once, he said, there were almost two thousand people in the village. Now only one hundred and fifty. "The young are leaving us." Of his own four children, only one remained in Kastania. But they had ten grandchildren, which was a good thing.

Then the inevitable question: "Do you have children?"

"We have a daughter."

"Tell your wife she must give you a son."

I obliged him with a translation and Annie laughed. Our life was too difficult to explain.

Still, I was glad Annie got to meet these two kind people. "Baucis and Philemon" was one of our favorites of the old stories. They were the aged Phrygian couple who welcomed two strangers into their home. Baucis cooked them vegetables while Philemon, her husband, prepared the meat. They also served their guests some local wine, noticing that as the meal progressed the jug remained full no matter how much they poured from it. At this point their guests revealed themselves as Zeus and Hermes, who had come down among mortals and had found no such hospitality anywhere but with this elderly couple. Zeus decided to destroy the inhospitable ones with a flood, but sent Baucis and Philemon higher on the mountain for safety. They looked down and saw the floodwaters below, only their poor cottage spared, but changed to a temple. When asked to name their wish, the old couple said they wanted nothing more than to remain in their home and serve the temple. And that was what they did until, at the end of their lives, they turned into two trees twined together.

This was the proper reward for piety and kindness to strangers. Neither Annie nor I had been graced with one lifelong marriage, but the image of two trees twined together was still a hopeful one.

8

Annie remained behind for a week to work with Marikaty, taking photographs for the book, while I went north to see Katerina perform with Seamus Heaney and say good-bye to my friends. Travel with all my gear was cumbersome, but at last I was back in the island bungalow, offering scraps of bread to Little Shit, who curled up in the sun by my door. On the gnawed table another of Katerina's friends had left a jar of yellow blossoms. Their dried pollen was scattered over the chipped paint on the wood. I was hanging up some laundry when I noticed a large gray rabbit sitting on dried bougainvillea blossoms in the little courtyard—trapped there by a barricade devised out of mats and furniture. It was shivering, either sick or wounded. I left it a bowl of water from which it drank immediately, then chopped an apple and tossed it a few wedges. It seemed to improve, so I left it and finished my laundry.

When Nikos and Ourania arrived, they told me how they had found the injured rabbit and tried homeopathic remedies of various kinds. Now Niko brought cream for its sores from a pharmacy, and even an injection of some kind, as well as such proper hare fare as lettuce and carrots. With the likes of Little Shit about, not to mention the neighborhood dogs, the rabbit's chances were slim.

At evening business hours I went out to the tourist police in Aegina town to get my papers in order before leaving the country. I had already visited several times the hot upstairs room where bored men in uniforms lounged and smoked amid heaps of paper stuffed in folders. They were vestiges of a bureaucracy that might have come as much from Sultans and Czars as anything else, and I could never imagine how the files they kept on each foreigner in their district could be of any use to anyone—except in the more ominous time of the Junta.

I had brought my six passport photos as instructed, and the bored but meticulous officer in charge slowly got around to telling me I was mistaken.

"We need seven photos."

"You told me six."

"We need seven."

"I don't have seven."

He shrugged. "Have you got any other photographs—in your bag, perhaps?"

I opened my book bag. There was an envelope of snapshots taken when I drove around the island with Philip and Sarah Ramp. In one, when I was still bearded, Philip and I stood side by side in the blue-walled taverna where we had eaten lunch.

"Will this do?"

The officer took the photo. "You know Philipo?"

"Yes, he's a friend."

Drawing a pair of scissors from a drawer in his desk, he cut my head out of the snapshot and handed it back to me.

"Now it has a window," he said, pleased with himself. He stapled my head into the residence permit and gleefully handed it over.

Then a last dinner with Katerina, who in a distracted mood said that if she had met me ten years before she would have eaten me up. She was recalling her favorite line from Maró, Seferis's widow, who at ninety said of some youth, "If only I had met him at seventy, I would have eaten him up and left only the little bones!"

"Good thing we met now," I said.

Later, when Annie and I had said our good-byes to the Fulbright staff and our friends in Glyfada, I called Katerina's flat but got no answer. It was just as well. Having no idea when or if I would return, any sort of good-bye would have been too hard.

I never did learn the fate of that sick rabbit.

XI

THE OTHER SIDE

. . . I sit at an old table writing my book,
visualizing the colours of the Turkish ships
appearing like phantoms in the fog; this
seems the best of times to tell a tale.

—Orhan Pamuk, *The White Castle*
trans. by Victoria Holbrook

1

Ten days after the attacks on New York and Washington in September 2001, I was returning to the States from Athens. In Rome, because we were switching airlines, my fellow passengers and I had to retrieve our luggage and pass through security before rechecking it. No one seemed to mind the security. While waiting I struck up a conversation with a silver-haired, mustachioed Greek-American from Cleveland, and we discovered that we had both recently visited Turkey for the first time. "It was beautiful," he said. "My wife and me, we had a great time."

I asked if it was strange to go there as a Greek.

"Nah," he said. "But my relatives in Thessaloniki, they didn't like it that I went there. They said, 'Why do you want to visit Turkey? It hurts us that you go.'"

I knew what he meant. Though some of my Greek friends were too polite to tell me what they felt, I could see them holding something back.

"My relatives," he said. "I'd tell them how can it hurt you? The Turks are people like us—why keep hating them? And they'd give me the whole history thing all over again. Four hundred years of domination. But the ones who did that to us are all dead."

"And 1922," I said.

"Yeah, the Catastrophe. And Cyprus—I heard it all. I told them it's crazy to keep all that stuff alive. Why can't they forget?"

We nodded agreement, but grimly, given the times.

"I mean," he said, "I was in Nam, I went to Viet Nam. My kids went there a while back as tourists and they called me up: 'Dad, it's a great place. The people are so friendly. Scenery's great. Food's great.' I think it's fantastic they could see it that way, and not how I saw it, you know? When I was a kid over there, I didn't get to see the beauty."

He was a good man with no interest in being bitter. I think of him as I begin this chapter about Turkey and crossing the sea back to Greece, and it seems that America's willingness to forget the past has sometimes been a blessing. Sometimes Americans are world-champion forgetters. But every now and then we learn of people who hate us enough to kill us. We can't remember why this is so, and we have to learn all over again about the world beyond the oceans.

2

As someone who loves Greece I found it ironic to glimpse Turkey for the first time on August 29. The next day would be *Zafer Bayrami*, a national holiday in remembrance of the defeat and expulsion of the Greeks in 1922. I will say more about this when I get to Izmir, but as I walked through Istanbul's ultramodern airport I wondered how my Greek friends would react to it. Later I would see the new Athens airport, and it would occur to me that these international zones are the banal faces countries present to each other—dueling airports—but they have little to do with the actual countries they represent.

One Turk I very much wanted to meet was the novelist Orhan Pamuk. I had just devoured *The White Castle* and much of *The New Life*, the latter of which begins, "I read a book one day and my whole life was changed." A passage I had read on the plane over went like this (in Güneli Gün's translation):

> I walked across the train tracks, took back streets, trampled on yellow autumn leaves stuck to the pavement. A deep feeling of optimism surged up inside me. If only I could always walk like this, walking fast, without stopping, if only I could go on journeys, it seemed I'd reach the universe in the book. The glow of the new life I felt inside me existed in a faraway place, even in a land that was unattainable, but I sensed that as long as I was in motion, I was getting closer. I could at least leave my old life behind me.

I was there with a colleague from Colorado College, charged with planning a course on the classical origins of theatre to be taught in Turkey and Greece in the spring of 2002. In addition to learning the lay of the land, we would work out logistics for travel with twenty students. My colleague, Jim Malcolm, was an actor and director, now retired from our drama department. A native New Yorker, Jim was gifted at making friends. This would come in handy when the world fell apart.

We drove along the Sea of Marmara toward the Golden Horn, past buildings and minarets that gleamed in the late afternoon light, the remnants of the city walls built by the Byzantine Emperor Theodosius II in the Fifth Century, then the older walls of Constantine. We entered Sultanahmet through a gate near the train station, and found our hotel a few blocks from Aya Sophia.

At the hotel we were met by Jim's friend, Evin Egeli, our glamorous guide, who would watch over us for our ten days in Turkey. Evin was a beautiful and cultivated woman, the widow of a prosperous Izmir businessman. She looked much younger than her sixty-odd years, and was also tougher than her smiling countenance suggested, having held her family together after her husband's death. That evening in an outdoor café we had a memorable introductory meal. We had *kalamari* and superb bread and tomatoes—the flavors of the Aegean in late summer, everything fresh, the vegetables and fruit picked at their peak, unlike the pulpy, warehoused or flash-frozen stuff Americans routinely eat. I had *barbouni*, a red mullet, and noted that the Greeks called it by the same name.

"Yes," Evin explained, "the Greeks are more sea-going people than we are, so all of our names for fish are the Greek ones." She was anxious that I should not have a grudge against Turkey, but I was already feeling quite at home. As much as I dislike being a tourist who does not speak the local language, so much of what I encountered that night was familiar to me. Not only the food, but also the oleanders leaning at my shoulder and the pot of small-leafed basil set by our table. And our after-dinner *raki* with its seductive sweetness and powerful impact—unlike Cretan *raki*, which is a more ferocious drink. I was mildly drunk and prepared to love the whole world by the time I tumbled into bed that night.

3

Evin could out-walk either of us, and she was hell-bent on showing us every mosque and monument in Istanbul. She knew her stuff, our Evin, and everybody in Turkey seemed to know her. Tanned, fit, tastefully dressed, stylishly informal and utterly commanding, Evin's very presence sent headwaiters and hotel clerks into paroxysms of attentiveness.

She could also be heartbreakingly vulnerable. Later I would see old black and white photos of her family when the three boys were young and her husband was still alive. He was a very handsome man whose death nineteen years before had forced Evin to take over her family's businesses. His people had come from Crete, hers from Bergama, and they made a glamorous couple with their movie star good looks. They were as happy and beautiful a family as any I could imagine. He had died of complications from rheumatoid arthritis, having sought treatment at the Mayo Clinic.

Evin had such light-heartedness, telling us with a mischievous laugh that her husband used to make a rule about when everyone should go to bed at night. But when he slept, she and the boys might sneak up and watch a movie on TV, and she would have to get the boys back to bed without waking their father. Or the time when some conservative business prospects came to their home in Izmir for dinner and infuriated Evin by their manners. They insisted on having separate tables for the men and women, then demanded a prayer rug so they could say their evening prayers. Evin was livid, and would only give them a bed spread, which she dropped unceremoniously on the floor.

In addition to its conflicts over religion, Turkey's economy has been in crisis. It was always a mild shock to deal with the currency, counting zeroes to be sure that a one million lira note (about seventy cents) was not a faded ten million note. The lira was then worth fifty per cent of what it had been a year ago. That, combined with ongoing corruption scandals in government, worries about the military, a hunger strike and terrorist attacks by Kurdish Marxists and other problems, created a depressive national mood. But the rug merchants of Sultanahmet were still doggedly inventive in their sales pitches, most beggars seemed to have been swept away or were cared for by families, the markets were jammed and bustling, cell phones rang or beeped, as ubiquitous as cicadas. Though we found signs of the conservative Islam in some women wearing the veil or traditional headdress and in amplified scripture readings in a few public places, much of Istanbul seemed as trendy as Southern California.

Newspapers were full of glum stories. In the *Turkish Daily News*, an English-language paper, I read a survey in which Turks expressed some faith in their president and armed forces, but virtually none in the police, the courts, Parliament, political parties and the media. The largest perceived threat to the country was the economic crisis, and the murder of prominent businessman Üzeyir Garih in a famous Istanbul cemetery had upset people almost as much. A full forty per cent of respondents reported feeling hopeless about the current situation.

The *International Herald Tribune* reported that "reality TV" had come to Turkey in the form of a program "pitting two middle-class couples against each other to see who can survive on the country's paltry minimum wage of eighty-four dollars a month. . . . Half of the country's 65 million people live on a monthly income of less than 290 million Turkish lira, far below the official poverty level of 688 million lira for a family of four." At that time, 290 million lira would have been approximately 214 dollars.

One night we took a cab to the Pera Palace Hotel near Taksim Square. Evin wanted us especially to see Kemal Atatürk's permanent suite, kept as a shrine just as he left it. Among the artifacts in the room, I particularly remember a framed letter from the Greek anti-royalist politician, Eleftherios Venizelos. It was in French, and it recommended Atatürk for the Nobel Peace Prize.

After dinner at a small cafe, we strolled on Istikal or Independence Boulevard past cinemas and department stores to Taksim Square, a business and tourism hub. Roughly ten days later, in Greece, I would read that a Marxist sympathizer with the hunger strikers had approached a police van in that same square and detonated explosives strapped to her body. She killed herself and two policemen, injuring some twenty others, including an Australian tourist. The Australian woman's arm was blown off. Fragments of the bomb lodged in her chest. She died a few days later. I read about it in Athens on the morning of September 11, so I was already in a strange, discomforting mood that afternoon when I walked into our hotel lobby and saw four Israeli boys staring at CNN.

Orhan Pamuk and Sim, 2001
PHOTO BY DAVID MASON

4

I had contacted Orhan Pamuk's publisher to see about meeting him, and from the bar of the Pera Palace Evin called the number I was given. Pamuk was staying for the summer on Heybeliada, one of the islands off Istanbul. The next night we took a ferry to the island, where we were met by Pamuk and his beautiful wife, Sim. She was a tall, sweet-tempered woman with the sort of beauty that beggared the emaciated models of world capitals, slender and effortlessly healthy-looking, and a gentle manner that immediately set one at ease. Orhan, who said he was "a nervous person" and who must be one of the hardest-working novelists alive, was himself a good-looking man, two years my senior (I was forty-six when I wrote this), whose glasses seemed at first to shield him from acquaintance. Soon it was obvious that he saw a great deal and was very friendly. A natural raconteur, he had us laughing most of the evening.

We sat outdoors at one of the restaurants near the docks, and Orhan ordered for us. Sim and Jim, as if it were ordained by the rhyme of their names, hit it off quickly. They were theatre people. In fact, Sim once acted in a production of *Lysistrata* in New York, and still yearned for the stage. When Orhan bragged about her high IQ, and we complimented her beauty, she smiled and responded, "I am a better actress than I am beautiful."

As it happened, the English translation of Orhan's novel, *My Name Is Red*, had just received rave reviews by John Updike in *The New Yorker* and by Charlotte Innes and others in several American newspapers. He was happy about these, fully and deservedly aware of his growing reputation abroad. He worked twelve hours a day now, did not take lunch, and ate out every night with Sim in a different café. They were celebrities on the island and had to spread their business around. One night, he told us, a small, obnoxious dog pestered him in one of the cafes. He remembered the Bunuel movie in which a man kicks a bothersome dog, and he wanted very much to kick this one. Instead he raised a bottle of water and emptied it over the yapping creature. The dog's mistress raised a stink about this, causing Orhan to lecture her at riotous length about the bad manners of certain dogs and their owners. At the climax of his lecture, he poured water on the lady's head as well.

While dinner was served, Jim commented on the hierarchy of waiters in Turkish restaurants. "Yes," Orhan answered in his richly accented English. "They are like American surgeons comanding their underlings, demanding their instruments. They present the food like a culmination of science!"

There was scarcely a subject on which he could not discourse with humor and invention, from the depressive mood of the country to its other civic troubles. He was not careless with his words. Turkey's entrance to the E. U. had been stalled not only by the objections of Greece and the economic crisis, but also by its disturbing human rights record, including the detention of writers critical of the state. Orhan had his share of troubles, though I suspect he was protected to some degree by his growing reputation abroad.¶

I wanted to ask him about *The New Life*, which I was still reading, fascinated by its surreal atmosphere. Looking back after September 11, I find the book's surrealism and violence almost prophetic and utterly realistic. Early in the novel, a man named Mehmet, associated with the book that changes people's lives, is shot and disappears under mysterious circumstances. This, too, happens near Taksim, and in the stunned aftermath the narrator notices a little boy nearby:

> A two-year-old kid wearing a beanie went by with his stylish and attractive mother.

¶   The political details of my account will seem dated now. Not only has Pamuk survived prosecution and won the Nobel Prize, but Turkey has moved closer to conservative Islam. The Iraq War has, to say the least, complicated everything.

"Mom, where did the rabbit go?" the kid said. "Where, Mom?"

I wondered if this alluded somehow to Lewis Carroll, and if the subsequent chapters were a journey down the rabbit hole into a Turkish nightmare Wonderland. Orhan replied that this was not his intention. Rather, as he wrote of such dramatic and violent events, he wanted to convey their ordinariness as well, or the impression one has that ordinary moments still occur in the vicinity of extraordinary scenes. It was a technique he had noticed in Hitchcock's films.

We also touched on his career as a writer, and how his father, who admired writers, had supported him in his twenties during the long struggle to create successful novels. Unlike some American authors who insist on their working-class roots, Orhan had no apparent qualms about acknowledging his prosperous background. He had an enviable acceptance of his gifts and enough restlessness to make each book different from the last, though I imagined critics would soon refer to a Pamukian universe as we do to a Nabokovian one.

On the ferry back to Istanbul we glowed with wine and the sense of our good fortune. I was falling in love with Turkey, wondering what it would mean for the book I was writing about Greece. Surely part of this was due to Evin Egeli and the spirit of Orhan Pamuk, who had written, "What is time? An accident! What is life? Time! What is accident? A life, a new life!" This semi-intoxicated rumination came from a fictionalized, surrealistic travelogue. It was as if Orhan had taken a cue from what Alejo Carpentier once said of Haiti: "I was discovering, with every step, the marvelous in the real."

Of course falling in love is only a stage—a pleasant one but not a full experience of a person or a place. I would have to learn more, and have since benefited from reading books like Stephen Kinzer's *Crescent & Star* and Mary Lee Settle's *Turkish Reflections*. A letter from Yiorgos Chouliaras, to whom I showed an early piece about Turkey, reminded me of the Stalinesque image of Atatürk one sees everywhere with his handsome visage and hypnotist's eyes. It was a cult of forced nationalism, and Evin's great pride in her culture was something altogether different from the "official story."

Obviously loving people is not the same as loving policy. Over time my love of Turkey is not replacing my love of Greece, but deepening it, maturing it, helping to make it real.

Evin and her brother Salih, 2001
PHOTO BY DAVID MASON

5

In Izmir we stayed at Evin's home outside the city. Hüseyin, one of her three sons, was an architect, and had designed and built a village of modern houses surrounding a garden and swimming pool. The homes were both solid and whimsical, a colorful meeting of Gaudi and Frank Lloyd Wright, lit from their big windows but somehow cozy, too, with their stone and wood construction. One night we joined Evin's brother, Salih, and his English wife, Sonia, for a meal under the stars. Salih, a man who exuded hospitality and kindness, was an exporter of Turkish foods. With his cropped gray hair, tanned features and white leisure suit, he seemed the epitome of the sucessful and worldly man. He was well traveled, and when he talked about Greece he was careful to let me know that he had Greek friends and felt sorrow at these international differences. "I don't think the Greeks are really Christian," he said at one point. "Nor do I think the Turks are really Moslem. There's something about this part of the world. Maybe we are pagan." His sister would no doubt agree, fascinated as she was by Cybele, the earth goddess whose cult originated in Anatolia. Hüseyin, an athlete and water polo champion, had often enjoyed sporting events with Greeks. While no one diminished the impact of the foreign occupation after World War I or the evacuation of the Greeks in the flames of 1922, I never heard a word of anger against them in our days with Evin and her family.

Ephesus, Priene, Miletus, Didyma—the ruins were impressive and moving, and certainly helpful for our work. One blessed day we did not go anywhere, just lounged in Evin's house, reading and writing while an early

Aegean rainstorm thrashed the olive trees outside and thundered over the roof. I was reading about that Greek word, Anatolia, which signified much of what became Turkey. Turkish has a word for Motherland that is accidentally similar: *Anadolu*—Bountiful Mother. Another allusion to Cybele, perhaps? There were so many ways in which Greece and Turkey had fed each other's cultures as well as antagonizing each other. So much intractable bigotry on both sides mixed with so much good will, compromised by official incompetence.

That evening before dinner, Evin drove us to Skala, the seaside village where George Seferis had spent much of his childhood. The Seferis home, built of stone on a narrow street, had become an hotel, flying both the Greek and Turkish flags, with a shrine to the poet above its guest book. The hallway below the staircase was said to be just as the Seferis family left it. The dark stained furniture, much like several pieces Evin has in her home, was characteristic of the Greek community of Smyrna before their evacuation in small boats while the city burned. Seferis himself had already left home for Paris when the Catastrophe took place, and his family was in Athens. But the loss of their home near Smyrna was a trauma they never forgot. As his sister, Ioanna Tsatsos, wrote, "National despair was annihilating us. We had surrendered Greek soil, become fugitives. Greece shrank, shrank, crumpled." It was all due to the Megali Idea, the "Great Idea" that Modern Greece could ignore geopolitical realities and assume its ancient borders. When one remembers that Atatürk was born Mustafa Kemal in Salonica, one can readily see how each side had populations on the other's soil. Even Turkey's great national poet, Nazim Hikmet, who was jailed and then exiled by his own country, had been a native son of Salonica, and had fought in Kemal's army. The result of Greek attacks and Turkish counterattacks was great suffering on both sides, massive exchanges of populations, cities and towns in flames. (The young Ernest Hemingway wrote of it in "On the Quai at Smyrna.") But for Hellenic identity the loss was agonizing. "The land of Niobe was lost to the Greeks," Tsatsos wrote.

Seferis never forgot his lost home in Asia Minor. His *Poet's Journal* records a visit to Turkey in 1950. On October 24th of that year, he saw Skala again from the deck of a passing boat:

> God have mercy upon our dead! Such air, such tones, such warmth, such light—they don't let you break away from them; they hold you, delay you longer and longer—this sensation of a bare autumn resurrection. My eyes, I think, are full; they have room for nothing else.

Perhaps he had this house in mind when he wrote his great poem, "Thrush." I will translate just a few lines of it below:

> I don't know many things about houses
> I know they have their lineage, nothing more.
> New in the past, like babies
> at play with the sun's fringes in gardens,
> they embroider chromatic shutters and glazed
> doors upon the day.
> When the architect's done they change,
> frown or smile or turn obstinate
> with those who left with those who stayed
> with others who'd return if they could
> or who disappeared, now that the world's
> an endless hotel.

The world's more an endless hotel than ever, I often feel. And tourism, as Paddy Leigh Fermor wrote, is a "gregarious passion, which destroys the object of its love. . . ." But what else can we do? Stay at home all our lives? Travel at its best is an attempt, an essay, and not all essays are trivial. I think of another passage from Orhan Pamuk: "I sat down somewhere next to a rock in the paradisical darkness and stretched out on the ground. Stars here and there above me and an actual rock beside me. I touched it with longing,

feeling the unbelievable pleasure of a touch that was real." We want that
touch, that reality, which is an awareness of being alive in the various world.

Our last night in Turkey was spent in the tourist town of Bodrum with
its yacht-filled harbor and market hustle. The next day we took a short ferry
ride to Kos, which Jim had once joked he would claim for Turkey when he
landed there. We had a few hours to see some of the island, where the bells
of Orthodox churches replaced the ubiquitous calls of the *muezzin*. But the
doves I had heard on waking in Bodrum sounded like the doves on Kos,
where I slowly regathered my rusty Greek and prepared to be a tour guide
myself. We had said our good-byes to Evin on the Bodrum pier. We took
a bus to a beach and rented chairs on the sand, looking across the windy
Aegean at white buildings on a dry Turkish hillside. How strange it was to
be using familiar Greek words with new shadings now that I had friends on
the other side.

It was an odd journey that night on the ferry to Piraeus because I had not
bothered to book bunks for us. So after dinner we stepped over the blankets
and stretched out bodies of other Deck Class passengers and claimed space
on some sofas in the bar. Jim stretched out, put on his sleeping mask, and
was soon entertaining our fellow travelers with his musical snoring. I got a
fitful two hours of sleep, tried to read and write, and at the first breath of
light outside the portholes, went up on deck to watch the sun rise, the blue
shades of land and sea going red by degrees. That was Anatolia behind us, I
thought. *Anadolu*. The land of the bountiful mother. It lay well out of sight
beyond the islands—back to the east, which the Greeks call *anatolí*.

XII

THE *MUEZZIN* AND THE DOVE

I wasn't made to live in paradise.

—Rachel Hadas

1

Arriving at Piraeus, Jim and I went to the B Class lounge where we had stowed our bags behind a row of upright seats. We were just about to leave for the disembarkation point when a shouting match erupted in the room. I was not wearing my hearing aids at the moment, and even if I was, I'm not sure everything could have been made out. A woman howled at the top of her voice. She was a ferocious, dark-haired beauty, a ranting Medea, turning her volume up and down for dramatic effect as she realized that nearly a hundred people were staring at her, her performance swelling with operatic brio.

Two handcuffed prisoners sat in the row ahead of her with sheepish expressions on their faces. They were apparently being escorted to prison. She had just noticed them there, or perhaps she recognized them—I couldn't tell. But it was clear that she was appalled to have two convicts seated in the same room with law-abiding citizens, especially in B Class. She slapped one hip five times in quick succession to demonstrate how instead these devils should be beaten."Jesus," Jim said, watching her with his directorial eye, "she's like Anna Magnani!"

We were watching a woman whose righteous anger had been transformed by performance, as if she had been wholly taken over by deep, irrational forces that could only be released in drama. Americans think of character as something fixed and discrete. Politicians speak of "the character issue," by which they mean the sex life of their opponent. But in Greece it was still a more fluid condition, or a mask that could be replaced by other masks as a moment's inspiration transformed you.

I was back in Greece for the first time in four years, eager to gauge changes in the country and weigh them against my first impressions of Turkey. This performance seemed an auspicious start. The enraged woman was dragged away by relatives, but she had made her impression. The prisoners paled and slouched down in their seats.

When we found a cab at Piraeus I wondered if the driver would prove anti-American, as I had been told all Greeks were since the bombing of Belgrade two years before. The man who drove us into the center of the city was jovial enough. I asked about the election planned for 2004, and he offered that it was time for a change. PASOK was finished now.

"What kind of change do you want?" I asked "Further left?"

"No, further right," he said. "I'm New Democracy. Mitsotakis. Don't misunderstand me. PASOK are not bad people. But we've had them for twenty years. We want a change."

"And the Olympics? Will Greece be ready for them?"

"Of course, but we want peace for all of the world. If the world is not at peace, Greece will cancel the games."

"Yes," I said. "Health and peace are everything."

"Exactly! Peace and health, peace and health!"

This was the ninth of September, 2001.

2

After a long lunch on September 11 we walked into the lobby of our Athens hotel, the Hermes, and saw those four Israeli boys staring at the TV tuned to CNN. An airplane had just crashed into a building in New York.

"That's the World Trade Center," Jim said.

"An accident?" I asked.

"Is terrorists," said one of the boys.

"No," said another. "Maybe is accident. Wait and see."

I had traveled widely that year, and had met Israelis everywhere—especially young people touring before or after their military service. The *Intifada* burned like a wildfire, as bad as ever, and one could hardly blame them for wanting out. Then, like millions of other people all over the world, we saw the second plane hit. "Terrorists," Jim said.

"Is like what we live with always," said one of the boys.

The rest of that afternoon and evening we stood stunned in front of the television. The lobby filled up as I translated gruesome statistics for those of the hotel staff who did not speak English. How many planes? Where did they crash? How many dead? In that lobby there were Finns, Japanese, Israelis, Greeks, Danes, and two increasingly grim Americans. Outside we saw fewer people passing on the street, and those who did pass had cell phones pressed to their heads.

We tried contacting our wives in America, and each of us worried about friends in New York. Jim was especially worried about Paddy Brown, his friend in the Fire Department. The moment the buildings collapsed he said,

"Paddy would have been in there. He was always the first to go in. I know my friend is dead."

I don't remember how or when we got through. I learned that my brother-in-law had not gone to work that day. Most others I knew worked uptown, but I wasn't sure where some former students lived. It would be days before I learned they were okay.

Jim had no news of Paddy Brown. He tried his friend's apartment and only got the answering machine.

Neither of us felt like eating, but we grew sick of seeing the same collapsing buildings over and over again. There was a good taverna half a block from the Hermes, a vestige of the working-class neighborhood near the Plaka, so we went there and I ordered a plate of beans that I could not eat. The young waiter, Marko, expressed his condolences. From then on everywhere we went there were condolences, or sometimes grim looks that seemed to be saying, "Now you know."

When I paid the bill that night, Marko's boss said to me. "*Demokratía.*" There was a bitterness in the word: democracy.

"What can we do?" I answered. "We are an open people. We must be an open people."

He shook his head. I don't know if this was a political opinion. Perhaps it was just the same disbelief I felt myself.

3

We rented a car and drove to Delphi. At the mountain village of Arachova I stopped for coffee, and the young woman there was watching CNN, so we stayed long enough for more casualty estimates from the talking heads.

I hardly remember our tour of the ruins, which I had visited years before. I do remember watching the BBC in the hotel room, then after dark stepping out on my balcony with its spectacular view down the valley to the Gulf of Korinth, and above me a placid array of stars. Somehow I could not put these things together in my mind. I could not imagine how the wreckage in New York and the silence and stars of Delphi at night could belong to the same world.

The tourist buses had left in late afternoon, and Delphi became one of the most beautiful towns I knew, clinging to a slope of Parnassus high above the oracle's sacred road. This was where they all came, the ancients, to ask the priestess what should be done to set the world right. They were answered in riddles.

Jim had tried calling his friend again to no avail. We were suspended there, still in shock. The purpose of our trip now seemed little more than endurance of scheduled days. Looking at the site of the *omphalos*, the center of the ancient world, was very strange in this new context. Eventually Jim decided against a visit to Palestinian friends, and instead booked flights to Crete and Egypt. I planned to visit Katerina and the Chalikias, then drive back to Mani for a few days before going home. We moved through these arrangements like men trapped in the same nightmare, numbed.

In Athens we haunted an Internet café in the Plaka. One afternoon I raised my head from the keyboard and realized I was surrounded by Americans, all trying to get news from home.

In 1981, when Ronald Reagan was wounded by a gunman and later John Lennon was killed, it was even harder to get news from America—at least in the village in Mani. One had to take the bus to Kalamata to find an English-language paper or magazine, and I had trouble absorbing details from Anna's TV until she explained them in simpler terms. But I remember the villagers asking us, "What kind of a people are you Americans? Why so many guns? Why so much killing?"

Twenty years later, I heard everything imaginable on Greek TV. It was our punishment from God for being a sinful nation. America was a police state where no one was free. It was our fate to be punished for bombing innocent civilians in Serbia. Now Americans would learn what it was like to be bombed.

Would there be war? Everyone was divided, just as I was about such a possibility. But there wasn't only blame for Americans; there was also sympathy. And there were grim jokes like this one:

"Where do American generals meet after September 11?"

Answer: "The Tetragon."

I learned new words like *tromokrátous*, terrorists. *Tromokratía* would mean something like "chaos state." I conjugated *thranó*, the verb "I mourn," for the first time in many years. A newspaper cartoon in *Eleftherotypia* showed the smoldering rubble in New York and bore the caption *"Evlepan oloi to 'Amerikaniko Oneiro'"*—Everyone saw 'The American Dream'."

4

I went to see Katerina and Rodney on Aegina. It was a hot day. Katerina's bicycle stood in the shade of the mastic tree. Things looked so much the same, yet I could feel the past years as if they lingered in the cicada-ringing air. The pistachios had all been harvested. Little Shit, that mangy cat, was long gone, replaced by other strays. Nikos and Ourania had left their bungalow on bad terms, and when I mentioned their names Rodney made the sign of the cross with two fingers as if to ward off vampires. Rodney now wore a pacemaker and seemed heartier than he had years before. My little bungalow was taken by a dear friend from Israel, an artist named Tamara Rikman, so it was agreed that Rodney would sleep in the extra room upstairs and I could have his bed in the library.

We spent that afternoon in the shade of a seaside taverna, eating and drinking. I had stuffed tomatoes and chilled retsina that was like liquid sunlight. Tamara and I went swimming in the bright, warm sea, but Katerina and Rodney remained at the table. Especially for Katerina, the mood of celebration swelled with the music of a nearby wedding party. She sang along with the music, throwing back her head and snapping her fingers as if to dance in her chair. She was in great spirits, full of gossip and jokes as we caught up on old friends. I showed pictures of my granddaughter, and Katerina responded as if she had been shown the secret of life itself. She wondered aloud about old loves and long-ago abortions and miscarriages. For a moment she became wistful. But she was happy for me, having this contact with children.

Tamara spoke of how hard it was to live with constant security crises, and I wondered whether life in America would ever be that bad. We all got a bit looped, as if the wine could really dilute our troubles.

A siesta, then a meal with more friends, one of whom brought his family of little girls. Then a bit of sleep. I couldn't bear a prolonged good-bye, and crept out early the next morning for the Flying Dolphin, leaving a note pinned under a wine bottle in Katerina's kitchen with a promise to see her in the spring.

5

Yannis and Popi were well. They had closed the laundry and were renting the ground floor of their building to two businesses, though one of the renters was giving them trouble, landscaping without their permission and failing to pay when the rent was due. The second floor was being converted to a flat they could eventually rent out. Alekos, meanwhile, had started working at the local golf club and was frequently downcast that he could not go swimming as often as before. Magda had come from America and was busy dealing with the problem renter. She had taken a leave from work, and would join her partner, Verlin, in Texas after this visit with her family.

That day we did not go swimming. Everyone had chores to do, and I desperately needed a nap. In the evening we visited Nikos and Anna, a lovely couple who lived in a comfortable flat with their son. Nikos traveled on business, and had recently returned with a bottle of *tsipouro*, the strong Macedonian drink, and we all got light-headed while he played an array of music from his CD collection, including the Gypsy *klarino* player named Yiorgos Mangas and a traditional wedding song entitled "A Cunt Up a Cherry Tree."

It was a restful evening with a family who would not have been out of place anywhere in America: relatively prosperous, well educated, suburban. Their son was taking sailing lessons. We spoke the back-and-forth Greeklish that becomes common on such social occasions.

"There are not many Americans who know Greek," Nikos said to me out of politeness.

The small, wide-eyed daughter of another guest had been watching me from her father's lap, and now she asked, "Why not?"

"Because Greek doesn't matter," Nikos answered.

Probably he saw evidence of such an assertion on his travels, but I imagined Katerina's reaction to such gentle pessimism. Someone's brains would be blown out—his or hers.

6

Back in the village for the first time in four years, I went straight to Lela's taverna. Petros was there, seated in the same chair and wearing his black beret. But his eyes were more vacant than before, and his goiter had grown. It bristled with whiskers. Lela greeted me and showed me to a room upstairs. When I asked how old Petros was, she said, "Seventy-eight. He's not old. He has something wrong with his mind."

She gave me the good suite at the end of the hall with a window overlooking the sea. We exchanged commiserations about the chaos of the world, then, clutching her apron in both bony hands, she left to prepare the evening meal.

After a nap I went for a stroll in the agora, recognizing faces and knowing full well that most villagers could not tell me apart from any of the other foreigners who came there. Their life was a continuum, made up of people who were present more often than not until they died, while I was one of those who pass through, leaving them nothing to cherish or regret.

I knew that Lisa had divorced Yiorgos, or at least begun the proceeding. There had been a card from Margarita with a cryptic message. She had read the Chatwin memoir I had sent her, and could only say that she no longer felt as attached to Greece as she had when young. There was an implication of something learned. Something catastrophic.

Now Lisa lived with her children in the basement rooms of her parents' house—the same place I had gone when fevered twenty years before. Kelly was ten, Kosta six, so she had one child in each of the most difficult grades in school, 5th and 1st. I found Lisa that evening in Marikaty's shop, where she worked. Marikaty had gone to Kalamata and would be late getting home.

Sitting among the tasteful jewelry and *objets d'art*, I caught up on Lisa's news. Things were very bad. Because of the divorce, more and more people learned that Yiorgos had mistreated her. Before that became known, her leaving was a scandal in the village. Most people had sided with Yiorgos. Other than Marikaty and a few young women, Lisa had no allies, and even one of Lela's sons had threatened to testify against her.

It did not help that Lisa was considered part American, the American bitch who ruined a beautiful local boy, the President of the village. Only Yiorgos was no longer President, and that too must be Lisa's fault. After the bombing of Belgrade it got even worse. One old woman stopped Kelly on a pathway and offered her candy and informed her that her mother was a whore.

"I'll tell you," Lisa said, lighting up one cigarette and offering me another. "When I found that out I went straight to that woman. You can say what you want about me, I told her, but don't you ever, ever touch my child again or I'll kill you."

Lisa was a slender woman, but there was nothing delicate about her. She could be formidable when she wanted to because she had been fighting to maintain her complicated identity all her life.

Yiorgos had more or less collapsed into passive complaint, jockeying for sympathy at every opportunity. He managed to put up roadblocks to the divorce and to many of Lisa's wishes. When Friend invited the children to have Christmas in Buffalo, Yiorgos refused them Greek passports. Until they came of age they needed their father's consent to leave the country, and he refused to give it, claiming the American might steal his children. Now Lisa was afraid to leave as well, in case Yiorgos could give her more trouble or attempt to prove she was a negligent mother. She did manage to get to Athens a few days each month to see friends and enjoy a little freedom.

When I left the shop that night I thought back on Margarita's card; were these the troubles that caused her to fall out of love with Greece?

7

More news of the village:

How Marikaty's business partner, Stratis, had died of the unnamed illness, and how she kept on with her shop, complaining that it was hard to keep buying the right things for it without Strati's impeccable advice.

How that younger Stratis, Stratis the Mariner, strolled to the end of the pier each night to watch the sun set. Still a dreamer. He rented rooms now, and one of his foreign guests painted a romantic mural outside his door. Perhaps she helped him forget about Eleftheria, who had left him years ago.

How Sotiris no longer pumped gas. Even after winning the lottery he had kept the station open. But he only had leaded gas, and the new laws insisted that he must sell unleaded. So he closed the pump and put up a sign telling motorists how many kilometers north or south they would have to drive for unleaded. One could still see him calmly riding his bicycle through the village or explaining the lottery to fascinated children.

How Anna was said to be increasingly bitter and getting fatter all the time, using a walker for balance. I couldn't bring myself to see her again.

I took it all in, made notes in my journal.

From an article in the *International Herald Tribune*, September 17, 2001:

What makes ants worth studying, if not emulating? For one thing, they exhibit something called swarm intelligence. That is, the framework of social insects is decentralized. Individually, the ant's actions are primitive, but collectively, they result in efficient solutions to complex problems like finding the shortest route between the nest and a food source.

The key to ants' efficiency is their ability to lay down trails in their communal travels with pheromone, a type of chemical. Over time, those trails result in a system of routing. The lesson, in short, is follow the pheromone.

Remembering how I used to watch the ants at Kalamitsi I wondered if this article explained the behavior of anyone I knew. Or the Taliban. Or humanity in general. Human beings, I wrote, "behave with complacency or hysteria. . . ." There seemed to be no middle path. I could have been thinking about peoples' love lives. Or about international catastrophes.

8

Paddy and Joan, just back from England, had me over for lunch. Their accumulated mail lay in heaps in the living room. Carcasses of dead moths littered the carpets. I was catching my friends at an inopportune time, aware that I shouldn't impose on them for long.

Both were in good form. Paddy sported a new pacemaker that he loved and a hearing aid that bothered him a good deal. He seemed quite vigorous, and spoke of swimming and playing cricket back in England every chance he got. Joan wore a patch over one eye and was as gently self-effacing as ever, intimating that Paddy called her "Long Joan Silver." One of her few concessions to age was a walking stick, which she carried about the house, trying to navigate with her one good eye. I recalled a postcard some years ago from Paddy in which he said that Joan had had a fall and had broken something—a rib, a thumb? Paddy's scrawl was worse than ever, and I couldn't make out the seriousness of her injury. It was nothing, Joan said—just a rib. She wouldn't have anyone talking about her little injuries. Both apologized for the disorder of their house and even for their ages. Paddy asked me not to watch him eating at lunch because he was embarrassed by his bad teeth.

Still, it set me thinking: how would the endgame be for them? My father's Alzheimer's kept such things in my mind, and the fact that Annie and I had her elderly mother living with us in Colorado. In Joan's case, her constant mental clarity made the slow breakdown of her body a source of inevitable embarrassment. Her dignity and presence of mind astonished me more each time I saw her. As for Paddy—well, who could imagine such a Byronic figure ever having to grapple with decrepitude? He had in conversation a clearer memory than before, perhaps due to better circulation, and I knew he was at work on various writing projects, including a *Paris Review* interview with Ben Downing. His charmed life continued in his ability to carry on, nearly always with good cheer, though I didn't have the heart to ask him about the third volume of his trilogy. One rumor held that he had been so depressed at the post-Communist mess of Bulgaria, the utter eradication of the world he strove to recall, that his book was thrown off course. Ben Downing had suggested to me that Paddy only needed a good secretary to put his papers in order and keep him on track. There was a time when I would have jumped at such a job, but now I had my own life to steer.

We started with *ouzo* and a bowl of *babaganoush*, and for lunch we drank a tart white wine from Neo Chori in the mountains and ate pasta saturated in boiling olive oil and garlic, with a carrot salad and *hórta*. For dessert a slab of brie, figs from their own tree and Greek coffee. All this was served out in the shade of one of the terraces by Riza, who had replaced Lela as cook.

In a little wall niche by the table was a beautiful marble goddess from Italy. I remembered it from years before, but had never learned its story. Paddy told of running out of gas on a drive to Rome many years ago, and meeting a farmer who had turned up the statue while plowing his field. He was able to buy it for a song. It was yet another example of the extraordinary good fortune that had attended him all his days.

As they readied themselves for a siesta after lunch, Paddy insisted I stay and nap in the living room and later swim at their beach—though I had told him I wanted to swim off the rocks as I had done back when Jonna and I lived in the little house at Kalamitsi.

I did take them up on the nap. The large sofas were a bit worn and dusty from their absence the last few months, but their living room was still one of the loveliest spaces I had ever seen. Books lay about, looking a bit wilted in September humidity. I picked up a volume of *The Hungarian Quarterly* and found a review of Paddy's *Between the Woods and the Water* that was gently critical of his attachment to the old aristocracy yet praised his "noble humanity." An apt phrase. And nearby I found *The Writing on the Wall*, a trilogy of novels by Miklós Banffy, newly translated and published in London with an introduction by Paddy. So he was working. That was good. To be eighty-seven and writing anything at all seemed beyond fortunate to me, and I doubted my own genetic fate would be so kind, assuming I survived the other disasters life sends our way.

Not wanting to impose, I crept out after my brief nap, leaving a note as I had done at Katerina's, only this time under an *ouzo* bottle. I walked to the little hut up the path and climbed over the gate. Now someone kept goats on the land and the weeds had been cropped by the flock. I went down to the edge of the sea, but the pathway to the rocks was blocked by a dense barrier of thorny sticks to pen the goats. It was really insurmountable, and with great disappointment I realized that I could not swim there. The goats watched me as if trying to think through very thick skulls just who I might be. They were like hosts at a tedious party deciding what to do with a crasher.

Praying with a Friend

That gecko panting on the whitewashed wall,
only witness in the little chapel
where I pay my coin and light a beeswax candle—
deference applied unasked for. Given.

Whatever gods have lived at Kalamitsi,
I know, as many locals do, the spring
now hidden by a thorny cloud of brambles.
it fed my garden once. I drank from it

the clearest water I have ever known,
medium of shade and other voices.

9

That night I had a good dinner at Lela's, though I was irritated by two Colonel Blimps at the next table who seemed delighted at America's latest misfortunes, going on and on about how meddlesome and litigation-mad we were. I entertained a fantasy of confronting them with a few choice bits of British imperial history, until I was pacified by a half-kilo of wine.

Later I found Marikaty in her shop and caught up on news of the village from her point of view. Yes, Paddy's pacemaker made him look ten years younger. And yes, things were very hard for Lisa and the children. And Marikaty's mother, Electra, had died. "It was peaceful," she said. "I was sad, of course, but if we must die it is better to die as she did."

Her daughters were doing well. Young Electra had finished medical school and was doing her residency in a village, and Alexandra was in business.

I saw gifts wrapped for new weddings on a table in her shop, and she remarked that new children had been born in the village, which was a very good sign. And I realized that this calm, philosophical and subtly active woman was a beautiful presence in the community, a voice of rationality, a bringer of culture. She showed me the courtyard of her house next door, which she had repaved with stones and decorated so it could become an outdoor art gallery—something inconceivable in the old Mani I had known with its survivalist mentality.

Others dropped by the shop, and there was much conversation about the attacks on America and whether we deserved them or not. Many people in the village were agitated, and I could see that nerves were rattled by the NATO jets that had scoured the air all day, probably from a base on Crete.

Nevertheless, Marikaty's tone was calming. She left me feeling that peace would prevail in the village. Its life went on: weddings, births, deaths. I thought of Electra's bones in the graveyard, her spritely personality and laughing eyes slowly giving up their hold on life, melting into the impersonality of earth. In a few years the bones would be brought to light again and given a name, part of the living memory.

Up before sunrise for my return to Athens, I heard a bat squealing outside my window, trapped by a cat in the yard. It was an eerie sound for the start of a day—a rude interruption of dreams. Again I felt that dread at the edge of consciousness—a fear that the world's violence was stronger than its love, that our good will was too weak in the face of so much enmity. When I had loaded my car, I found Lela at work in the kitchen, paid my bill and said goodbye. She wished me safe travels as we kissed. "I don't know letters," she said, "but I have seen things and I fear for the world. Be careful on your journey."

She could have been sending me off to the ends of the earth.

I drove north across the Pelonponnesos, then through the snarled streets of Athens to Glyfada, left the car, and spent my last afternoon and evening with Magda and her family. I felt as though I had crossed time as well as space, as though every day of my journey had been a year and my family in America would hardly recognize me.

As it happened, I interrupted a family argument in the Chalikia household. Magda had confronted her father about his financial naiveté, his fear of reporting inherited property to the tax authorities, and Yannis had taken great exception to her questioning of his authority. It was embarrassing for all of us. Magda was relieved when my arrival gave her an excuse to get out of the house.

We went to the bay and swam with the nudists, and I tried not to be angry at the chatter about Americans—how we cared only for money, how moralistic we were. I let Magda come to my nation's defense—our nation's, since she was getting dual citizenship—and tried to release the nausea I felt in the pit of my stomach. I tried to let the sun and sea do their therapeutic work.

Leaving the village, and also late that night leaving my dear friends in Gly-fada, felt less raw and emotional than it had in the past. My eyes were full, but I was privileged to witness lives outside my own. These were people I loved as I loved my own family. And along with this love came the almost proverbial letting go. Somehow I didn't need to own the story any more. I only needed to see it through.

Partway through a journey one thinks less about what one is leaving, more about what one is coming to. After so much travel in recent years, staying at home seemed a luxury beyond dreams. I returned to a country at war, streets filled with cars flying American flags, a bizarre jingoism. More than ever I knew my own family and my own land were crucial to me. Yet all the way home I felt the Aegean sea salt sticking to me like a second skin.

XIII

WINE AMONG FRIENDS

It is good to see places where one has been
happy in the past—to see them after many
years and in different circumstances.

—Lawrence Durrel, *Reflections on a Marine Venus*

1

"If you go to Lemonodassos," Paddy once said to me, "you must give our love to Kyrie Andreas, who owns the taverna."

He had offered me this assignment five years ago in 1997, but I had yet to fulfill it. This time I was sure I would finish the job. First, however, I had to survive three weeks leading seventeen students through Turkey and Greece. I had first gone to the Aegean as a "child." Now I'd be a leader of "children."

I don't actually like to travel. I don't like buses, planes or schedules. I hate reservations. I hate phone calls. I hate tickets, luggage, airports, the furniture in airports, even the air in airports. I hate travel in groups, waiting in lines, crowds of all kinds. But the truth is, organized groups will sometimes stumble into a different sort of luck than one finds on one's own. So it was with "the children," as Evin called them.

We were lucky to have a group without major drug addicts or street-fighters. Some of these young people had never traveled overseas before, and were genuinely awestruck at this brave new world, while others could discourse on air quality in Beijing, taxis in Mumbai, body-surfing in Baja. Though a few were students of sun-tanning more than of ancient drama, all were tolerant and open and curious in ways that made me proud of them. Two or three were better versed in drama and classical mythology than I, so the intellectual aspect of our journey was not a total loss.

I had the pleasure of seeing Istanbul through their eyes, watching young American women wrestle with headscarves in order to enter mosques. The poor things also dealt with frequent harassment, from the stares of old men at a taxi stand to the ubiquitous shoe blacks shouting for lira to the cat calls of merchants in the bazaars.

"Come children," Evin called at each stop, shaking a wooden rattle, and I would count to make sure I had the right number and gender: fourteen women and three men who apparently fell into brotherly roles more often than they would have liked. I knew we were safe, yet with so much responsibility on my shoulders I sometimes envisioned every danger from run-of-the-mill harassment to Al-Qaida kidnappings.

They adored Evin. At sixty-seven, she marched them through the sites, lectured them on the bus microphone, ran them up acropolises and through bazaars as if she were training a soccer team. They adored her energy and her laughter, though one or two could be heard to whisper about that "god-damned rattle."

With the help of a contact at the American Consulate in Istanbul, Evin arranged for us to visit the drama school of Müjdat Gezen, a graying actor who was described to me as "the Walter Matthau of Turkey." Under the mistaken impression that we were VIPs, Müjdat and his students treated us to performances of dramatic scenes, including a vigorous, rhythmical chorus from *Antigone* in Turkish, followed by a buffet of food and drink with folk music accompaniment. All of it was utterly professional, staged in what appeared to be a converted house in which the huge number of students would have had to work patiently in crowded conditions. Moved by the performances and powerful music in that plaintive, oriental minor key, my students and I threw ourselves into this gathering, unplanned on our part, as best we could.

Our new Turkish friends believed that we were performers rather than a literature class, and invited my students to perform. The crowd cleared space for them in front of the little stage. I could have predicted what happened next. How often do Americans initiate sing-alongs, only to find out that no two people in any group know the words to the same songs? They made a brave attempt at "American Pie," but even that petered out after the first chorus. They were saved from acute embarrassment only by our host, who saw they were in trouble, clapped his hands like a Sultan ordering figs, and restarted the folk musicians on the stage.

Before we were swept onto the sidewalk to meet our bus, Müjdat gave me an armload of his books, including a Turkish version of *Hamlet*, and gifts were bestowed upon all the American guests, who were stunned by such generosity. They had seen mosques and monuments, but this was their proper introduction to the Turkish people.

2

Leaving Istanbul this time I was more impressed by its sprawl and bad air, though the latter was in part a mist that rolled in from the sea and gathered in little valleys of half-finished buildings. Empty concrete shells, signs of the economic crisis, stood everywhere.

In Bursa we lingered at the silk market, finding ourselves surrounded by dozens of laughing schoolchildren who wanted to practice their English. They were small and thin, wearing school uniforms, and they giggled like *geishas* at every word we spoke. But their friendliness moved me, and I would have spent even more time scribbling stanzas of Robert Frost into their notebooks if our schedule had allowed. My students helped me choose a scarf for Annie—the heaviest gift I intended to carry—and we were off to Çanakkale, the town across the Dardanelles from the Gallipoli battlefield.

We got there April 26th, the day after ANZAC Day, but there were still plenty of Aussies and Kiwis packing the hotels. The Gallipoli campaign of 1915 was yet another example of the phenomenon started at Troy—the quest to control access to the Black Sea. Winston Churchill's obsession with opening a Balkan front assumed that a corrupt and weakened Ottoman Empire would capitulate rapidly, leaving Germany without an ally in the Middle East. Churchill didn't take into account the budding nationalism of the Turks and the military acumen of Mustafa Kemal, who reportedly told his troops, "I am not ordering you to attack, I am ordering you to die." His soldiers held their ground at great cost, forcing that other empire, the British, to withdraw.

Though victorious at Gallipoli, the Turks were on the losing side of the war, and were promptly punished by the Treaty of Sèvres in 1920, allowing the occupation of their land by Greeks, British, Russians and others. But Turkish nationalism grew rapidly under Kemal's charismatic leadership. At Çanakkale one felt the power of a place in which national identity arose for three peoples: Australians, Kiwis and Turks. I had been in New Zealand with Annie not long before this journey, and remembered the paintings hung in peoples' homes of ANZAC ghosts haunting the Gallipoli battlefield. Now, half a world away, I felt the strange nausea that gripped me when history neared with its roll call of the dead.

3

After Ephesus, Aphrodisias was hushed and unblemished. In such places I entertained brief fantasies of living in the ancient world, entering a city on marble roads, seeking the shade of the walnut trees, the poplars and plane trees. Sunlight and white Carian marble and the perfumed agora. I had always thought of the ancient world as a frightening one, full of conflict and bloodshed, but there must have been peaceful epochs as long as any I had known, at least for those lucky enough to live in certain places. Aphrodisias seemed such a place. Of course Alexander came and the Romans and the rebellions were many and ruthlessly put down. But there must also have been days when even a poor man or woman could luxuriate in the beauty of a moment, the sensual pleasure of other people in simple dress, the painted statues and shadowy colonnades. The Greeks were right to see our existence as a precarious one. We were the toys of forces we could still hardly comprehend, and our deaths would come without reason and in myriad forms. Most of us were anonymous except to a very few, and knowing this could teach us to strive for awareness of every day of life, every flavor, every look, every touch of the beloved, every word that gave savor to the tongue.

The tourist bustle of Bodrum was more bearable this time because we embraced our identity as tourists and hired a boat to take us out where we could swim. Evin and I sat mostly in the shade while the children sunned on the upper deck. Later we spent hours wandering the medieval castle by the city's quay. It had been turned into a museum, and in one room of the Snake Tower, a display devoted to fertility symbols, I noticed a plaque bearing a poem that fully comprehended the Greek view of life. It was by T. Oguz Alpözen, Director of the Bodrum Underwater Archeological Museum, and it went like this:

> DO NOT TURN YOUR BACK ON LOVE
> FEMALE OR MALE
> SOONER OR LATER
> YOUNG OR OLD
> YOU WILL TASTE DEATH

I couldn't have distilled the lessons of the course in clearer terms.

4

It was hard to say good-bye to Evin, but it helped that I had to usher the students through Turkish customs, onto the small ferry to Kos and through Greek customs on the other side. There we met the bus that took us to our hotel, and I explained to *ta paidiá*, as I now called them, that our pace would henceforth be slower. It was Holy Week. I wanted them to experience Easter just as they had the *muezzin* and scripture readers on the other side of the water. I gave them time to read and swim at a beach on the east side of the island, and on *Megáli Paraskeví* we made sure to watch the bier of Christ, the *epitáfios*, born through the streets to the town square. Each church sent a separate funeral procession, some with marching bands, until the square was packed with jostling, excited people.

We were to board a ferry to Piraeus at 3:30 Saturday morning—a special run scheduled for the holiday weekend. But when, after little or no sleep, we arrived at the pier in the dark, a German propped against a wall in his sleeping bag told us that the ferry would be hours late. We had already sent our bus away, so "the children" huddled with their luggage, some of them sleeping like spoons out of the breeze, others laughing off the drink they'd had that night until they tentatively dozed. I paced the pier all night, watching over them.

At dawn they gathered on the quay's edge to watch the sun rise over blue Anatolia, a bank of clouds turning redder until the sun bled through and spilled onto the waves. Later, on board the *Daliana*, they would see the sun set over Greek islands that I tried to name from a map spread open on my

knees. Many islands were like jagged slabs of some ancient desert incongru-
ously deposited in this summery sea. I was sleep-deprived, but happy out in
the salt air. We had booked cabins this time, but I spent most of the long
voyage on the upper deck, reading or talking with those who could stay awake.

By midnight nearly everyone on board was asleep, either in cabins or in
the bar. There were very few passengers, and that changed little with each
island port of call, the little towns lit up, some with strings of lightbulbs at
quayside resaturants. Only one student, Kirk, stayed awake with me on deck.
He was a bright young man who had once been a missionary in Brazil. We
could barely make out stars beyond the ship's lights, but could clearly see
lights of villages out in the windy darkness. Whether these were islands or
the mainland I could not tell, but the time of night caused me to think we
must be off Sounion, the cape southeast of Athens.

Suddenly two whiskered men joined us on the deck, swinging beer cans
and joyfully crooning the liturgy into the wind. One turned to me, shouting,
"*Christós Anésti*"—"Christ is risen!"

"*Aleithós anésti*," I answered. "Truly He is risen."

Right on cue, skyrockets flared and burst above the constellated lights
on shore. It was midnight.

The captain must have put a microphone next to a radio, because we were
treated to a broadcast of the singing from Athens, a full-throated celebration of cantors and priests over the ship's loudspeakers. I dashed through
the ship, wondering if I should wake my students. In every passageway, on
every deck, the singing filled the hull, but most passengers were dead to the
world. *Let them rest.*

As I climbed back to the upper deck and the wind caught me, I turned
toward the wake, startled by the ghostly presences of gulls rising and falling
outside our light. On such a night, with such music in the air, to find these
winged scavengers persisting against the wind, doggedly following our mea-
gre lights, was haunting. Were they flesh or spirit? Was this an anunciation
or merely a crowd of refugees seeking a free meal?

The whole encounter damned near made a Christian of me.

5

When I had seen my students off at the end of our tour of Greece, I took the bus to Glyfada, where I rented a car. I planned to drive back to the village, saving a few meals with Katerina for my last days in country. Rodney's health was failing, and it was unclear when and where we could meet. First I had to see the Chalikias, which would not be easy. It had been an agonizing year for them. Yannis had surgery for cancer, and then quite suddenly doctors discovered a malignant tumor in Popi's jaw. Her surgery and treatment had disfigured her beautiful face.

Magda was at the house with Verlin—like her a psychology professor. Alekos had not yet started seasonal work at the golf club—a job that improved his English, among other things—and a cousin was still visiting, trying to enlist Alekos in a scheme to sell phone cards. So we were a large gathering at the living room table for the midday meal.

As Magda led me into the kitchen to greet her mother, Popi became teary-eyed—her reaction whenever anyone saw her present state for the first time. Yannis had come through his treatments well and seemed much his old self—he would soon start swimming again at eighty-five. But Popi's illness had been a profound shock. She was still on a liquid diet and often sat apart from company as if ashamed.

After the meal, the cousin left and Alekos explained to me that this hair-brained scheme with the phone cards was not going well. He had contacted owners of dozens of *períptera*, the kiosks that sold every item imaginable, but his cousin was unhelpful with publicity and expected Alekos to finance his own advertisements. Alekos was waiting for a call from the golf club. It was hard to be at home and unemployed, but Magda and I advised him to stick with the real job—which would start soon enough. He pored over the lists of kiosks he had already contacted and worried aloud about what they would think when he couldn't come up with ads for them. "That's it," he finally said. "*Teleíose*. It's finish!"

Footloose for the time being, he was able to join us for nude bathing at the *limanáki*. The sea was clean and refreshing, especially now that the hot summer weather had arrived, but the two paleskins, Verlin and I, had to be careful lying in the sun.

The next day I was late getting on the road to Mani. By the time I reached Korinth it was already mid-afternoon. I could stay on the highway and be in the village well before sundown, but my promise to Paddy weighed on me. I had neglected it too long.

I drove south through the rolling hills of the Argolid, the forests and well kept farms and small villages that still had their own bakers—one of the prettiest regions on earth, where in the heat of that day shepherds sought shade in the olive groves. The heat fairly radiated from the golden grass, and the shade seemed to pool under the trees.

My map was vague about back roads, and at times I steered as much by the sun's position and my sense of where the sea must lie as any of the crude directions I had brought along. At last I descended the pot-holed track down to Galatas, the seafront town opposite the island of Poros. Paddy had described the Kardassi Taverna to me—how one parked at a little church and walked up through the lemon groves. And how behind the taverna there was a fountain and little waterfall. He had first stayed there in 1935, renting a room from the family. Andreas would have been a boy then, so it was his father Paddy remembered talking to and singing songs with.

Now there was a roughly paved track through the groves for Andreas's truck as much as for customers, but I kept on till I found the little church, got out and walked stiffly uphill in dappled shade and birdsong. I found the blue walls of the taverna just as the last midday customers were leaving.

Under an open roof, an old woman ironed sheets at one of the tables, while her husband cleared the dishes.

"Kyrie Andreas?" I inquired.

"Yes. Who are you?"

I gave my name, adding, "I'm a friend of Patrick Leigh Fermor, O Michali, who stayed here long ago."

At once he extended a hand. He sat me down, talking happily of Paddy and Joan, then brought me a glass of fabulously fresh lemonade followed by Greek coffee. As he heated the bríki of coffee on his stove, I spoke with his wife.

"Who are you?" she asked, and I went through the friend-of-Paddy line again.

"Who?"

"O Fermor!' Andreas shouted from the back. "The writer. He stayed here three months in the summer of 1935."

"So long ago," she said. Then of her husband: "He remembers. I don't."

She was clearing out one of the little huts below the terrace, making room for visiting relatives—hence the laundered sheets. But she had a bad arm and needed help moving the furniture. After she had stitched a clean sheet to one of the mattresses, Andreas and I hefted it inside and threw it on a crude bed frame, both of us huffing at the weight. We fixed up a few other beds, and he showed me an oil lamp backed by a little mirror that Paddy wrote by at night more than sixty-five years ago.

"It was very good that you came," said Kyria Kardassi about my little bit of help.

I responded that I had only come to bring them greetings from Kyrie Michali in Mani, where I hoped to see him soon.

"You have far to travel," said Andreas. "It will be midnight when you get there."

So it was. After a long, bleary-eyed drive I made it to the sleeping village and, finding Lela's full up, rented a room from strangers that night, and ate bread and cheese and drank a few glasses of wine while writing in my journal. The next morning after a good breakfast I found Marikaty in her shop, and she bought me an *ouzo* and *mezes* while she had coffee. "Of course," she said, "you can stay with me."

Paddy at Kalamitsi, 1997
PHOTO BY DAVID MASON

6

She moved me into the guest room by the front door of her eighteenth-century house, and that afternoon while the shop was closed we sat in the shade of her courtyard, catching up. She was having the house repaired and repainted by a marvelous new addition to the village, a Polish immigrant named Specek who lived with his wife in the small, top-floor apartment of Friend's house. He had already expanded the basement of that house into a lighter and more comfortable home for Lisa and the children. Now he was at work on the woodwork and wrought iron at Marikaty's. One sign of Specek's good humor was the tiny wooden bridge he had fashioned to cross from an earthenware jar to one of her marble counters in the courtyard; this was to facilitate the travel of the ants back and forth from the soil in the jar. I liked him immediately for doing that.

While he worked slowly and carefully at replacing a rotted door jamb we talked together—three different nationalities, all communicating in Greek. It must have been like that with traders in the ancient world. Swallows swooped and sang above our heads. *They are migrants too*, I thought.

Marikaty's book with Friend would soon be out, she hoped. The first publisher had gone mad and been hospitalized; the second was slow, but it appeared to be happening. And Alexandra would be married in the fall. She wanted her house to be in good shape when the guests arrived.

That evening I found Lisa in the *plateía* by the church, sitting with friends under the eucalyptus trees while their children played. These were her closest allies, the other mothers with young children. I still thought of Lisa herself as young though she was forty, an edge of toughness in her voice.

Her divorce had come through in October, but at precisely the wrong moment the judges had gone on strike, so there were more delays. Now in May it was up to Yiorgos to sign the papers, which he put off doing. She was still dependent on her father, but hoped to have work soon and find her own place to live.

Would she want to leave the village?

No, never, she said, looking at Kosta running like a wildman with his friends in the evening light. This was an ideal place for children. Though of course she had to tell her children to stay clear of certain men in the village who were known predators. There were only five women they could trust other than their mother, she told them. She had to be vigilant.

After she closed the shop, Marikaty and I made a late dinner and watched a movie on TV, finishing the Chalikias' wine. We noticed the ads on TV were, as she put it, *"ta misá ellinibá ta misá anglibá"*—"half Greek and half English." I told her that my friend Katerina, whom I would see soon in Athens, would be enraged by such cultural change. I wished these two friends of mine, both dynamic women, could meet. It seemed my motive for connecting friends was the same one that underlay this book—wanting to connect, wanting the people I had known to join in some imaginary circle rather than remaining scattered in experience. In Athens Katerina and I would meet twice, once near Lykavittos and once at *O Platanos* in the Plaka for leisurely meals, and as always it would be as if no time at all had passed, though news of Rodney's health was not good. In the shadow of the Acropolis, the passing years of our own lives were little more than the blink of an eye—or the wink of an eye, I should say, since Katerina was as full of jokes as ever. "You're a lucky man," she had said to me once. A lucky man. I turned the phrase over, somewhat fearful of being jinxed by it. Lucky in my friends, my marriage. Lucky in so many things. Let it be so, just a while longer. I had been lost so many years. Who or what could I pray to now but the god of shrugged shoulders? The god of *who the hell knows?* Give me the years to do my work, I would say to that god. Please let it be that I don't screw up my family, that I live a while longer in such light and humility and love and friendship. Let it be so.

7

That year my last full day in the village was spent at Kalamitsi with Paddy and Joan. She had had another fall, and had seriously cut her head and lost a lot of blood. Paddy's hearing was bad enough that he was oblivious to her shouts, and the help were absent. Riza had gone round the bend when her only son declared that he wanted to join the priesthood, and she had quit. She was replaced by two younger, less experienced girls, one for days and one for evenings.

A friend was staying with them—Miranda, who had known Paddy since childhood and now found herself commanding the situation as temporary caretaker. She had found Joan and stanched the wound and cleaned up the mess. When I arrived, Joan was reclining on a sofa. I bent to kiss her and could tell she was frailer, but this had no effect whatsoever on her sense of decorum: "Do fix yourself an *ouzo*, David. Paddy will be back with the mail any moment now."

When Paddy strode in with a young man's vigor, his good looks only slightly caved in by age or overgrown by his shrubby brows, we took our drinks outside with a tray of *mezes*. The faintest breeze ruffled leaves in the ilex trees and nudged the cypresses full of singing birds. I conveyed greetings from Kyrie Andreas, and that took Paddy back to one of his happiest summers.

Miranda joined us, having walked back from the village while Paddy drove Dapple Gray. She had once been married to an Algerian revolution-ary with whom she had a daughter. He was assassinated in 1964, and there was something horrible about how she had to go out and find his body in "a charnal pit."

"I'm bi-polar, you know," she announced at one point. "Manic-depressive. I can't help talking this way, and besides that I've been drinking all day. . . ."

When she had run off to check on something in the kitchen, I remarked to Joan that I had only seen Miranda's manic side. "Yes," said Joan dryly, "so have we. We're rather worried about the other half."

Growing up, she had several stepfathers, among them Rex Warner, the poet and translator, and the painter Nikos Ghikas, whom she adored. It seemed to be one of those slightly batty English circles with plenty of ambiguous sexuality. As a girl she was introduced to another writer I admired.

"Him?" I said, slapping my forehead. His memoir of childhood in England had once been a favorite book of mine.

"None other. He seduced me. I mean I was willing, but I was a girl, I was ugly and he took advantage of me."

"Oh no!"

Another ikon of innocence shot full of holes.

This came out when we had returned to the *hayati* while Paddy and Joan napped. Miranda was jazzed, as "the children" would say. She was energized. While I excused myself for a quick lie-down, she dashed off to help in the kitchen.

I must have slept for an hour or so. I woke with Paddy leaning over me as he jostled my arm. "Dave? Dave? I say, do you fancy a walk?"

"Of course," I said, unsure how I had been beamed to this particular time and place. "I'd love to."

He grabbed us a couple of hats and sticks and we stepped down the path outside the wall to where Dapple Gray awaited us in the shade.

I'm sure Paddy was a splendid driver when young but at eighty-seven he sat behind the wheel like El Cid tied to his horse. He drove with the gas pedal on the floor though he never got out of second gear. As a result, the car screamed like a banshee as he jerked it around bends in the road.

On the ridge above Petrovouni he pulled off the track through the olive trees. We did not walk far, perhaps twenty minutes, Paddy keeping time with his walking stick like a Whitehall barrister. He glanced at his watch frequently, as if keeping strict account according to a doctor's orders. Still, think of it. Eighty-seven and able to get about like that. Even at a fraction of the physical specimen he once was, Paddy was utterly admirable. Assuming I lived so long, I would be drifting into la-la land before I was eighty, with someone wiping my bum and feeding me through a straw.

God of the shrug, give me time.

Farmers had recently burned slash from the olive trees, and at the end of our walk my trousers were striped and smeared with ash that had clung to the scrub. The heat of early summer radiated from the grass and wild sage. It was almost time for the cicadas to start their whirring. For now, utter stillness. Hardly a breath of wind. The crunch of dry vegetation underfoot amplified by my hearing aids.

"A swim will feel good after this," Paddy said. "Are you game?"

"Of course."

He whipped Dapple Gray down the mountain road, found me an extra pair of trunks in his room, and sent me off ahead of him to the sea.

The water was calm, buoyant with salt. Wading in from their gravel beach, I swam out around the rocks to the point where I used to dive in the old days, and there I treaded water for some time, looking ashore as if I expected to see someone I knew stepping down the slope. We had picked capers from a bush there—Wolfie and Isy and Jonna and I, twenty-odd years ago.

By the time I swam back, Paddy had made his way down the stone staircase to the beach. He carefully entered the water, balanced by a walking stick in his left hand, a huge boulder at his right. When he'd gone deep enough he cast the stick aside and gave himself to the sea. I watched him swim for perhaps twenty minutes, and when he emerged we rested briefly on the stony shingle.

I could see the pacemaker's little mound at his clavicle, and on his left bicep a magnificent old tattoo of the naked *Gorgona*, the mermaid who, according to one tradition, was sister to Alexander the Great. When I complimented him on it he told me how Seferis had loved the *Gorgona*. If a fisherman caught one, the story went, she would ask, *"Pou eínai o Megaléxandros"*—"Where is Alexander the Great?"

And the fisherman could answer to save his life, "*O Megaléxandros zi kai vasilévi*"—"Alexander the Great lives and reigns."

It was the ultimate parable of modern Greek identity.

8

Richard, an English lawyer, and Vanna, his Italian wife, joined us for drinks that evening, whiskey and soda on the terrace. Richard and Vanna had built a house nearby, and they were very good neighbors, introducing Paddy and Joan to movies on a VCR they gave them—another example of people watching out for them. That night Richard brought a tape of Truffaut's *Jules et Jim.*

Paddy had changed to a white shirt and looked refreshed by the swim and the walk. "Nothing better," he said about it. He was in great spirits, bothered only by a blackbird that kept singing away in the tree behind his good ear, so he couldn't follow all of the conversation. I had earlier shown him my own hearing aids that could be adjusted with a little pad of buttons I carried around. It was supposed to hook onto my belt, but I kept breaking the plastic tab and had resorted to carrying the damn thing in my pocket. Still, it was useful for cutting out background noise. Hearing is partly a matter of concentration on other people and, if necessary, reading their lips. Annie always joked that I was not hard of hearing, just hard of listening. It was a writer's vice.

I wore the same smoke-stained clothes, but no one seemed bothered. Joan joined us for a while, then excused herself to lie down, accepting help from Miranda.

This is how they'll do it, I thought. *The childless couple. They have friends. People who love them and would never want to see them in a home.*

They would keep their dignity and grace as long as possible.

"Paddy is a young soul," Miranda had told me. "Joan is an old soul. She always has been." The description was perfect. With her long, angular frame in a caftan, Joan moved slowly through that house. She was older than Paddy, literally and figuratively. She was wise—always reading, always listening, rarely putting herself at the center of things. She was as beautiful as any human being I had ever known. Paddy, the obvious matinee idol, dashing and talented, would be anybody's pick for a friend. How lucky he was to have found Joan as a companion in good years and bad.

That day I had tried to say to Paddy what I felt about his work, how important it was, how important to me he had been. I couldn't know whether I would ever see them again. Perhaps he sensed how much it meant to me to spend those hours with him, and when the other guests were gone he insisted I stay to dinner.

Miranda, Paddy and I sat at the table in the living room, one lamp between us, eating fried eggs and potatoes and drinking more wine. Miranda gave him orders, taking care of him as a daughter might, and he recalled fondly how he first met her when she was a little girl. There was something about it he was trying to remember. A mouse. Yes, a mouse had died, and this wee girl was performing a funeral for it, a ritual burial.

"But it wasn't just that," said Miranda. "I felt guilty. You see, I've only just remembered. I killed that mouse."

"No," Paddy said. "It died on its own in a field."

"I killed it," she said. "Or I think I did."

"What do you mean you think you did? If you killed it, you'd remember."

"But I don't. I don't remember. It's something I repressed. It's only now coming back to me."

"Nonsense."

"What?"

"I said nonsense!"

"But it's true, Paddy. You're so innocent you don't believe I could have done it. But I did. Or I think I did."

"You can't kill a thing and not remember it."

"Are you sure?"

"Of course I am. Absolutely sure. If you kill a living creature, something with life, you do not forget. You never forget."

"How do you know?"

"What do you mean, how do I know? I don't want to talk about it."

"Have you killed?"

In the lamplight Paddy looked shaken. "Yes I have."

"Have you killed people? You mean in the war?"

"Oh, don't let's talk about it. It's too horrible."

"But we should talk about it," said Miranda as a nurse might to a small boy. "It's good to talk about it. I'm just remembering something I did as a child and repressed."

"You can't mean what you say."

"But I do mean what I say, Paddy. The world is like that, and I'm part of the world, I can't deny it." She turned to me. "What did T. S. Eliot say—mankind cannot bear too much reality?"

"Yes," I answered, no longer at ease in our small circle of light.

Paddy's hands moved, agitated, in front of his face. We had all had a lot to drink. Miranda was firm with him out of caring, I could see. But at the same time I thought, *Oh, leave him alone. He has borne his share of reality. Let him be.*

It was late. I fretted about Marikaty wondering what had happened to me, and since I didn't have the phone number of her house I said I should go. Paddy became very worried about my safety walking the paths in the dark. He suggested I stay the night, but as is too often the case with me I felt I had to press on, keep going, meet my obligations.

Give me time.

With her habitual practicality and way of taking care of people, Miranda volunteered to escort me to the road with a torch that she could bring back to the house.

It was agreed, but I did not want to say good-bye. I never knew when I would be back, whether I would see them again. Paddy meant the world to me—not as a monument, but as a friend who taught by example a love of life. I tried not to be grim about going.

Before we left I knocked on Joan's door to say good-bye. She reclined on her bed with the reading light on, a volume of Yeats sprawled open beside her. Again she apologized for her age, her frailty, and again I tried to convey that I was simply in awe of the way she carried on. "You're heroic," I said.

"You're sure you won't stay?" Paddy asked as we shook hands at the door. "I worry about you falling off a cliff out there. It's very dark, you know."

He was right. A haze obscured the stars and the moon had not risen. With two torches, Miranda and I could just find our way up the path and through the lighted yard of Poniereas's new hotel. When we said good-bye and embraced at the edge of the road, I told her how happy I was to know that such friends were looking after Paddy and Joan.

"It's what we have to do," she said. "The alternative is unthinkable."

Then I was back on the road, the only sound the slap of my sandals on pavement. Past the older hotel on the hill. Past the lane to Friend and Margarita's house where Lisa and the children slept. Past Stratis the Mariner's to the gate for Marikaty's courtyard. The lights were out, but Specek had removed the front door from its hinges to work on the wood, so I walked into the quiet house where my friend slept.

An open house in more ways than one.

Time. Give me time.

Postscript

I go back in a different way now—less the child-romantic, more the friend. I see Paddy, Lisa, Marikaty, Alekos, Katerina and others. I go back to the village, hoping to catch up on the news.

In 2006 Paddy had tunnel vision and wore an eye patch, just like Joan. She had died the previous year but he soldiered on. He said if he didn't wear the patch he saw double. People began to look like Picasso paintings. He was trying to tape a reminiscence for the anniversary of the Battle of Crete, but the illegibility of his own handwriting flummoxed him. We ate dinner together, but did not swim or go for a walk.

Later a letter came describing a trip to Albania, with lateral divagations into the lore of Ali Pasha and northern Greece.

His spirit was undimmed last October when I lunched with him again, having brought a colleague to meet the great man. Hearing was a problem—his aid was being repaired, and when I tried to show him mine he had to hold my hand and stare out of his good eye in cyclopean fashion. To facilitate conversation we sat beside him on cushions. "Yes," he said patting the cushions on either side, "cuddle up."

The sea washed the rocks below the veranda where we dined, and when it seemed time to part and leave him to his siesta I could see he was ready for it. We left him at his bedroom door, where he said he intended to go "straight into the arms of the appropriate god."

My friend and I stopped on the path back, climbed over the crumbling stone wall by the cistern and walked the land I had once gardened. It was no longer a goat pen, and we were able to clamber down to the rough volcanic rocks. I couldn't resist a swim.

The sea was delicious, bright and warm and clear. As I dried on the rocks I used a cell phone to call Jonna in St. Louis, where she lived with her second husband.

"Guess where I am," I said. I told her about Paddy and the swim.

"You bastard," she said.

The connection was so clear she could hear waves washing against the rocks. It was as if she became that young woman I once knew, talking to me from the next rock instead of halfway around the globe and I was capable of listening now. Time folded and the past came into view and we talked like old friends, though we had not seen each other in decades.

When I showed my friend the interior of our little hut at Kalamitsi we could see the lime and paint I had applied, preserved out of the weather's touch with the remnants of screens on the windows and the meager shelf and the now unstuffed and mouse-infested mattress where Jonna and I had been boy and wife. I nearly wept.

There had been more news over the years. Rodney Rooke was dead, Katerina inconsolable. Yannis and Popi were dead, Alekos living in the family house. Lisa lived on in the village, her children growing. Miraculously, she was running a bar with her ex-husband, Yiorgos. Marikaty was in the village half the year, a grandmother now. The place had grown, a tourist destination with hotels and new electrically lit pathways among the old towers.

Across the Aegean, Evin had remarried and was very happy, though the Iraq war and Islamic fundamentalism seemed not to bode well for Turkey.

Nearly everyone was better off, but that was before the bottom fell out of markets all over the world, before the riots in Greece when friends emailed they could smell the tear gas in their neighborhoods.

My life in America is with Annie and our family. We have built a new house near a park called The Garden of the Gods, and as I write this I can see a flowerbed where Annie has been digging. This is home. My work is in America, yet how deeply colored all of it is by Aegean friends. Their lives go on apart from mine, and at the final parting all that is left will be love. It does not matter who remembers.

Still, those were beautiful days in the village, sitting on Friend's balcony with Lisa, sipping wine and watching the swallows swoop and dart over the rooftops. There was a lot to catch up on, and I can't help wondering now what else has changed.

April 2009

The little house at Kalamitsi, 1997
PHOTO BY ANNE LENNOX

The Bay of Writing

And I with only a reed in my hands.
—George Seferis

The reed, dried and cut, could make a pan-pipe
on an idle day. I say the word again,
kalamus, that early pen, from breezy
leaf to leaves of nervy writing—Sappho,
Archilochos, their fingering lines,
a silent music till our voices find it.

In retrospect I walk among those trees,
polled mulberries no longer home to silkworms,
the crone-like olives, upright cypresses
above the hammered metal of the bay
called *Kalamitsi*. There the lazy hours
watching the ant roads through the summer straw

taught me the frantic diligence of mind,
the way it ferries breadcrumbs and small seeds
fast fast to its storehouse in reedy shade.
The way the hand rests on an open book
I've disappeared into, takes up a pen
and traces letters in a trail of words.

Kalamus, Kalamitsi, bay of reeds,
music of everything I have not written.